Not there yet

Wandering home with an amateur vagabond

Kevin Barron

First published in 2014
Copyright © Kevin Barron 2014

The moral right of the author has been asserted.

Maps, cover and internal photographs by Kevin Barron

ISBN 978-0-473-37981-0 (Softcover)
ISBN 978-0-473-37982-7 (ePub)
ISBN 978-0-473-37983-4 (Kindle)
ISBN 978-0-473-37984-1 (eBook)

5

Front cover: Salar de Uyuni, Bolivia

To E
For coming with me

"Tis but a banging of the door behind you, a blithesome step forward, and you are out of the old life and into the new!"

Kenneth Grahame, *The Wind in the Willows*

Contents

Preface

Moving to another country is an excellent opportunity to see somewhere else on the way. This book mainly covers travels around two such moves. The first was when I went to live in Australia because of family connections, the second was when my Kiwi girlfriend and I went to live in New Zealand.

On the Australian trip, even as I started those two years of travel, I felt that I was going home, for if you intend to return to where you began, you are already on your way back.

New Zealand was different. Originally we went for the duration of a two year contract my girlfriend had been awarded. At time of writing, we are still there.

As with my earlier book, *Into the blue*, the content varies in subject matter, length and style. There are descriptions of journeys and of people; there are simple anecdotes. I have changed the names of some people and I apologise to anyone who may feel they have been misrepresented.

Leaving Home
1997 – 1999

I had made some shorter trips to the US before, but spending much of my two months staying with friends combined travel with the insights of someone who lives there. I went from summer to winter to travel in New Zealand and from there to live and work in Australia. The honourable grandmother *is adapted from an article first published in the Canberra Times in 1999.*

Leaving England

My manager had heard a rumour that I was leaving to go travelling. I was non-committal. I told him I had been saying that for seven years. He asked if I would commit to staying for another eighteen months.

"I can't promise you that any more than anyone else in the company could," I told him.

He pondered for a moment.

"You're not married, are you?"

"No," I said.

"Do you own your own house?"

"No."

"You've got nothing to keep you here, have you?" he said, realising for himself that he could not tempt me.

"No." I was smiling now. I felt a power over this empire builder who was fighting his way up the corporate ladder. I made no promises, but as it happened, I stayed for another eight months.

A few weeks before I left, I stayed with my brother in Sussex. We walked along the chalk landscape of the Seven Sisters. White cliffs, green grass, blue sky: this could only be the shores of Britain. At his cottage in the village, birdsong and clip-clopping horses' hooves in the lane outside wafted through the open window as I lay in the bath. The smell of roast dinner came up the stairs, accompanied by the sounds of Vaughan Williams' arrangement of *Greensleeves*. Things could not have been any more English. I nearly wept.

The day I moved my belongings from my home in Nottingham to my parents', I drove through Derbyshire countryside of a rich, spring green. England, my England. And I was leaving.

So why was I going? My mother had asked me that. For a change, I said. To see some new parts of the world, have some experiences, see old friends, get to know relatives, take photographs, stimulate some writing and because I had run out of stories. She nodded understandingly. After all, she had left Australia for two years herself, met my father and settled in Britain.

I had not left myself enough time to do everything I needed. The night before, I was throwing things I would be taking in my backpack in one pile and things which would be posted to Australia in another.

An old friend was giving me a lift to London. I was pleased about that. I had dreaded the departure from the station, the waiting for the train. I had been bad tempered all day as my parents tried to help me. They were not getting in the way, I was just upset and that was the only way I let the emotion out. The parting was brief, teetering on a cliff of emotion.

My friend and I were silent in the car for a while. I think he sensed I needed some space. Then he started to talk about leave takings and the importance of family, before gently changing the subject. It was a pleasant, unhurried drive.

I stayed with friends in Ealing before a morning flight out of Heathrow and I enjoyed the beer, Italian food and the company of good friends. I was feeling sentimental and the letter which my mother had sneaked into my bag and which fell out while I was getting ready for bed did not help things.

We flew over Ireland; it was all fields. Then we were over the sea. The next land visible through broken cloud was Canada. As we crossed the eastern shore of Lake Michigan, I could see Chicago's skyscrapers rising from the urban plain.

In the Twin Cities

The queues at Immigration in Chicago were long. I asked if I could go in and out of Canada under the visa waiver programme.

"So long as the Canadians let you in," said the large young woman. "Or out again."

O'Hare airport was spacious and modern. I was assured my bag would be sent to my next plane; I doubted there would be enough time. I had some trouble in the toilets where there were all sorts of unfamiliar gadgets. There were plastic seat covers which sprouted over the toilet seats like an encroaching alien fungus. There were radar taps which noticed when your hands were under the spout and started to pour water. Before I had seen someone else do it, I had been looking for a knob or a button. Soon these would become normal, but then, they were proof that I was in a foreign land.

Arriving at Minneapolis, there was no sign of my friend Jim, so I went to the baggage carousel. I suspected my pack would not be there and I was still waiting when Jim strolled up. Jim and I went back a long way. We had met in the former Yugoslavia eleven years before. This was the guy I had swashbuckled with through Turkey, drunk beer with in Sheffield and whose car had broken down on the back roads of Wisconsin one dark night. We simply picked up where we had left off.

We drove across town. It was so different to my staple off season European trips. It was hot, the streets were wide, the cars were big, the buildings flat and boxy and there were overhead traffic lights. We collected his girlfriend Martha and went for pizza. Our waitress was helpful, friendly and efficient. It is a job which is taken seriously: they want a tip.

"That was quite disgusting," I said as I passed her a plate that had been licked clean. She looked troubled.

"Don't mind him, he's English," explained Martha.

Their apartment was comfortably cluttered, with boxes, books and files piled on shelves and cabinets and a desk. The Turkish stringed instrument which Jim had carried around various countries was hanging from one of the beams. I met the rest of the family: Skunky the cat who was old, scrawny and bad tempered, and Pippin the dog, friendly and excitable. They had found him along the lake shore the previous year, had meant to advertise him as having been found, but became too attached to him. We later discovered he became strangely excited when anyone mentioned Duluth.

My backpack arrived, we talked and at 4am British time, I gave up trying to stay awake.

We drove over to Jim's parents' to pick up a more reliable car than their own and drive down the Mississippi for the day. They were unsure which route to take. His sister Laurie knew a good one.

"It's very pretty and it goes through the hills and winds around and it's real interesting."

We bumped into his step-father outside.

"Hell, don't go that way, it winds too damn much. Take the freeway."

Later, on the winding, interesting route, traffic was light and the day was hot as I looked out at trees with the fresh bright leaves of spring. We drove beyond Redwing and took a walk into the forest towards the river. Floods out west, caused by a sudden thaw, had drained off into the Mississippi and it was only just beginning to regain its natural level. The approaches to the bank were still waterlogged and we could not reach the water's edge. We had been walking through the trees for some time when Martha suggested we should be looking out for ticks which have a habit of dropping out of the branches onto unsuspecting ground creatures such as ourselves and burrowing into warm, sheltered parts of their bodies. I rolled my sleeves down, turned my collar up and wished I had taken my hat out with me.

"Ooh, I've got one!" exclaimed Jim, hurling it away.

Already imagining the tiny creatures drilling into our brains and soft fleshy parts, we searched frantically through our hair, behind ears, in armpits and down our shirts. Martha found one, then another, brushing them off before they had time to delve. We drove away, still inspecting. Martha found another one. Once more I could feel the parasites digging into my nervous system and I joined the other two in a renewed frenzy of hunting.

We stopped for lunch at a diner on the river and had thick shakes and curly fries, then went in search of a scenic overlook. It turned out to be on private land at a flower nursery. I was pushed out of the car to charm them with my accent. The owner was suitably charmed and allowed us into their back garden to admire the view. The Mississippi lay in the broad valley, a layer of trees thrown over it. Straight ahead, cutting though the river bluffs was the valley of the Chippewa River. As we looked, a patch of sunlight slid across the trees.

We drove on through Wabasha, eventually crossing the river into Wisconsin and ducked off into back roads that took us deep into rolling farm country. The farms were clusters of wooden buildings, a farmhouse, barns and a silo or two, all shaped like Dutch barns. The colours were rich and soft in the early evening sunlight.

When we reached Redwing again, we noticed a trail going up the bluff. The low sun turned the rock to gold. From the top there was a view across a tree-covered plain with patches of water between the trees. Back the other way, the lights were just coming on in the town. I was reminded of narrow boats at home and explained that they were not allowed to sail after dark.

"I'm sorry?" asked Martha, thrown by my accent. "Did you just say something about – Say lofty duck?" Confusion was increased on the drive home when I discovered another couple of ticks sparking a flurry of probing in our warm, dark places.

The next day was Sunday and, following a lazy start at a café reading the paper and doing the crosswords, we drove to the outdoor museum at Murphy's Landing where a baseball game was being played to 1850s rules. The teams were the Quicksteps who specialised in 1850s rules and big moustaches and the Minneapolis Saints who specialised in 1990s rules. And won.

Afterwards we wandered around the old buildings in the sunshine. Volunteers acted out the parts of the townspeople. A trader and blacksmith were good and gruff, but a lad in a shop had trouble staying in character, as did a gunfighter in the street who seemed to be the fastest mobile phone in the West.

We went to the cinema in the evening. It was just like being in the cinema at home and I had culture shock all over again when we walked outside and I realised I was not.

Jim took me up the Foshay Tower. In 1929 it had been Minneapolis' tallest building at a massive 32 stories. Wilbur Foshay had been impressed by the Washington Monument, but felt it needed a few windows. This tower took in his improvements. We went up to the viewing platform and looked at the glass towers surrounding and dwarfing it. I scanned the streets with the powerful telescopes which gave me superb views of the moles on people's faces far below.

The state parliament was a big domed neo-classical building in marble. It was full of people talking, using mobile phones and walking around like extras on American television shows. We got in the lift with the representative of Duluth.

"It's warm up here," he said.

"Closer to the sun," I suggested. He shook his head.

"Hot air."

We watched the house in session. No one was listening to the speaker. They chatted and played with their laptops. There was more order in the Senate where a weary looking security guard called Hank X Patterson showed us into the public gallery. Finding out I was British, he told me they had me to thank for their drawn out parliamentary system.

"Only kidding," he said.

I had realised he was.

"Only kidding," he added. Twice.

Jim took me to Minnehaha Park to look at the falls, which cut right into the heart of the city. The river smelt of the sea. Jim pointed out a small island covered in mature trees.

"At the height of the floods, there was only about five feet of trees showing on that," he said.

He dropped me at the Art Institute where I spent the rest of the afternoon. There was an exhibition by Chihuly a glass-blower. Having lost an eye in a car accident, he lacked depth vision, so supervised a team of blowers. There was a video of him working, designing the sculptures with bold, messy sweeps, using his hands or a brush, squirting straight from a bottle or even spilling coffee into his design.

The sculptures were amazing. There were great chandeliers like Medusa heads, wild and curling. One was orange, another a pale blue. There were big dishes like flowers and a room with a glass ceiling where so called rejects were laid.

"I'd like a ceiling like that at home," said one woman.

My favourite exhibit was a stage set for the Seattle Opera. There was a black polished floor against a black backdrop. Five green and glittering tree trunks twisted up to the ceiling and seemingly down into the polished floor.

"I detect an accent. Where are you from?" asked the driver of the local bus when I went to meet Jim in town.

Jim and I sat in a bar across the street to wait for Martha to finish work. A guy was sitting near us quietly smoking and drinking. Suddenly he recited an amusing, lewd little rhyme, stood up and went to the toilet. When he came back, he kept interrupting us with jokes and stories. It was monologue without an awareness of an audience. He wandered from jokes to politics and it became impossible for us to talk. And besides, it was time to go to the Museum of Questionable Medicine.

It was full of quack medicines and bizarre machines. There was a phrenological machine which told us our characters from the bumps on our heads and there were others which were simply boxes covered in knobs and dials which were designed to look like they did stuff. One had been filled with tar to give a weighty effect. There was a story of a man who drank radium impregnated water for the good of his health until his jaws dropped off. When they dug him up seventy years later, his remains were still warm.

The next day, I explored downtown on my own. I did a walk along the river, crossing a great stone bridge which had once carried the railway around the milling district. This was the part of town called St Anthony after the favourite saint of an early pioneer. There was a waterfall which was retreating so quickly they had to halt its movement with concrete. A building was being knocked down nearby. A crane with a steel grab would tear off chunks of building and drop them to the ground while a brave man in a helmet standing nearby hosed down the rubble to settle the dust.

I watched a cop directing the traffic, throwing his whole body into his work with authoritative enthusiasm. Then I hit the Skyway, Minneapolis's city within a city, linking the first floor of most buildings to protect the locals from the heat and the cold which the climate hurls at them in roughly equal parts. There were restaurants and takeaways and I was spoilt for choice. A sandwich or a meal would cost the same, but offended my sense of value because I only wanted a sandwich. But there was also the terror of not knowing what I wanted. The queues moved quickly. "Chicken on rye with mayo and avocado and a dash of German mustard." Everyone else knew exactly what permutations and combinations were on offer and what they wanted. It was all so slick, the way people found trays, condiments, salad dressings and sauces. I would never have time to ponder the options and decide before I was trampled under a stampede of busy Minneapolitans. I took so long deciding on an outlet that the busiest time was over and the pressure was reduced, but I was still momentarily confused by the assistant asking me "wheatorwhite?"

At the History Museum in St Paul, I compiled a list of famous things from Minnesota. In no particular order: Jolly Green Giant foods, Sears (which started there before moving to Chicago and joining up with Roebuck), softball, Hiawatha, Jesse James' Northfield raid, Lindbergh, F. Scott Fitzgerald, Kellogg, Lew Ayres, Judy Garland, the Andrews Sisters, Charlie Brown, Bob Dylan, the Mary Tyler Moore show, Prince, Garrison Keillor, General Mills and Betty Crocker, the shopping bag with handles, Burma Shave, 3M, Tonka, Jessica Lang, Shelley Long, Bill Murray (who owned the Saints baseball team), Unisys and Honeywell.

In the evening, we went to a retirement party for two teachers from the school where Martha had worked. She had only been there for a year, but from the reception she got, seemed to have been popular. Having been introduced, Jim and I melted into the background most of the time. One man introduced himself to us. "Terry Kreitzler," he said briskly in a way that made me think he had also clicked his heels and bowed slightly. He was in his late fifties or sixties, his hair was thin and slicked back and his skin was suspiciously tight and brown for a part of the country that had just hit spring. He wore a cream suit with padded shoulders and a collarless shirt with a brooch at the neck. Martha explained him afterwards. His mother had been a good and famous senator and they were making a TV movie of her life. He had managed to wangle an executive producership and a bit part and liked to think he was well on the way to Hollywood, seeking school gossip in exchange for news about who Glenn Close was sleeping with.

Our next port of call was a bar where the Annual Bob Dylan Impersonation Contest was being held. Some of the contestants were good, but one not only did one not sound anything like Mr Dylan, but had the lack of judgement to think that an event so tongue in cheek was the best place to sing a tribute song he had written himself, incorporating song titles at salient points. His parents applauded excitedly.

A pretty, dark-haired girl asked me the time, commented on my accent and started to chat me up. She had travelled and could not wait to go away again. She lost interest when she discovered I was not living in Minneapolis and was leaving the next day. I went back to the others.

"I'm staying another week," I said.

"Who with?" grinned Martha.

I boarded the Greyhound the next morning, being offered drugs on my way into the terminal, which did nothing to counter the horror stories I had heard about bus travel in the States. The journey was over ten hours through uninteresting scenery. I sat next to a young lad who was reading the Iliad and who would splay his palms in a kind of twitch. Nearby a young white couple smooched and gazed into each other's eyes. More blacks got on at Milwaukee with some cute little kids. We had a change of driver too who was also black. We were driving along when he smelt a cigarette. The culprit was a lanky black guy who was returning to Chicago after failing college in Minneapolis. He had twice held up the bus while he sauntered back late from a rest break. The first driver, a blustery white guy had had no effect. Our second one was different. When he smelt the smoke, he slowed down and put on the interior lights.

"Put out the cigarette," he said. "Put out the cigarette or I'll drop you right here on the highway. We'll be there in fif-teen minutes, what's it to be? Here or downtown?"

There was a muttered reply from the back.

"What?" demanded the driver.

"Downtown, I wanna go home man," the answer came, louder.

"Cool," said the driver. "So do I."

When we arrived at the terminal, the man at the back swaggered down the gangway chanting "Gangsta, gangsta, gangsta. Anyone from Minneapolis on this bus can kiss my ass."

19

Canadian interlude

At the Greyhound terminal in Chicago were three young Amish lads in black hats and blue shirts, black waistcoats and dark blue trousers and boots. You could tell from the size of their forearms and the way they filled their shirts out that they were used to manual work. A family were to be on my bus, grandparents, mother and daughter.

We set off at midnight. I sat next to a boy of about eight. He was travelling with his mother and brother from California to Detroit to join his father who had been working there for a year. This was their third night on the road.

"Where are you from?" the mother asked.

"England," I replied.

"She was asking you which state you were from," said the boy.

"I'm from England," I repeated.

"I've never heard of a state called England before," he said.

"It's not a state, it's another country."

He didn't want the window seat, which was fine by me because it meant I could lean on the window, but he did end up sprawled over me for most of the night so I felt quite paternal by the morning, despite his poor grasp of geography.

In Detroit, the mother suddenly went mental: she just wanted to be off the bus and was stroppy with the kids and smacked her head on the luggage rack.

"Goddammit sonofabitch!" she exclaimed. I could almost see the elderly Amish wince.

We got a new driver, a Canadian. He was completely different from the security guard types expecting trouble like the American drivers were. I wanted to call him Uncle and give him a hug. The remaining passengers were also milder and once over the border everything felt more civilised.

I was met by Tammy who I had first met in Belgium. We headed north for the three hour trip to Algonquin. As we were filling up with petrol I was eating a banana and turned on the seat to talk to

Tammy who was filling the tank. I leaned on the partly open door which gave way and I slipped out, ending up in an ungraceful heap on the ground. She laughed. Another cause for amusement for her was in Huntsville where we looked for something to eat.

"Let's go to that first place we saw. It looked quite amusing," I said. She thought that sounded very English and used it on me mercilessly all weekend.

The forests opened up around the car and soon we were in Algonquin. We set up the tent at Mew Lake. In the night, wolves howled and crickets chirped loudly. The next day we hired a canoe. As we pushed away from the jetty, it started to rain heavily, easing a little once we were out in the middle of the lake. Paddling was hard work; a little like digging. Around the main body of the lake, there had been a few holiday homes, but further out was just nature with birch and fir coming down to the water's edge. We paddled slowly and quietly looking for wildlife, but saw only a loon and a woodpecker.

It started to rain again. Then it became heavier. And then it somehow became even heavier. There hardly seemed to be a spot on the lake not being hit by a raindrop. I started to laugh. I asked Tammy what the national anthem was, so we paddled down the lake, all but underwater, singing *Oh Canada!* at the tops of our voices.

We dried out around the fire that evening over dinner. The sky cleared and a few stars appeared between the trees. We went to sleep to the sound of Tammy's hiccups.

The next morning, we went for a bushwalk around Cache Lake. As we set off, we saw some B movie aliens out for a stroll. They were dressed in hooded white smocks with black netting screens hiding their faces. They may have looked ridiculous, but it kept the blackflies at bay.

Across the middle of the lake were the remains of a railway line which was built at the turn of the century. At its height, trains carrying logs, grain and troops would pass by every twenty minutes. The line had gone and nature was quickly taking over. We climbed a hill for a view. The lake lay below us, containing a small tree-covered island. The park rolled away all around us, trees as far as the eye could see. We carried on through the trees. We saw squirrels, furiously patting the ground as if they had lost a contact lens, toads, chipmunks, bluejays and woodpeckers.

We discovered an interesting ecological fact from an information board. Moose were decreasing in numbers in some places and this was because of the deer. The deer had a worm in their spine, which did not harm them, but came out in their faeces. Snails ingested the faeces and were then accidentally eaten by the moose that ate the leaves on which a snail may happen to be sitting. The worm attacked the nervous system of the moose, affecting their ability to move and they eventually starved. In Algonquin however, moose numbers were increasing. This was because the protected forest in the park was becoming more mature and providing less food for the deer, so their numbers had decreased, which meant less infected droppings. As if to demonstrate, on our way out of the park, we saw a moose. He stood posing for us on his surprisingly long legs, then calmly walked off into the trees.

The rooms in Tammy's flat were colour coded. The living room was yellow, the dining room red and the bedroom blue. However, both the bathroom and the kitchen were white, so I wondered if she ever got confused about which room she was in.

I went to the local park which was brimming with people and chipmunks, wandered around the nature trails, and noted the country's confused influence in selling both "fish and chips" and "fries". Then I joined Tammy and her friends Birj, Bob and Sandy at a pub for an epic contest. It was between Donovan Bailey, the Canadian Olympic 100m champion and Michael Johnson, the US Olympic 200m champion. It was a hugely hyped grudge match about which of the two was the world's fastest man. It comprised a race over 150m with a half a million dollar appearance fee and double that to win. As a 200m man, Johnson's strength was the curve, but Bailey took him on it and was into the straight. But then Johnson, already behind, pulled up with a muscle problem. The bar went berserk. Everyone was on their feet, cheering, doing high fives and whooping. Throughout the replay, a man at the next table kept saying *"Good*bye! *Good*bye!"

The girls were made to list their four guidelines for men. Bob laughed and said that these "guidelines" had previously been "rules" but had weakened over time. In no particular order, a man should be employable, have his own place, have his own wheels and of course must be attractive.

It was a hot night and I slept with the window open. I woke at about 3am to what sounded like two people talking at the foot of my bed. They were men's voices and I realised that they were standing out on the deck not far from my ground floor window. From the sound of things, they had been at a club.

"Steve saw you first and then I just had to come over and talk to you."

"You were just the best looking guy in the place."

And so they continued. This was fascinating, but I needed some sleep. And then they began to kiss. This went on for some time until where there had been words, there were moans and then strange slapping noises. This was none of my business. I didn't want to hear this. *They* didn't want me to hear this...or maybe they did. I quietly closed the window.

The next morning, my walk downtown, took me through Portuguese and Italian neighbourhoods. Men sat at tables talking and playing chequers. On the metro going back I saw a poster which read: "I hate you. Now feed me." At the bottom it said: "(See. Subway posters are so captivating, you'll even read one written by a cat.)"

That night, we watched the election coverage on television. There were interviews with voters which ran just like the ones had at home before I left: people not knowing what the main parties views were on major issues, the young feeling like they were being ignored. In the end, the liberals won again with a slim majority but a very uneven showing across the country compared to Quebec and the prairie provinces who voted completely differently.

I caught an evening bus to Buffalo and had my bananas confiscated at the border, but at least I had the friendly customs official. In front of me was a Korean girl with a less than perfect grasp of English who was confused by the other official's questions and especially his jokes. At one point, she thought he had finished asking her questions and she started to go.

"Oh you're going now?"

"Yes," she replied.

"I never said you could go now."

"Oh."

"It's okay. You can do."

I had a wait at Buffalo bus station. I spent some time with Annie. She was 29 and on her way to Martha's Vineyard. She spent a lot of time travelling in the developing world where it was cheaper. She moved from part time job to part time job and, not surprisingly, was quite self-assured. She somehow managed to combine this with a diet that had become completely organic over the years. She taught me backgammon which she said was a very good travelling game because it required a little brainwork, but not too much. She won all three games. But I am now able to alliterate that I was taught backgammon in a bus station in Buffalo.

After she had gone, I watched other people. There was the skinny, wizened guy with a big nose who was catching a bus to Rochester and kept trying to cadge cigarettes. In the end, he was asleep when the bus left. I tried to rouse him without success. Then there was the fat, waddling man who button-holed a young guy and preached to him non-stop for ages. And there was the burly cop with the shaven head who looked like he was ex-army. I wondered about the stories buried in these strangers.

The next morning saw us cruising through the Adirondacks, the forested hills of upstate New York, on my way to the south.

A brief spell in the South

Savannah was unlike anywhere else I had been in the US. It was what the Deep South was supposed to look like: stately wooden houses with grand porches, flowers everywhere, great oak trees with twisting branches dripping with Spanish moss. Down on the docks were the old traders' buildings, now converted into bars, restaurants and gift shops.

Outside one pub, a black guy sat on a bucket accosted me and played some rhythm and blues on his harmonica. He began sitting down, then, carried away, stood and writhed with the music, looking at me intently with bulging eyes as if to convince me he was really putting his heart into it.

I gave him a dollar and he asked for another because the egg sandwich he wanted was $2.50 and he already had 50 cents.

It rained all afternoon and evening. In the hostel I got talking to a Swiss language teacher about accents and as if to prove a point, a Northern Irishman came in. He was Mike and spoke quickly and indistinctly. He had spent five years in the army and then, when sick of being shot at, he had become a warder at the Maze prison and was riot trained. He said he had been walking through town and thought he had seen Clint Eastwood. Given Clint Eastwood was making *Midnight in the Garden of Good and Evil* in town at the time, he probably had. He had a huge sense of humour and whenever anything slightly odd happened, he would sing the first few notes of *Duelling Banjos* as a warning of Southern weirdness.

An Australian called Matt joined us. He had been a mate on a research ship near South Georgia. He was tanned, wiry, laughed like a drain, did not drink, practised meditation and loved surfing. He had heard that the place to be was the town's yacht club, so after dinner, he drove us there in his hire car. The joint was already jumping with people in their twenties and thirties. Most of the women had long permed hair and too much make up. It was fascinating to watch people.

We started talking to some women on the next table. One, a database designer, said this was as good as Savannah got. Most of the other bars were strip joints. She was bored with Savannah but showed little enthusiasm to move. Matt kept trying to inspire her with thoughts about life, but it was as if no one had asked her before and she did not seem to understand what he was saying or why it might matter.

We started dancing. A Michael Jackson song came on and, with no signal obvious to us, the whole dance floor started line dancing.

Over the top of the beat I could just hear Mike humming the opening notes of *Duelling Banjos*.

Running on empty

I felt ill in the evening, the urge to vomit came and subsided and I was tired. I was to wish I had been sick given I had a forty-five hour bus journey to Denver ahead of me.

My bus for Charlotte left just before midnight from a dark and dubious part of town. I had been given a lift there and my bowels had begun to signal to me that something was imminent while I was still in the car. The terminal was closed, so I could not go before boarding. Once, on the bus, the heating was oppressive and did not help me feel any more comfortable. I used its rest room almost immediately and several more times before we reached Charlotte. Whatever food poisoning I had, having failed to come out the way it went in, was making its way out the long way round.

Arriving in Charlotte, I settled down in the dingy terminal to wait for my early morning bus to Atlanta. Within minutes I felt the urge upon me again and I found the toilets. I went again and then again, having to lug my pack with me each time.

In Atlanta, I had about four hours to wait, but gave up on the idea of exploring the downtown of pointed skyscrapers in favour of staying near the toilets. By this time, there was not much substance to what was coming out of me. A television in the terminal played videos of *Sanford and Son*, the American version of *Steptoe and Son* and just as much of a classic. It was heart-warming to see a roomful of strangers laughing together. It was different to how it happens in a cinema. Perhaps because it was television, it felt like a great big living room and for a short while, we all became family.

Once on board the bus to Nashville, it was not long before I felt the now familiar desire to make the acquaintance of its restroom. My first visit was prolonged as I was racked with cramps. It was neither a comfortable nor a dignified situation. The bus shook from side to side, I would clutch at my belly as pain stabbed through my gut. The close heat of the airless cell was thick with the smell of the chemical toilet and inches away, on the other side of a thin plywood wall, were people with an intimate knowledge of how long I had been in there. Emerging at last, I noticed smirks from the trio on the back seat. On my second visit, I grinned at them and told them it would not be the last time.

Lavatory visits became less frequent when it occurred to me that the water I had been taking to prevent dehydration was simply going straight through me. By the third visit, to my relief, it had turned to explosive wind. I wondered how much of my tuba concerto could be heard by my friends on the back seat.

At Chattanooga, just over the Tennessee border from Georgia, we took on a local woman on her way to see her boyfriend in Minneapolis. She listened to the woman sitting next to her for some time who talked about the various forms of treatment that had been used on her following accidents ranging from slipping on hot wax to being in a car crash. I joined the conversation when they asked to see my pocket atlas so they could see where they were. The Chattanoogan said she really liked the English accent even though when she listens to two friends from Manchester talking at home, she couldn't understand what they were saying. Her own accent was such a slow drawl, any anecdotes became shaggy dog stories. Once, in a bad blizzard, she had followed a trucker up a big hill. He had bought her kids ice cream and she said "He was a super-sweetie", but in her own beautiful accent, it sounded like "soper sway-dee", which was much better.

The vegetation took on a tropical lushness under the grey sky and it became dense forest as we drove into the hills that break the weather that comes from the north. We changed buses in Nashville and two of my friends from the back seat sat nearer to me. He was a streetwise-looking guy from Miami in a goatee, shorts and baseball cap. She was pretty, slim and Latino with almond shaped eyes.

We crossed into Kentucky and I listened to Goatee talking to two other guys. One was a truck driver who also raced rigs. He and his friends were self-financing and considering they were up against business sponsored competition, he reckoned they didn't do too badly. The third was a lad who was about to leave the air force. Conversation moved onto military matters: the trucker had been in the army. It became a conversation about guns and tanks and ranges of weapons. Appropriately, we passed through Fort Campbell, home of the elite paratroop regiment the Screaming Eagles.

During the night we drove through Paducah, past the confluence of the Ohio with the Mississippi which we followed to St Louis with its distinctive arch. From there we headed west across Missouri via Columbia to Kansas City. I was surprised that Kansas City was in Missouri and not even on the Kansas River as the one in Kansas actually is. Kansas itself was pastureland as we entered it and went through Topeka, the state capital. Huge grain silos with their tall central tower looked like aircraft carriers dotting the landscape. Thanks to the movement of the bus, they appeared to sail through patches of woodland. Meanwhile, the driver slid back his window and spat.

We passed through St Mary's with its convent, large number of churches and shops selling Christian art. There were fewer trees and the land became low rolling hills. We paused at the small town of Russell which proudly proclaimed itself as "Bob Dole's home town!"

Undulating plains gave way to flat grasslands. To our right, the north, a storm was brewing and the sky was a deep, threatening bluegrey. There were flashes of forked lightning and a strong gust of wind rocked the bus. Then a strange rainbow grew at the base of storm. It began as a whitish glow on the horizon, at first only its edges rainbow coloured before it became a broad arc across the sky.

There were antelope on the plains when we crossed into Colorado and night had fallen by the time we pulled into Denver.

People of the Wild West

I managed to approach the Grand Canyon so that I only saw it at the last minute.

"Oh my God," I murmured as my jaw literally dropped. It was spectacular. It was beautiful. It was huge. There were precipitous drops into the main canyon which was filled with buttes and other rock formations. There were plateaux part way down and a million smaller gorges entering the sides. And on the other side of all this, the land was flat for miles. Flat, with this immense gaping chasm gashed into the ground.

At a viewpoint, a man was looking down on some sheer sided buttes deep in the canyon. He told his wife how it had occurred to him that no one had ever been on top of them.

His wife was so impressed with his thoughtfulness that she told their young daughters what their father had said.

"But you could get there by aeroplane or helicopter – "

"Or parachute – "

"Stop being silly!" said the father crossly as his great idea was ground into the dust by the innocence of imagination.

A group of Japanese girls asked me to take a group photograph of them. Then they wanted a group photograph with me in it. "You handsome," one explained. A few minutes later, I bumped into two of them. One rushed to have her photograph taken with me alone, putting her arm around me.

I met a man in Flagstaff who was a retired attorney from Pittsburgh. He had been stationed in Germany with the US Army. He said he had married the general's daughter. I asked how he had come to meet her.

"I was the general's bodyguard."

There was a Californian staying in my dorm room who seemed to be there long term. He had a quiff, wore cowboy boots and carried a Bible. When he came in late one night, he muttered over and over to himself. Then he climbed into bed, sighing deeply. "God I'm so sore," he said. Then he started to say his prayers.

I frequented the Hong Kong cafe. The cook was Chinese but his wife who served was a large Native American. She had a young, podgy face and a pronounced limp. Her voice was high pitched and, when thanked, she would respond with a simple "Mm*hm*!" On the last night, her son was helping her to clear the tables. He was very small and wore blue overalls, a black fireman's helmet and a red cloth backpack. He looked quiet and inscrutable and as he shuffled by, he would look at me with an expression which was a mixture of melancholy, self-consciousness and indifference.

The driver on the Greyhound bus across the Mojave Desert was a cheery soul. The toilet on board was out of paper. Just before we left Barstow, he stood up and brandished a toilet roll above his head.

"I've got some toilet paper! Don't take it home."

In Laughlin a Chinese man had looked at my camera and had been pleased that we both had an Olympus, but his was newer. Waiting at Los Angeles Greyhound station I struck up a conversation with him. Although we had little common language, I had an atlas and he had a dictionary. He was from a city near Beijing and was visiting friends for five weeks. He had just come from some kind of big party in Wichita, Kansas. He was a singer. Opera? I asked because he had done a few sweet notes as explanation. He pointed to a word in his dictionary which meant "in vogue, fashionable, popular". A Chinese pop singer! I asked if he was famous. He laughed. Only in his home city, he said.

At the farmers' market, an old guy was giving away samples of his popcorn.

"Oh no," said an elderly lady when offered some. "It gets stuck in my teeth."

"Well take 'em out and wash 'em, that's what I do," he replied.

Redwood country

As each passenger filed on to the bus, the driver took their ticket, tore out the stub and passed it back. I had a 60 day travel pass which looked very like a normal ticket but had to remain intact to be valid. As he looked at it, he looked as if he was going to automatically tear it out.

"Don't tear it!" I said, preferring to risk a mistake than the fuss of sorting out a replacement pass.

"I wasn't going to take it!" he snarled back, not hearing what I had said. I felt that any explanation would take too long and would not be accepted with any good grace. He had the look of a man who felt that getting out of bed on the wrong side each morning was in his job description and it was the only part of the job in which he found any satisfaction. I apologised and let it pass.

A family with a couple of children went and sat at the back. As soon as everyone was on the bus, the driver went straight to the back and read the kids a lecture on how to behave and what he would do if they didn't. From the way he said it, you would have thought that those kids had already been misbehaving for hours.

Leaving San Francisco behind, we stopped at Oakland over the Bay Bridge to take on some more passengers. A Greyhound employee helped a fragile old lady onto the bus and sat her down at the front.

"This lady's 94," she announced to the bus.

We all murmured our admiration and for a moment I thought there was going to be a round of applause. A woman in her forties boarded and sat across the aisle from me. The driver growled a few more times and gave us an excuse to talk about him. She had done the trip a number of times with him driving.

"He's a grouch," she said. "One of these days I'm going to complain about his attitude."

Later, when some seats further up emptied, she moved down the bus towards the front. She realised she had been issued with the wrong ticket. The driver made her buy another ticket which she

32

thought was too expensive. He said he would give her a receipt so that she could complain to the company but he had no choice but to go by the fares sheet. He was not impolite when he said any of this, but he was rather abrupt. Suddenly, the woman started to complain about his attitude. Not knowing that resentment had been building towards him for several journeys, the driver could only assume she was referring to this occasion.

"I'm going to complain," she said.

"You go ahead," he told her.

It calmed down then until the lunch stop. Neither the woman nor the driver was on board, but two other women started to discuss the matter. They too were familiar with the driver from previous trips and agreed the poor woman had been made to pay far too much. At this point, the 94 year old lady entered the fray and she wasn't having any of it.

"He wasn't rude, he was po-lite," she said. "I was brought up not to judge the colour of a person."

"So was I," said the other woman, shocked at being called a racist just because the man they were talking about happened to be black. She seemed to realise the potential of a rather nasty escalation of the discussion. At this point the driver came back on board and the old lady continued in his defence. This made everything a little embarrassing and the woman managed to quieten the old lady with a simple "Yeah, right."

The rest of the journey passed without incident as we wound through steep sided valleys of conifers and into Bigfoot country. Some road houses had hairy beasts planted outside.

At Arcata, Janice collected me in her new white pickup. She was the friend of a friend who had joined us for our annual cricket tour in Scotland the previous year. She was in her late fifties and had a large wooden house outside town on the edge of woodland. Her husband had died four years before and, living alone, she had come to occupy only a small part of the house. The rest could easily house guests or be used when her son came up from Los Angeles with a band to use the recording studio in the workshop beyond the house.

The next morning we went to the local sewage farm. It was something of an ecological triumph. An area of marsh was formed on the site of the town dump. The solids having been removed, the sewage was left in ponds where the natural vegetation filtered the waste. It also provided a recreational area of paths and excellent bird-watching opportunities.

We joined a small group which went out each Saturday morning. There were seven or eight in the group, and the leader, resplendent in floppy hat and fluffy white beard, told us that this was a bad time because it was between migrations. But we saw willets and other waders, great herons and snow herons and a night heron absolutely intent in its staring into the water.

The birdwatchers were at least as amusing as the birds. In their hats and beards and binoculars, they looked as if they had gone to a fancy dress party as birdwatchers. And that was just the women. Later, we saw an osprey and some turkey vultures. I gained a little credibility by having been within a few feet of a puffin.

Leaving the walk, we drove back into Arcata. The town, built around a green, called the Place, seemed to still live in the sixties and seventies and even the students at Humboldt University were doing their best to be the flower children for the nineties. It looked like a permanent festival.

A farmers' market was being held and we bought peas in their pods, carrots, tomatoes, peaches and delicious sweet strawberries, then sat on a bench to eat them and listen to the band in the middle of the green who were playing jolly folk music from central Europe. Later, we had lunch back at the house: crusty bread, topped with delicious tomatoes, sliced cheese and fresh basil.

We drove north up the coast to the fishing village of Trinidad. It swept down from the cliffs to a little harbour, the water dotted with white boats. Anglers were gutting their catch on the pier and a couple of seals were swimming languidly nearby. On a rock near the pier, a gull was sheltering her two chicks under her wing while her mate shouted threats to other gulls which landed on their rock.

At Patrick's Point State Park we gazed out at the calm, blue sea from one of the many rocky headlands on this coastline. A couple of brown pelicans flew below us, low over the water to the lagoon a few miles away up the coast.

The next day, Janice told me about her pets. The cats were Borden and Maruchek. Borden was white and considered herself to be elegant. She liked the sound of my tin whistle and would follow me when I played it. Maruchek, or Maru for short, had been named by a Polish guest of Janice's. He was affectionate and had been rescued from trick-or-treaters one Hallowe'en by Janice's daughter. Kailai was a big, fluffy, pale brown dog. He was three-quarters wolf and was named after a peninsula in Alaska. Maru and Borden were frightened of him, but he was actually a big softy. He was not allowed in the house, although the cats were.

Once, Janice had gone on holiday and a friend had come to look after the animals. One day, a young cat had appeared. He had been keen to be let into the house, but the house-sitter would not let him in. She did give him some food however and so he kept coming back. When Janice came home, she decided to keep feeding this new cat, but still would not let him into the house because she did not want to upset Borden and Maruchek. The new cat came to be called Agrippa. This is how it happened.

He made friends with Kailai who was rather surprised but happy to have a friend around the place because the other two still kept clear of him. Sometimes, Kailai and Agrippa could be seen curled up asleep together. Janice saw that the two had made friends and wondered that if he could worm his way into the affections of Kailai, maybe the two other cats would also accept him. So she started to let him into the house. Agrippa took it all in his stride and acted as if it was nothing unusual, but the other two would hiss at him.

Soon after Agrippa was allowed in, Maru and Borden hatched a plan. They would ambush him and beat him up, so they took up positions, one on either side of a door that he would have to walk through. Agrippa came along, walking without a care in the world, but as he approached the door, Janice saw that despite sensing something was wrong, he carried on going, as cool as you please. As he walked through the door, he looked neither left nor right. Borden and Maru watched him walk by and neither moved. They had had their chance, but failed to take it. Their hesitation had shown their fear and Agrippa knew there would be no going back now.

He had been still a young cat at the time and as the months went by, he grew large and solid, larger than either of the other two. So now Agrippa thinks he is in charge and that is why he is called Agrippa, after the Roman Emperor. He walked around the house as if he owned it and sadly is not above a little bullying of the other two, but he and Kailai stayed friends.

We drove north to redwood country. Swifts were nesting in the beams of the State Parks information office, little heads squawking from inside bird-cement homes stuck above our heads. We decided on a circular walk through Fern Canyon where some of the film *Jurassic Park* had been made.

The trees were well enough spaced to leave room for plenty of thick undergrowth. Janice showed me some sorrel. Its leaves were green on top and a reddish purple underneath. It was edible and tasted sharp, like an apple. Trees were coated with moss like velvet and the forest floor was dry through lack of rain. Winters used to be a constant drizzle in which the redwoods thrived. But the climate has changed so that when it rained, it poured which was not good for the shallow rooting trees.

The trail wound up a few hundred feet through the trees and skirted a slope. The wind was towards us and as we rounded a bend, we startled a small doe and her fawn. They skittered off around the next bend. The wind was still in our favour, so we crept up on them. As I peered around the next bend, they were already standing, looking. I froze. The doe stared at me, her eyes big and dark in her small pointed face, her large ears angled to catch the smallest sound. I stayed still and she even took a step closer to me. Then she lost interest and started to look around for food. I moved very slowly, being careful not to make any sound, one step, two steps closer. She looked up sharply. I stopped. There was nothing for her to notice, so she went back to her grazing again. I edged forward a few more steps and once more she turned and looked. "I could have sworn that tree was further away a minute ago," she seemed to be thinking, then shook her head in reproach at the foolishness of her idea and went back to looking for interesting leaves to nibble. We continued this game of statues for about twenty minutes, me edging closer and closer to her until I was only about fifteen feet away, crouched on the ground. Eventually she ran off into the trees to join her offspring, who had already realised it was all strange and run away.

We realised that if we could surprise an animal designed to notice the approach of predators, we could also surprise a bear or a cougar. We decided to make much more noise as we walked.

The trail was longer than we had been expecting and sign-posting was poor. I had a compass which set us at ease as we realised we were still going in the right direction. We started to descend and head west, to the coast where the trail ran back south along the edge of the forest and the base of a bluff. It started to rain.

Janice had said it would not rain. Trusting the local knowledge, for the first time ever I had taken my waterproof out of my pack and Janice did not have hers with her either. The rain fell steadily. It looked like it would keep up for the rest of the day. "It never rains in California, the girls don't they warn ya. It pours, man it pours." as the song goes.

We were walking at the foot of the bluff on the edge of a narrow strip of forest that climbed up the steep slope below the cliff face. On our right was the sea and between the two, a stretch of grassland about a hundred yards wide. We had been walking for some time when up ahead in the mist of the falling rain, we saw a herd of elk. They were spread across the width of the flat land. Signs around the park warned "Danger - Wild Elk". They were large animals, nearly the size of a horse. In this herd, not only were there the naturally protective mothers with young, but also some frisky young bucks scuffling with each other. We decided we should not attempt to walk through the middle of them, but the only way around was through the dense bush on the left.

This out-flanking manoeuvre involved scrambling through the rain-soaked vegetation and we were soon drenched. When we had rounded the herd, we made our way back out of the bush. A lone elk stood right in front of us, watching me, quietly chewing. "Hello," I said. It did not reply. Looking back, the rest of the herd carried on, oblivious.

Driving out of the forest, we had to stop for a huge stag to cross the road imperiously in front of us. A little further down were more behind some rocks on the side of the road. Most of the animal was invisible so they looked like people hiding behind the rocks wearing false antlers.

Grandad's farm

It was a clear, sunny day as I set off from Taupo in New Zealand's central North Island to hitch to Turangi which I thought was the closest settlement to the volcanoes. My research was not very good.

I had been walking for about an hour and was just becoming disconsolate when a van pulled up driven by a couple I recognised from the backpackers'. They were going to the mountain, was that any use to me? No, I'm going to Turangi, I answered. They wished me good luck and drove off. As I watched them pulling away I wondered what I had been thinking. They were going to the volcanoes. They were ideal. I would have had transport the whole way, rather than wondering what to do next when I got to Turangi.

I kicked myself, but let it go. I decided this was part of the right attitude to travel. I felt that people who plan in detail are not travelling in the right way; they merely see obstacles to their plans. The better way of looking at things was not to see problems, but to really see opportunities. There must have been a Reason for this and all I needed to do was to go with the moment and all would be revealed.

It took about two minutes for The Reason to show up. He was called George, but he said everyone knew him as Grandad. He had just dropped his wife off at Auckland Airport where she was flying back to England to visit her mother.

The son of a Northampton chicken farmer, he had arrived in New Zealand 35 years before when he was 19. He had hitched around the country, picking up work until he found himself working for the electricity company on pylons. It paid well and he had nothing to spend it on, so he saved. An old school friend of his, who he had really fancied, was visiting her uncle on a sheep farm. She invited him to visit. She still did not fancy him, but he found he had fallen in love with the farm and stayed on to work as a shepherd. He went back to England for a visit when he was 22 and realised he no longer wanted to live there. Instead, he met Diane, married her and returned to New Zealand where he bought his own

38

farm. He later sold that and bought another and sold that and bought another, moving around the country and increasing the size of the farm each time. When I met him, his daughter and three sons each had farms of their own and he was extremely happy. He had just collected three English lads and dropped them off to work on some of their farms, something he does each year.

"Why are you going to Turangi?" he asked.

"I don't know," I replied. "I'm trying to get a bit closer to the volcanoes."

"You could come and help me on the farm," he said. "It's beautiful around Taihape."

I was unsure how serious he was. We arrived in Turangi. It looked like I had made a mistake wanting to go there as the mountains were nowhere in sight.

"It's beautiful around where I live," he said again. "Green hills, the river. Beautiful."

"I'm beginning to lose interest in Turangi," I admitted.

"So come with me," he said.

We drove past the snow-covered volcanoes on the way, the perfect cone of Ngarahoe looking like a pile of sugar. We stopped first at the old farm where he still lived, then went on to the one he had just bought. The new farm had left him out of pocket by $25,000. Both were in beautiful settings. The old farm was on the flat with hills on either side. A field away, the valley dropped away to steep clay cliffs and the Rangitikei River meandering below. I preferred the view from the new place however. It looked down the valley between the hills and over a line of trees to the Ruahine ranges beyond, topped with snow in an even line below the ridge.

Then we drove south to Feilding to help Gran, George's brother's mother-in-law. She was moving up to the north east of the country, but when we arrived, she was out, and looking through the windows, nothing seemed to have been packed. We drove back into town and went into the Lotto shop. George perused the different scratch card games.

"How much money do I need? Twenty-five grand wasn't it?"

So he bought a game card for that amount. He didn't win, but I admired his pragmatism. We were a bit peckish, so went to a cake shop run by a small Chinese man. George inspected the produce.

"What's that? Oh. And what's that? How much is that then?"

We decided on apple pies. They were $1.85 each.

"Two dollars for those two."

"Two dollars? No, they are $1.85 each," he responded.

"No. Two dollars," insisted George.

"Three," said the Chinese, catching on.

"No. Two," said George.

"Go on," I said, "He's haggling now. Play the game."

And so we agreed on three dollars.

We tried Gran's place again, but there was still no sign of her. Maybe she was doing the rounds of the old people's homes, saying goodbye to her friends, thought George. But we would need to know where they were.

"We'll ask in the Lotto shop," said George.

"They won't know in there," I said. But they did. There were seven in town and they even knew what streets they were all on and off we went in search of them. When we found them, we cruised past slowly, looking for the car. Some of them were harder to find. We had to ask a few more people where the streets were.

"You know what's going to happen," I said. "All the rest homes are going to get turned over in the next few days and we're going to be prime suspects."

We tried the house again. We asked the neighbours, then we went to the pub, drank a couple of pints of Guinness and tried the house one last time. There was still no sign of Gran so we drove back to the farm.

We had a big roast dinner with some of the neighbours. Conversation roamed around a variety of topics. They talked about Maori land claims and how the government brings up claims that no one had considered contesting. They talked about how the three households had once shared a single telephone line and how each had had their own ring. George had made free calls to the UK for years by giving a false number before they stopped him. He justified it by saying that they had promised to give them their own lines in 1993 but it took four years to happen.

We moved onto the referendum on the new superannuation and discussion became quite heated. And then, suitably warmed up, it was time for the All Blacks – Wallabies rugby union test match. With my Australian heritage, I had to support Australia but, to everyone else's delight and my embarrassment, they were trounced.

I was up before George the next morning, which was most unfarmerly of him. He surprised me by preparing a healthy breakfast of kiwi fruit, muesli and yoghurt and then we drove off to the new farm where we met up with Jan and Harry. Jan, a thorough country girl, worked for George occasionally and Harry, her partner, was a local teacher and hailed from Sunderland. We were herding heifers onto a couple of cattle trucks which would take them to George's daughter's farm. They were all first time mothers and some had already calved. One calf was stickily brand new and another heifer gave birth while we were moving them. In the end, we rounded up the heifers and went back for any stray calves. Some of these were old enough to be frisky and difficult and it took some patient work to tackle them. Kneeling on the neck of one calf as we carried it on a trailer up to the road, I had an interesting combination of shit, milk, snot, mud and other goop over me. I was glad George had let me borrow some clothes.

I have usually been a little timid around cattle, but decided I had to be brave around these farm folk, so went to it with enthusiasm, shoving them (the cattle, not the farm folk) and shouting at them like I had been a farmer for years. I shouted at the dogs too. "Fay! Geddoutovit!" for example was one I learned from George, and it worked too. Fay was a good cattle dog, but did sometimes wind up some of the more rebellious cattle. Rose on the other hand was useless but enthusiastic. She was old, grey-nosed and hang-teated. She wanted to be helpful but had lost all method or discipline and simply ran around barking excitedly and worrying the cattle. George caught her and chained her up to a fence where she looked on sadly. Waggles was the third in the doggy trio. He was a fox terrier and although really a house dog, he liked to pretend he was a cattle dog, at least from a safe distance. He loved to be petted or to sit with George on his quad bike as he zoomed around the fields.

Next we turned our attention to the sheep. They were grazing around the river bottom and they needed to be brought up the steep bank to another paddock at the top which would be a much better place for them to lamb. Harry and I herded them up the hill and afterwards, back in the farm house, Jan whipped up some scones and they told me I was a natural stockman, knowing how much of a distance to keep from the animals. I have to admit I was dead chuffed.

In the afternoon, George and I turned to his three barrels of home brew which needed bottling. We set up a production line where we filled the bottles, added a teaspoon of sugar then capped them. We did 198 pints. His garage was full of crates of beer. He regularly brewed enough to keep himself and all his kids fully stocked. We completed the day's work by cross-checking his tax returns, then rewarded ourselves with some beer. And then one or two more, which we accompanied with a rather tasty beef stew I concocted from things I found in the cupboard.

I was up first again the next morning. George said it was because Diane was not there to kick him out of bed. The day's first job was to move a mob of cattle up through a couple of paddocks to some pens where George could delouse them. I took them up some of the way, then Fay came to help. Rose had to be chained up again. It was a good job that they were dehorned because Fay had a habit of picking fights.

From one pen, the mob of sixty-four was moved into a fence corridor in groups where George would spray delouser along their backs, then I would let them into another pen which gradually filled up with the mob. At one point, I let through a couple which had not been de-loused yet because I thought they had been done. George had to push through the mob to get to them, which he was unhappy about. I felt like I had let everyone down and was no longer a natural stockman. Afterwards, we let them back into their old paddock and moved the electric fence line along a few metres to give them some kale and swede to eat.

George and I went to put out some extra feed. Hay bales were piled three high on a trailer. I had to cut the strings on top of the bales then pull the string off. As George drove the tractor up and down the paddock, I pushed sections of bales out onto the grass.

Jan meanwhile had spotted a problem with a couple of ewes who both had prolapsed vaginas. We caught the first one between us. Her vagina was brown and swollen and apparently there was no hope for her. Trapping her between his legs and twisting her head around, George stood over her, sharpening his knife. I was interested to see how I reacted to what was going to come next. As an eater of meat, I had never seen an animal killed.

He slit her throat, blood spurted onto the grass and she lay kicking for a while. I was relieved to see that I took it in a way that meant I did not have to give up eating meat. Then we went looking for the other. Hers was not as bad and George pushed it back inside. But there was puss, so she went too after all. We threw them onto the back of the cart, the legs of the second still in spasm. We took them to an offal pit which contained a pile of old timber and the stretched skin carcasses of two cows. The sheep's heads were lolling from red, ragged necks. George slit each sheep up the belly and their innards spilled out. The second had a perfect lamb inside which could have been saved with a caesarean and nursing. It would have been due in about three weeks. The other's lamb was long dead, bloated and brown. All ended up kicked into the pit. The carcasses were bent over the trailer bar to break their backs then loaded onto the back of the trailer. We sat on the back with the two headless bodies bobbing about from the bumpy track.

"That one's looking at you," I said to Jan.

"Thanks," she said.

They were hung on a fence where they would catch a frost and he would not forget them. They would become dog food.

We had to drive back over an electric fence. The trick was to kick your leg up onto the wire then tread it down with a gumboot. The wire slipped under my boot and up my leg towards my groin. George and Jan laughed as I leapt off, fortunately missing the electric pulse. George continued to wind me up as he revved the tractor's engine and waited for me to open a gate.

"You country folks, always in such a hurry," I tutted. "You ought to learn from this city boy to slow down and take it easy."

Before I left, Jan drove me up to the highest point on the old farm on the quad bike, Fay and Waggles running along behind. We could see down the valley towards the line of snowy hills and up the other way was Ruapehu, the volcano which is the North Island's highest mountain, still just lit by the sun. All around, steep hills rose and fell.

George was right: it was a beautiful place.

A night at the Hilton

We watched the sun set over the Tasman Sea. A streamer of cloud stretched diagonally to the horizon, ending at the sun. It looked like a comet tearing across the evening sky.

It was dark by the time we drove into the small town of Blackball and pulled up outside the 'formerly the Blackball Hilton', peering into the poorly lit street to read the name. It was an ancient, shabby wooden structure with a balcony around the first floor. They had had to add the 'formerly' after a lawsuit with the Hilton hotel chain.

The entrance hall was freezing. A couple of darkened rooms led off and a worn red carpet went up the staircase. It was much warmer in the bar where a few people were sitting and a fire was heating the room. The fireplace was the only brick part of the building. Smoking was banned for fear of burning the place to the ground. Atmosphere peeled off the walls, along with some of the wallpaper.

Marg, Nipper and I were shown to a dormitory upstairs which was also freezing. An electric radiator sat near the door in a vain attempt at heat creation. It was hot to the touch, but the heat itself seemed to be huddling next to the radiator for warmth. We dumped our bags and returned downstairs where it was filling up.

A group of touring actors were putting on a play. They were unemployed and had decided to write and perform a play about unemployment. At least one was a political activist who had found herself in prison for her pains. Blackball was an appropriate venue: it had been the site of coal and gold mines and the New Zealand union movement had begun there. But the coal and gold was gone and there was only a little fishing left on the coast nearby.

I was just buying the first jug of Monteiths when the play started. What the actors lacked in professionalism they more than made up for in enthusiasm. They talked about the closure of rural post offices, privatisation, lack of public transport, big business, the growing importance of money over people. For a moment, I

44

thought I was at home. Afterwards they invited comments from the audience.

By the time the play was over, the pub was packed. The kitchen started to serve meals. We sat with a couple from nearby Greymouth. He was a farmer, she a teacher. Every year they hosted an epic party, they told us. It was a themed fancy dress to which the entire neighbourhood would come and get hideously drunk. The next morning, people would be found everywhere; inside food troughs or pieces of farm machinery.

Then the band came on, a couple from Nelson calling themselves Cutty Wren. Kate and Clayton were the Bonnie and Clyde of folk music. Kate was blonde and looked like she had done a thing or two in her time as did Clayton, but in a goofy kind of way. He was scrawny with a growth on his chin that was too short for a beard and too long for stubble and had a mouthful of teeth like a medieval graveyard. I soon discovered that, like me, they had been brought up on the songs of the Clancy Brothers and the Corries.

Their performance was relaxed. They were local favourites and Blackball was their favourite venue. A character in the audience with a beard, a beret and a large stick with bells on heckled the singers, claiming, amongst other things, to have had sex with Clayton.

"You were crap," Clayton shouted back.

They had a couple of Celtic drums or bodhrans, which they weren't always able to play because Clayton had his guitar and Kate would play her whistle. Marg and Nipper kept hassling me to offer my services, but I wouldn't go. Eventually, when they had finished their first set I went and had a brief, shy chat to Kate. When they started again, she came over with a bodhran and invited me to join them.

The pub was rocking. Spoons were issued from the kitchen to the entire pub so that everyone could join in and those who could fit in the space in front of the fireplace danced wild and diabolic jigs. The man with the beret banged his stick on the ground in time with the music.

The Monteiths was going down a treat. At some point, it turned midnight. At another point Kate announced that they were now playing on their own time, but they were having too much fun to stop. A string broke on the guitar. They rolled out an easy stream of gags until Clayton had fitted a new one.

Towards the end, I sang a few songs, as did a couple of others. To my surprise, people came out of the audience and asked me how to play the bodhran. Marg and Nipper were highly amused at my new Diva status. One of my disciples was the driver of the steam train at the nearby Shantytown outdoor museum. He said to come over and ask for him the next day.

The bar closed sometime in the small hours. We talked to Ken, a Samoan who had been in the play. I made him sing some Samoan songs for us. They were beautiful. Kate and I returned the favour by singing *Arthur McBride* which, if not beautiful, was at least lively.

Those of us remaining were herded out of the main pub into a hexagonal annex so the owners could go to bed without interrupting the party. Pints and a couple of guitars were taken with us. An odd young bloke strummed one of the guitars and sang a strange and intense song which made me glad I wasn't alone with him. An earnest young woman talked to me about how interested I would think tourists would be in booklets of vouchers giving them deals on local attractions. I found someone else to talk to who was prepared to be more frivolous.

On the other side of the room, Nipper was being talked to by a tall man called Blondie. He was bald on top, but grew it long at the sides. She was looking a little uncomfortable, so on my way out to relieve myself, I leaned into her ear and asked quietly if she was okay or did she need rescuing. She said she was okay, but apparently it wasn't much of a whisper because Blondie heard, as did Marg on the other side of the room. He became concerned that she thought he was harassing her and went home. The white knight strikes again.

Outside it was a clear and frosty night. Clayton joined me in watering the garden. I looked at the stars. Orion was standing on his head. He had obviously had a few too many as well.

The actors were in the same dorm as we were and many were already asleep by the time we stumbled in, a few hours before daylight. We crept around in the dark. Ken appeared, put the light on, then climbed into bed.

"Someone switch off the bloody light!" he suggested.

A few hours later, the troupe were up and off south. Downstairs I made porridge and talked to the hotel owners. Apparently it had been a particularly good evening, even by their standards. Outside we could see distant snow-capped mountains. We would be

46

amongst them by evening. Kate and Clayton came out to see us off and we hung around chatting, not wanting to end our Blackball experience so soon.

A few days later we met two blokes who had arrived in Blackball the evening of the day we had left. The pub had been quiet for a Saturday night and the landlady had explained to them that the Friday had been a big night. The town had obviously still been nursing its hangover.

Okarito smoke out

It was dark when we turned off the road to little Okarito on the coast. We were alone in the hostel, an old converted schoolhouse. It was cold and, in a reversal of gender stereotyping, Marg set about trying to get a fire lit while I cooked dinner with the not very warm electric bar heater to keep me company. Marg wasn't having much luck because the wood was damp and soon the room was full of suffocating smoke. I opened the front and back doors to clear it and eventually it drifted out, replaced by the freezing night air so that we were worse off than we had been when we'd started.

We warmed up a little with our pasta sauce, but then Marg eyed the fire with renewed enthusiasm. I watched with growing sadness as once more, smoke filled the room and had to be cleared at the expense of the paltry heat from the fire and cooker which had built up and which followed the banished smoke into the Antarctic night.

The room was just beginning to warm vaguely for a third time when my heart sank as, match in hand, Marg made for the fireplace again. The wood was no drier than it had been on the previous two occasions, so naturally, we were once more enveloped in a choking fog. It seemed I had a choice between choking or freezing to death. In the end, the warmest place was our bunks, where we chatted.

"What's the stupidest thing you've ever done?" asked Marg, which in the light of the evening's events was an interesting question.

"Umm…" I said.

Marg claimed she waited three hours for my answer, not realising I had gone to sleep within seconds of starting to think about it. She was unable to go to sleep, later blaming it on me as she waited for my answer. So at 3am she went outside for a walk under the star-filled sky.

Extreme sports

We were ready for anything. We had been up into the mountains and seen the glaciers change colour from bluewhite to gold in the evening sun. We had seen the pink snowglow on the peaks after sunset. The night had been clear and cold and now the new day was greeting us with seemingly whiter snow, higher mountains and bluer sky than ever before.

We had given ourselves the whole day to make the short journey over the Haast Pass to Wanaka. Marg said she would drive and was feeling happy and raring to go. What beautiful sights and adventures would New Zealand show us today?

At a one lane bridge we pulled up to admire the view. A couple of blokes had parked their Landcruiser near it and were taking photographs. As I walked by them to take my own, I muttered "Bloody tourists stopping in the middle of bridges." They grinned. Behind me, I heard Marg quipping that we would be sure to bump into them a few more times that day as she found out that they were also heading for Wanaka. Sure enough, a mile down the road, we both pulled into another parking space from which Mounts Cook and Tasman could be seen, looming above the forest. We introduced ourselves. They were John from Christchurch and jolly Andy, his English cousin over for a holiday. Andy was happily snapping photographs and we made some rude banter about cameras and telephoto lenses.

"See you in a hundred metres!" they said and pulled off.

John was ahead and driving faster than we were, but we passed them taking photos in Bruce Bay looking at the Tasman sea. We honked our horn as we sped by. We opted to stop a little further on at tranquil Lake Paringa. Its still water was a calm contrast to the spectacular mountain view just over the treetops. Andy and John drove by and beeped at us. Black swans glided silently over the dazzling water.

We were just preparing to drive off again when the boys drove back the way they had just come, giving us another beep and a wave as they did so. Margaret, meanwhile, was really enjoying her driving. She was very happy.

"Do you feel safe with my driving?" she asked.

"Yes," I replied.

"We'll soon see about that," she said and suddenly we were all over the road like a slalom. Then we lost it, skidding and starting to slide sideways. Trees and ditch were coming unstoppably nearer. And I was angry. She'd been mucking around and now we were going to damage the car. No, it was worse than that, I decided as the branches and the edge of the road closed on us with a helpless inevitability. We were going to go into that ditch and we probably wouldn't even be able to reverse out because it looked both steep and deep.

We came to a rest, nose down and with my door against a tree. I turned angrily to Marg. I have no idea if I was going to say something, but she saw the look on my face and read it so clearly she reckoned I could have bottled that look and sold it. Immediately and in a frantic tremble she said "It wasn't me!" Later inspection of the road showed loose gravel and the area was shaded too, so there was probably black ice. Lack of rubber on the road showed that she had correctly kept her foot off the brake and the fact that the car was still facing roughly forwards was evidence of how she had steered into the skid.

Despite all that cool thinking, she was now about to go to pieces. We wondered afterwards why we reacted so differently. She was the one who had felt the control disappear. I was probably too busy being furious to be scared, but I also remember realising as we skidded that we would be unhurt. The tree must have absorbed some of the impact.

Seeing how shaken she was, I became completely calm. I couldn't get out of my door because of the tree right outside, so I gently told her it was okay and to get out of the car.

"But what are we going to do?" she said sounding lost.

"I don't know," I said. "We'll figure that out when we've got out." I persuaded her out and we climbed up the ditch. "The boys'll be along in a minute," I said.

A few minutes later, a van drove by. I flagged it down. The driver was a chopper pilot and flew deer out of the mountains that hunters had shot. We took our packs from the car and put them into the back of his, then he drove us up the road to the Wilderness

Lodge Motel. He was a local from Haast, the next town, and he called up Eammond, the local mechanic. I thanked him for his help and he drove off.

The motel manager too was kind. He let us into the lounge and plied us with coffee and biscuits. I made sure Marg got some sugar into her. She was thinking too much. I was still surprisingly calm and telling her not to worry or blame herself. I think my signs of shock were that I had to urinate copiously several times over the next couple of hours, but that could also have been the coffee.

The manager came back in.

"You've got some visitors," he said.

And right behind him were John and Andy. Seeing their concerned faces was like meeting two old friends again. They had seen the car and several other cars had stopped to check as well. Seeing we were safe, the inevitable jokes appeared. It turned out that Andy had put his camera down on the roof of the car and then they had driven off. We had seen them going by us twice because they had gone back to try to find it but never did. If Andy had not left his camera there they would have been ahead of us when we hit the ditch and they would have been wondering why we never met up with them in the pub that night.

Eammond arrived and we drove back to the car. He was a short, broad man with a red, practical face. He wasn't chatty, but he wasn't unfriendly either. He was simply going to do his job and get us out of the fix as well as he could without making any judgements. He drove beyond the bend and put an Accident sign out to warn coming traffic so we didn't become the start of a pile-up. The motel manager had told us there had been six other crashes there in the previous six weeks. It was a relief not to be unique. Marg took the second sign in the other direction. She was still rather vacant, still staring at the car and thinking about what could have happened.

Eammond had a Rangerover and a trailer. He tied the car to the trailer and pulled it out of the ditch. It came out easily and we inspected it. Stuck in gear, a few dents underneath where we had hit lumps of concrete coping. Then we drove on to Haast. We were all quiet at first, but when he found out what I did for a living, we had a chat about the new computer system he ran his garage on.

We drove by the boys on our way and they pulled in behind us at the garage and offered any help they could. We didn't think there was much they could do at that stage. We would either have to stay the night in Haast, or if the car was okay, we would get to Wanaka and see them for a well-earned beer. They were just about to leave when Eammond emerged from the workshop, wiping his hands.

"You might need those jokers," he said.

He had the car up on ramps. The main problem was where the coping had hit underneath. It had bent part of the chassis, including part of the gear mechanism. He could fix it, but he would need a couple of days and the permission of the hire company. They weren't much help. Jamie, the friendly lad we had dealt with was unable to do anything until his boss came back from holiday, so we were going to have to sort ourselves out. We squeezed into the back of the Landcruiser with all our gear and continued over the Haast.

On the eastern side the scenery changed. From the lush, dense rainforest crowded against steep mountain walls, the land was quite suddenly much drier with less vegetation. The valley widened out and there was Lake Hawea. The mountains no longer loomed over, but stood back to be admired as part of a panorama.

As we drove into Wanaka, John said we may as well stay at their place, a holiday home they had in the town.

"We'll do dinner," we said. We had a yearning for red meat after the day's events and we cooked up prime beef with mushrooms and red wine and washed it down with beer and more wine and sat around until late, telling jokes and stories and marvelling how days can turn out.

The world according to Mark

At the backpackers' in Te Anau, I got talking to Mark. He told stories in a monologue so that you could only respond with "well I never" or "really, that's terrible!" He had incontrovertible opinions and thought Australia was going downhill because the Aborigines were getting too much money and owned everything.

He was tall and wiry with a tangle of hair and a face that had seen many suns. Born in London, he had left for Australia when he was six and had been there for twenty-eight years, living all over and working variously as a plasterer, tree feller and who knows what else.

He had had a rough life. For example, while living in Darwin, he had broken his leg in two places and the "fucking cunt of a doctor", who spent all his time at the private hospital anyway, would not put any pins in it because they cost too much. His plaster was only supposed to be replaced when it wore out, which was not a pleasant thought when you lived somewhere as sweaty as Darwin, so he would rub it against a concrete step so he could get a new one every six weeks. His doctor advised him to pour meths down it to ease the itching, which would then evaporate immediately. His wife bought white spirit by mistake which burned his leg into a long blister. They had to remove the plaster to sort it out and he twisted it in the night, moving the bones and causing them to not quite meet. They offered to re-break it, but he thought "fuck that". He still limps sometimes, he said.

Another time, while working on a cattle station in the Northern Territory, a big wooden beam hit him in the jaw, very nearly killing him. The station nurse stitched him up because they refused to chopper him into town. She had never done it before and not only had he felt the anaesthetic injection scraping his jaw bone, but he had felt the last five of the eight stitches she gave him, which had not been enough for the cut he had and all of which had fallen out four days later.

His last few months had been interesting too. His girlfriend's young daughter set fire to some clothes in their wardrobe with a cigarette lighter she was playing with. When he tried to separate the burning clothes from the others, he had caused a draft and the whole lot caught fire. They had lost them all and had not been insured. Then his girlfriend had run off with a younger bloke, taking the car which was his but in her name and only had $200 left to pay. He tracked her from Canberra to Newcastle where she was surprised to see him. I was unsure quite what had happened next, but he said that one reason he came away was to avoid doing something he might regret. He had brought $500 to bring away with him and lost it somewhere en route. He said he had been living off a $100 bill which he had brought over as a present for his son in Christchurch. By this time I was losing track of the different threads of the story which were opening up.

He had done some good road trips in his time, such as when he and a mate had taken two weeks to get from Darwin to Melbourne for a wedding, stopping at every pub on the way. When he was 16, he had been hitching from Adelaide to Townsville for Christmas with his family. He had got a lift with a student and on the way they had helped a woman with a puncture change a wheel. She was so grateful she told them to stop at her pub in Cloncurry where they had ended up being given free beer all night. One bloke offered him a day's work, but he turned it down. When he woke up, he was in the back of a ute being taken out to the cattle station. He herded on a motorbike for the morning, spotted cattle in a chopper for the afternoon and was driven back to town with $180 in his pocket: a week's wages.

When building at Uluru, he and his mates had a good relationship with the local policeman, so they were surprised when, after a night on the turps, he appeared behind their car, flashing his lights. They pulled over and waited. Eventually one of them got out of their car to see what the policeman wanted. The policeman said he was "completely fucking pissed and could they drive him home?" So they drove him to the station and put him to bed in one of the cells with the door unlocked.

Another story was about a mate they had discovered outside a hotel wearing only his sandals. He had gone to bed in what he had thought was his room. Later a woman had come in and snuggled up with him, realised it was not who she thought it was and had started screaming. He had got up, put on his sandals and left.

Mark stayed up because someone had been stealing from the kitchen.

"I only go to bed for two reasons and that's to fuck and to sleep and I wasn't going to do either of them."

He seemed like the kind of bloke who would give you his last dollar and indeed he happily let Marg borrow his only jacket when we climbed Mount Luxmore the next day.

Down on the farm

After a week staying with respective friends in Wellington, Marg offered me a lift north in the hire cars she was taking to Auckland. Bright sunshine reflected off the dashboard. We got into Rangitikei country with the gorge visible from time to time across the fields and the Ruahine Ranges in the distance. I had arranged to stay with Janet, the farmer I had met in Taupo a few weeks before.

I had been at the Huka Falls and had overheard three women wondering if the Waikato was New Zealand's longest river.

"Are you a Kiwi?" one had asked me.

"No, but I think it is," I had replied. I knew because the driver of the previous night's InterCity bus had given a bit of a commentary. "It's 393 kilometres," I added. We had chatted a while longer and one of the women, Janet, told me she owned a sheep farm near Hunterville and I could stay for a while if I liked. I had wanted to work on a New Zealand farm and told her I would probably visit as I made my way back north.

We found her farm north of Bulls, but there was no sign of Janet. We were greeted by loud barking from the working dogs in their kennels and by two domestic dogs. One of these was Chloe, a ponderous, solid, little white dog with a sweet, ugly face and a mad, jumping fox terrier called Milly. Chloe lost interest after a while but Milly did not, continuing her excitement for the half hour it took for Janet to appear. She had a lamb with her, floppy and near death which she gave to us to bottle feed while she put the kettle on. Marg and I said goodbye. After that, Janet got me some old clothes out of a wardrobe and I started work.

My only experience of working on a farm had been on George's a few weeks before. This was to be more intensive. For a start, lambing season was in full swing and secondly there was Janet's situation. George had come from a large farming family whereas none of Janet's children were farmers and none helped her on the farm.

I bottle-fed some lambs in the stable. When that was done, I stood on a platform attached to the back of the tractor with Winkle, one of the working dogs, as we drove up the track onto the hill out the back. We collected a few dead lambs up there. They were like floppy, woolly toys. There had been a hailstorm the week before and afterwards Janet had found seventeen dead lambs which had crowded into a tree stump for shelter. There was a bunch of ewes in a small pen which had either deserted their lambs or they had died. We caught each one, Janet doing most of the catching. Then she would test to see if they had any milk. If they were dry, she would spray them with a blue mark, but if they had milk, they were still able to mother orphaned lambs and she would truss their legs and tie them onto the platform. Winkle was still sitting on it and ended up looking out forlornly from behind a wall of trussed ewes and dead lambs. The lambs were still useful for their soft fleece and were left out near the road to be collected.

After checking the hill paddocks on both sides of the valley, we left the ewes in the shearing shed near the railway line, then crossed the tracks to where the beef cattle were being fattened. We moved the electric fence a metre or two to give them a little more fresh grass.

By this time it was dark, but we could still work in the shearing shed which had a light. There were nine pens, each containing a ewe and each was given a lamb. The lamb would not smell like hers, so a special spray was squirted on the ewe's nose and at the base of the lamb's tail, where she would sniff, to confuse her. Then we had to get the lamb to suckle. This was easier said than done because the ewe sometimes objected and the lamb usually had trouble finding the tit. (I use Janet's word as the earthier terms for such things seemed entirely appropriate, especially as they originated amongst the Anglo-Saxon peasantry. It's a farm. They *are* tits and muck *is* shit.) The ewe could be pacified by a knee jammed into her neck against the side of the pen. Sometimes she would sink to the floor and have to be heaved up again.

By the time we had finished with the ewes, it was 8pm. A leg of mutton had been slowly roasting and over dinner, Janet told me about her recent life. Her husband had left her for a younger woman about six years before. At first she had gone to pieces and moved to a nearby town for a few months. Then on a whim, she went to Western Australia and spent a year working on a couple of large cattle stations, one 360,000 acres, the other a million. There, she had not only enjoyed herself, but had also regained her confidence. She came back and decided to run the farm on her own. Friends and family telling her she would never manage it only hardened her resolve. Two of her children lived nearby, the other worked in a goldmine in Western Australia.

The combination of a lack of sleep, the quiet of the country and a bit of hard work the previous day meant that I did not wake up until 9 o'clock. Janet had been up for hours. Embarrassed, I threw on my clothes, bolted a couple of slices of toast and hurried to the shed to make sure the lambs were fed from their foster mothers. I met Janet on the way and after feeding, we wrestled a few more sheep in a pen. Next I shifted a heap of wood, then chopped it up for the fire where guts are cooked up for the dogs. After a welcome lunch, I made the ewes feed the lambs again, then it was onto the back of the tractor to move fences and cart around big bales of hay and plastic wrapped silage for the cattle while the tractor slipped around in the mud.

A couple of Janet's friends dropped by. As usual, the working dogs in their kennels started barking. Janet's response was to roar "Geddoutovit!" and they would stop instantly.

Janet found one of the ewes with twins was dying so she drove it up to near the house. Do not try the following at home. She slit its throat, cut into the ewe's stomach and pulled out the two lambs which were covered in a yellow slime. I stuffed the goopy creatures into a canvas bag and hurried them up to the house where there was a crate. This had been recently vacated by one which had died in the morning. I wrapped them in towels, gave them a little milk and left them to sleep.

I cooked roast pork and many vegetables for dinner and talk wandered into the depressing world of politics, war and religion.

While we were eating breakfast the next morning, a strange bloke walked up the gravel. His boots and the bottoms of his trousers were muddy and he looked and sounded intoxicated. He muttered about running out of petrol and a drunken night somewhere. He wanted to go to Hunterville, so she told him the way. Once he had gone, she phoned a couple of neighbours to let them know there was a strange man on the prowl. She was glad I was there and had made myself visible. The house was always wide open and the keys always in the truck. Once when she was still married, seven biker types had unpacked themselves from a vehicle claiming they wanted some sort of nut or bolt for their car. When the girl amongst them had asked to go to the toilet, Janet had been concerned because she would not be able to watch them all. Not knowing what kind of nut they wanted, she had gone to fetch her husband. Unlike Janet, he had been in bed, but had heard the cattle grid announcing their arrival and had retrieved the shotgun from its hiding place. He had told her if there was any trouble to hit the deck. The unexpected visit had ended without incident, but living isolated could be unnerving at times.

Checking out the lambs, I found that one ewe was on her side in her own muck and could not stand, but the lamb was still able to suckle when she was lying down. I noticed she had milk dripping from her udder, but not her teats. She turned out to have mastitis, so we let her out and put the lamb in the stable until we could find it a new mother. I had become covered in shit moving her around so it seemed appropriate that my next job was to shovel shit in the stable.

While Janet was on the dead run, she found a ewe and lamb that had had their eyes pecked out by gulls. Both were still alive, so she put them out of their misery. She saved another lamb whose mother was unable to stand. It is a nasty world out there, so I tried to make it better by cooking a stir fry for Janet and her visiting daughter.

"What do you know about pruning trees?" Janet asked the next morning after I had fed the lambs and moved the electric fence.

"Whatever you teach me right now," I replied.

The orchard comprised three apple trees, a couple of plums, a quince and a number of seedlings. Janet had not had a chance to prune them for a long time and they were beginning to grow too tall. It was one of a number of jobs that had been taunting her, but for which she didn't have the time. I had Milly and Chloe for company and all I had to do was throw sticks for them every now and then. Despite the fact that Milly always leapt off with great enthusiasm, Chloe got there first each time. This was because Milly would become so excited she would just run anywhere, whereas Chloe would trot in a sensible way straight for the stick. But then Milly would go bounding after her and grab the stick too. Chloe would usually let go at this point, because she was a simple old dog who couldn't really be bothered to tussle more than was dignified.

At one point, Chloe actually pretended to see something more interesting somewhere else. Milly, not wanting to be left out, dropped the stick and gave chase, whereupon, Chloe collected the original stick and brought it back to me. They were like a double act and I laughed out loud at their antics.

The early evening brought Janet's mother, daughter and daughter-in-law, who in turn brought cake and conversation for an hour or two. The cake was in honour of Janet's sixtieth birthday in two days' time. They had had plans to go out for a meal, but the granddaughter was sick so they cancelled it. After they had gone, Janet said she liked things simple on her birthday anyway. She didn't like a fuss. "We'll just have scrambled eggs," she said.

"We will not," I responded and prepared cold pork with sautéed potatoes and leeks in a white sauce. Janet reminisced about a trip to Europe in 1990 with a working horse called Reservation that they had entered for show jumping events. At an international event in Denmark, there had been a shortage of between-event entertainment, so they had suggested her husband have a shearing race with a former Danish champion. Tony had beaten him hands down. They had used old equipment that did two sheep in five minutes. She said that a good shearer with modern equipment could do three or four sheep in a minute.

I had thought to leave for Napier the next day, but over the mountains it was wet and windy and as Janet said she could still use me, I decided to stay. I was rewarded with glorious sunshine. I sang as I finished the pruning and talked to the dogs. Milly would jump up at me and sometimes Chloe would waddle over and be humbly grateful for the attention. I loaded four woolsacks of clippings and four big branches onto the back of the truck and started on one of the hedges.

Coming back from moving the electric fence in the evening, the sun had just gone down and I looked over towards the bridge and got a twinge of homesickness for stone bridges and greens, hills and trees which were similar but different.

That night I made meatballs with mash and a beer and onion gravy that was copious and tasty. I was enjoying the opportunity to cook again after more than three months travelling and it was a pleasure to cook for someone who would not have made the effort for herself. Janet showed me a couple of books, one of great rail journeys, one of great road journeys. I had done only a few of them and they were perfect itchy feet material. Place names leapt out from the pages: Kathmandu, Baghdad, Samarkand…

I dreamed of my old job and woke up feeling worried about going back to work in a strange environment. Getting up, I wished Janet a happy birthday.

Back in the stable for my first job of the morning to inspect the one lamb left. It had started lively, taken sick, then perked up, but that morning, it would not take more than a few sips of milk. The rest I had to slowly pour down its throat. Then I moved the fence and did some maintenance work around the house and garden. All of these jobs I was doing, she told me, were ones which had been preying on her mind and causing her stress, but which she did not have the time to do herself. She told me I had eased her stress as she had not had her usual migraines. She once had a young woman backpacker work with her for a year.

Her son and daughter-in-law were supposed to be coming over, bringing fish and chips. They phoned at about 5.30pm saying they were just leaving. The sun had gone down behind the hills and Janet remembered she had left a ewe tied up, which was a good reason to do a dead run. With Winkle and me on the back, we ploughed through the creek, almost slipping back down the mud on the far bank. Several dead sheep and lambs later, we found a mother who was cast. A leg and a head were sticking out of her rear. I thought they were dead, but we went over and while I immobilised the mother, Janet pushed back the leg, pulled out the lamb, cleared the membrane and mucus from its nose and blew into its nostrils. It stirred.

"Good boy!" she exclaimed. She could tell the ewe was going to desert the lamb, so we trussed her and took her to the stables where we could keep an eye on them both.

I had showered and Janet was still sorting things out when a host of people descended on the house. It was a surprise party, bringing food and drink. I went and changed again into the smartest clothes I had with me. Almost all the visitors were farmers and all were local, so there was a great supportive, community spirit. We chatted and ate and one woman read out a poem she had written. Janet was touched, more so because it was the first party she had ever had as an adult. So much for not liking a fuss, I thought.

The next day was my last on the farm. I had heard the weather was set to improve further north and it was time I was on the road again. I fed the lamb, shifted the fence and saw a calf had been born overnight. I went and opened the gate so that Janet could drive in some more bales in the tractor.

"There's a new calf," I said. She didn't respond. "Looks like a new calf was born last night," I tried again. She still didn't respond. Oh well, maybe it was only exciting to a city boy, I thought. She drove the bales into the field.

"Oh, there's a new calf," she said. "Why didn't you tell me?"

Janet and the dogs drove me into Hunterville to catch the bus. It had been a great six days. It can be hard for visitors to get behind the tourist brochures, but I felt like I had given back a little to the country in helping out Janet. She was a woman of guts and determination and I was glad I had met her.

Firestorm

My alarm had gone off and I was dozing before I forced myself out of bed to go to work in downtown Sydney when frantic shouts began to float in through the window. It seemed to be Deb from next door. The calls began to sound like "Jasper! Kevin!" and "Fire! Back bedroom!"

My flatmate's bedroom is on fire! I thought as I leapt out of bed, although *my* room was the one at the back and I was clearly not on fire. Still, I opened my bedroom door expecting to see smoke coming out from under Jasper's even though there wasn't the faintest smell of smoke. Jasper's room was clearly not ablaze either.

Maybe it was the house that backs onto us! I pulled on my jeans and started downstairs, had second thoughts and rushed back upstairs and put on a tee-shirt as well then rushed back downstairs again. I could see smoke coming from the rear of the neighbour's, which was about five yards away across the back yard. I didn't have my keys on me to open the back door. By this time, Jasper was up.

"Get the back door keys!" I called up to him. He came downstairs and saw the smoke.

"Where are the back door keys?" he asked.

I rushed upstairs and got my own.

Flames were coming from a tall metal box beside the bathroom. One of the house's occupants, English Emma, had been in the shower and was standing outside in her dressing gown with wet hair. The flames had burned a hole in the fence. It was a good job there had been rain recently and the fence was soaked.

Rob from next door had a small fire extinguisher. Opening the valve, he sprayed foam in his own face before he managed to gain control of the flailing nozzle and point it straight at the fire through the fence.

I picked up our little garden hose, turned on the tap and moved towards the blaze. The hose was ridiculously short and I pulled it off the tap. Jasper put it back on and, with my finger over the end, I managed to make it reach to the fence where I trained it on any smouldering wood.

For a moment, we thought Rob had managed to put the fire out. Then it came back.

"I think it's gas!" he said.

Jasper went into the girls' house to try to find the gas tap and turn it off. I suspected he was also spurred on by the hope of seeing one of the girls in a state of undress.

I continued with my feeble hose and as I stood, I pondered. If this is gas, I shouldn't be standing here. I should be a couple of blocks away. But that would be like leaving my post. I stayed where I was.

I was so focused on what was in front of me that I hadn't really noticed the sirens of the fire brigade as they tried to cut their way through the rush hour traffic. Suddenly there was a huge roar.

It's exploding; now it's time to go, I said to myself.

I calmly put down the hose, turned off the tap and went inside. But once inside I looked out to see the cause of the roar: the fire brigade had arrived and had brought a real hose.

And so it was that with adrenalin soaring through my veins and ready for a serious dose of physical action, I set about making my sandwiches and caught the bus to work.

The Melbourne cab driver

I had missed my plane. Once on board the next flight, I resigned myself to being late for my meeting. There was nothing more I could do. Arriving at Melbourne Airport, I took a cab out to the suburbs. The driver was Vietnamese.

In Vietnam, he told me, the party officials were peasants. They felt intimidated by anyone who seemed more intelligent, or dressed or acted differently. He knew of people who had been made to cut their hair or take off their tie. Most books were banned except a short list of recommended works. But people would keep their other books and swap them secretly. He said the whole population was under a cloud of gloom, like the sun had stopped shining for them. So he fled the country.

It was 1979 and he got to know someone who had a boat. It was a river boat the width of a flatbed truck and carried about 50 people. Within 10 hours of setting sail, all three engines had stopped working and for the next two or three days, they drifted aimlessly. Then they saw a ship, a large Thai fishing vessel. It came alongside and pulled them all on board. The crew gave them water and cigarettes. He looked over the side at their little boat. It seemed insane that they had tried to cross the sea on it. It looked like a toy car beside a real one.

But after an hour, the sailors separated the men from the women. They were told to strip and were searched. Some of the sailors went down into the boat and ransacked it, looking for money and jewellery or anything valuable. Then all the men were put back on the boat and it was towed from the ship at the end of a rope. The women were kept on board and their screams could be heard through the night.

"We knew what was going on, but there was nothing we could do. I was lucky because I was single, but for those with wives or daughters, it must have been very hard."

In the morning, the sailors dumped the women back into the boat and cut it loose.

Now they had no food and water and were still drifting. To make matters worse, a storm blew up. One moment they would be high on a wave and would be able to see the waters all around, the next, they were down low. It went on into the night and they thought they would die.

But the morning brought an easing of the storm. The women pulled themselves together and started to clear up. He had a lot of respect for them after what they had been through. The men were given new hope and had a look at the engines. One was a motor mechanic and with his help, they got them working again. They started to sail in the direction of land.

They sighted another ship. The women said they would rather die than be caught again, so they steered away from it. They realised the gap between them and the ship was increasing: they were no longer being followed. They soon saw the reason why. Across the horizon lay a strip of land; they were entering Malaysia's territorial waters.

They were unable to steer properly and were heading straight for a rocky coast. They sailed closer and closer and he could see they would be driven against the rocks. He said he would stand at the front and tell them when to jump out. Fifty metres from the cliff, they all jumped. The boat was smashed, but they were washed up on the shore. No one was lost. At low tide he went back to look at the cliff. The water was four or five metres below it another few hours and they would never have made it.

They were found by some local people and the police put them into a refugee camp. It was like a prison. They had no idea what was happening in the world outside and they were not allowed out. There were no languages they understood on the radio.

During those two months, delegations would come from the US, Canada and Australia to interview people. Eventually Australia gave him a stamp of approval. He was to spend another month in a camp in Kuala Lumpur before he flew out, but he was happy: he knew he was leaving.

In Australia, he spent the first few months in a hostel. He received $50 a week, all but $10 of which went on food and accommodation. He learned English and went looking for work. He was soon taken on by a factory making extrusion mouldings where he was to work for 17 years. After 16, he was offered redundancy but he turned it down. He regretted it a year later when he changed his mind. He did not like the way the company was going. His wife had given up work to spend more time with their nine year old daughter and three year old son. He worked six days a week in the cab. He had seen little of Australia because when he was younger he had preferred drinking and discos.

I do not know why he decided to tell me his story. Perhaps he told anyone who would listen. What I do know is that being late for work no longer seemed such a hardship.

Down the Great Ocean Road with Jack

Jack was excited at the prospect of a trip. Kara and I put the happy red setter in the back of the car and set off from Melbourne. We took the inland route west through pretty, green country and stopped in the small town of Winchelsea where there was a pub by a flooded creek. An old red tractor sat rusting in the water and a couple of weary field guns and a cart waited patiently in the sun like old men.

Some miles later, we turned left and south into rolling hills. Looking back over the plain there were little conical wooded hills dotting the horizon. Old volcanoes, Kara told me. The country looked almost English as we wound down lanes and eventually emerged at cute little Port Campbell by its bay and beach. We let Jack out for a bit of a run. This was the tourist base for the Great Ocean Road and we duly set off to cover the sights. Twelve years earlier I had tried to cycle the Road, starting from Warrnambool further west along the coast, but it had proved too far for my aching rear and I had turned back.

Our first stop was London Bridge, a wide, flat stack with arches. A few years before it had been joined to the mainland but one arch had collapsed, surprising several tourists who found themselves stranded on the wrong side and had to be rescued by helicopter. Further on we came to the Loch Ard gorge. The land by the coast was moor-like before it crumbled away sheer into beautiful limestone cliffs of golden brown. In places, the sea was a rich dark blue, elsewhere it was a lustrous steely colour under a low grey sky.

Finally, we reached the Twelve Apostles, a series of sea stacks which form a line of sentinels guarding about half a mile of coastline. I heard a woman say "It's taken us forty minutes to get here."

"Well it took me 12 years," I said. And it was worth it. They looked wonderful, majestic, magical. There was a hint of mist creeping amongst them and into the inlets. I gazed at them and a light rain fell. I put my arm around Kara and thanked her for taking me there.

The road became very windy. Jack sat attentively in the back seat, looking out the front and leaning into the bends. Every now and then she would come and stand between us in the front, which tended to get in the way of the gear stick. "Jack in the back," I would say and she would retreat.

The road went a few miles inland, into the hills and forests. Every now and then we would snatch a view from the top of a hill, sometimes with a farmhouse nestled into a valley surrounded by the dark greening of trees at dusk. The hills came right down to the shore and the road hugged their feet. Valleys opened right onto the coast, streams emerging from bush-filled glens.

At Fairhaven the houses were well separated from each other but within a short walk of the beach. It was dark by the time we arrived. Jack recognised the place from previous visits and capered excitedly. When it came to bedtime, she wanted to come in with us, but I insisted she sleep outside the bedroom, so she dutifully curled up at one end of the long living room.

I woke in the middle of the night. Jack was barking and making a growling, whimpering sound. As I lay there, I heard a voice outside the room. It was a man. My blood froze. I turned to Kara, but she was still sleeping. I listened again, listening hard, desperately straining my ears into the silence. Then he spoke again, presumably to the dog.

"It's all right. Calm down."

There was an intruder in the house! What should I do? There was only one thing *to* do: go out and face him.

I put the light on. Still Kara didn't move. I fumbled on a dainty dressing gown, then, heart pounding, threw open the door and turned on the light.

My eyes raked the room for bandits and burglars, but it was empty apart from a happy dog. I could not believe it.

I searched the house. I looked behind the breakfast bar, I looked in all the bedrooms, in the wardrobes and the bathrooms. Nothing. Jack scampered along with me. We went downstairs to the back door. It was still locked. I opened it, holding on to Jack's collar. She barked twice into the darkness. I did not know what she meant, but so far as I could tell, there were only the three of us in the house.

I went back to bed, leaving Jack outside the room once more. She was whimpering again. I lay there with enough adrenalin going through me to stop a small tank. I had no idea how I was going to get to sleep.

Five or ten minutes later the storm hit. It sounded like it was going to take the roof off. Huge gusts of wind hammered at us straight off the ocean. Great, I thought, this is pure Hollywood. The house is smashed to tinderwood and in the wind and the dark and the pouring rain an axe murderer waits for his moment.

Exhausted, I fell asleep. In the safer light of morning I realised that Jack had probably been whimpering because she sensed the storm coming. My imagination had done the rest.

"Thanks for looking," said Kara. "But what would you have done if you'd found someone there?"

I thought about that for a moment.

"I have no idea," I decided, but I could probably have overpowered anyone while they were laughing at me in that dressing gown. We let Jack in and she curled up on a blanket on the floor and went to sleep.

After breakfast, we took Jack out onto the beach and threw a stick for her to fetch. Kara watched me bounding after the dog with some bemusement.

The wind was cool but the sun was warm. It was a beautiful beach several miles long. At one end of the white sand were the hills and at our end some cliffs, topped with a tall white lighthouse.

We sat down, watching the sea. Jack kindly brought us a couple of dead fish and sat between us.

We tidied the house and put some Cadbury's chocolate fingers in the front of the car and set off. The biscuits had melted and reset into one giant biscuit, so we ate chunks of them.

We stopped at Anglesea golf course, famous for a mob of kangaroos living on the greens and stood in the trees along the fairway to watch them graze. Golfers strolled amongst the animals as if they too were part of the wildlife.

When we got back to the car, Jack was sitting in the front looking pleased with herself: the rest of the biscuits were gone.

A couple of hours later and we were back in Melbourne. And just as she had been excited by the prospect of a trip, this time Jack was excited at the prospect of home.

The honourable grandmother

The lad with the didgeridoo saw her on the far side of a group of people, smiled, then went over and shyly introduced himself to her. It took her a moment to recognise him and another to comment on how much he had grown.

"They still talk about you back home," he said.

That was the kind of effect Maureen Watson had on people. I first met her at the National Folk Festival in Canberra and everywhere she went people would stop and talk to her. Some had met her before, one had been in the forces with her brother, others had just heard her speak and wanted to talk to her. She had time for them all.

Maureen was the daughter of a Kungalu woman and a Birrigubba man. She was a Murri, one of the Aboriginals of Queensland. At 67 she may have had white hair, but her skin was smooth and her face could be a picture of childlike joy and mischief.

She was a proud woman with five children, 24 grandchildren and four great grandchildren. A difficult life had left her with angina and diabetes, but she had time for people when they needed her and especially time for her family. Very active in affairs of the indigenous peoples, she took any opportunity to make people think again about themselves and in doing so, to question their relationship with Australia and its original people.

Her parents were chained and whipped for speaking their own language and as a result never taught it to her: it was a matter of personal survival. She married young. They lived on a big station where her husband worked as a stockman.

One evening she was out with her first baby son, quietly talking to him. The moon was big and bright and she told him how one day he might live on it and she would go to visit him in her spaceship. She did not hear her husband walking home across the rough grass, but he had heard her. "What's that nonsense you're talking, woman?" he demanded. "Living on the moon and spaceships. You're out of your mind!"

It was to be typical of the stories she would continue to tell throughout her life to the many children in her family, but his reaction to it also turned out to be typical. It took 17 years for all the children to be old enough for her to leave him.

At the age of 41, she and her sister went back to school in an attempt to matriculate, but she had to drop out to tend one of her sons who had contracted meningitis. Her months of care paid off and he made a complete recovery.

Her sister, who had continued at school, encouraged her to sit the exams at the end of the year despite her lack of study. "She'd have been the only black dot in that snowfield, so I decided I'd at least keep her company. And of course I couldn't resist having a look at the questions." As a result of looking at the questions, she went to university.

After two and a half years, she realised university was not taking her where she wanted to go. Instead, she began to put the oral tradition of her people to wider use. She became a storyteller and speaker. She would go into schools and speak at festivals. Word went around and she became busy and eventually even known internationally.

She enjoyed going to schools. She would tell stories, do workshops, sing songs. I have rarely seen someone generate so much affection, especially with children. By the time she left a barbecue, she had names and addresses of all the children and was going to find each of them Aboriginal penfriends. She made time for them and they were drawn to her.

She also realised that young minds are ripe for education. She encouraged children to be "wisdom seekers". She remembered a recent occasion where a young girl was puzzled about land rights. Had not Captain Cook discovered Australia and claimed it, the girl had asked.

"That's a nice watch," Maureen had replied. "Give it to me. I've just discovered it, it's mine. And that's a nice book. I'll have that too." Naturally the child protested. "But didn't you just say you can have things you find? You can't have it both ways." She said that she looked at the room full of children and could see the message was getting through. She tried to challenge her audience without alienating them.

She would teach her own children the myths and legends, bringing home books for them. "My youngest son ended up with a stack a kangaroo couldn't jump over." But he claimed that they were no longer relevant to him and his mates. They didn't go out and hunt or dance in a corroboree. They wore T-shirts and joggers, they rode bikes and skateboards. "Where are we in those stories?" he asked.

So she looked for other books. "I found that you could come from almost anywhere in the world and find a story about yourself and your people that enabled you to feel okay, unless you were an Aboriginal. The only stories were the ones where the children wore practically nothing but body paint. It was like looking in the mirror and seeing everyone else except yourself."

She started telling different stories, where the children may hunt echidna when they are on holiday in the bush, but when they come back to town, they eat Weetbix and go to McDonalds.

Maureen sees this lack of identity for all Aboriginals, not just children. "Aboriginal people have a different perspective on things. When a white child is born, the mother is laid on a table that was probably made by somebody from a white race. The doctors and nurses around her, the first faces which that child would see, would be white faces like her own. Also the first voice she would hear, the first hands that touched her. And she goes to school: the people who built the school, the architect, most of the teachers, most of the books, the shops she passes, the people, the statues in the park.

"She would be getting these messages which would be telling her with every breath she takes that she comes from a race of people who have achieved worthwhile things, who have made a worthwhile contribution to their society. This is the message she is getting every single second of the day.

"When an Aboriginal is born, the first face we see is a face that is from a different race. The first hands that touch us, the first voices we hear, the shopkeepers in the street, the taxi drivers, the books, the newspapers, the clothes we wear, the houses that are built. That's why I feel I must hold up the mirror for black reflections. It's like we are invisible."

Some years before, she had been doing a film-making course with other Aboriginals. When she set up the camera, the tutor told her that it and the crew would be visible in a mirror. Maureen challenged her. "But I want the audience to see black hands on the camera and a black head inside the headphones."

Maureen believed in balance. There are many other races in Australia now. If they consider themselves to be Australian, if they are proud of it, then the Aboriginal culture going back thousands of years is theirs too, she said, because it is of the land which they call home.

But she felt this sharing should also involve respect. In Brisbane once, she came upon a white girl busking on a didgeridoo. It is an instrument which women are forbidden to play but the busker said that she had been given permission by elders in the Northern Territory.

Maureen pointed out that if she had been given permission to play in the Territory then she should go and play there, but in Brisbane she was offending the local Aboriginals. At this point the girl told Maureen to mind her own business.

She was amazed by the growing support among whites for Aboriginals. She could not help but be surprised when a white person was kind or polite to her. Yet she also believed that Aboriginals fill a need in white people. "If there were no Aboriginals, white people would need to invent us." She felt they have become a good cause rather than simply people.

Many people, she felt, forget to see the common humanity behind the black face. "It's about human compassion. 200 years ago, parents still taught their children to care. If I see a child crying for a dolly she's dropped, or a dog run down in the street or heavy rain break off the petals of a flower, I feel compassion."

"We are all ancestors," she said. "Remember that where you put your feet on this land, someone else has put their feet before you and others will put their feet in future years." She believed that most people like to think of themselves as good. They want people to remember them well and they will be remembered by their actions.

"We should all try to be honourable ancestors."

A wedding to remember

It was an odd wedding. For a start, there had been no invitations and the bride had asked my cousin Mel if she would invite a couple of her friends. I was passing through Brisbane at the time so filled the gap well enough.

Because I was on my way to Asia, my backpack did not contain clothes appropriate for a wedding, so I borrowed a shirt, tie and trousers and felt under-dressed.

It was being held in the Botanical Gardens in Brisbane at the foot of Mount Coot-tha. There was a groomsman at the gate, a chubby young bloke who, from the look of his sweating red face, had run there from the city centre. He was wearing a grey suit and brown hiking boots. I no longer felt so under-dressed. We found our way to a little clearing in the gardens, surrounded on three sides by a small stream and walled in by trees and bushes.

Andy the groom was there but looked stressed.

"Hi guys," he said. "The car going to fetch Tina has had a crash." We were about to look concerned when he quickly added "She wasn't in it yet, no one's hurt, but they've got to get another, so she's going to be a little late."

We looked at the other guests. Some were in suits while others were in jeans and open necked shirts. One attractive, willowy young woman was in a long, translucent white dress, but the glamour was spoiled by the bra strap stretched across her open back.

The wedding celebrant had been fidgeting somewhat and finally had a chat to Andy. Firstly he pointed out that he had been told that the wedding was at 2pm when it was actually at 2.30pm. Secondly, he had to leave because he had another wedding to go to.

"It's okay," Andy told us after he had gone, "he said he'd come and do it at the reception."

Minutes later, Tina arrived, completely unaware that the wedding had been postponed. She walked up the garden equivalent of the aisle looking demure and lovely with her bridesmaid beside her. We watched as Andy went over to explain. For a moment, she looked upset, but she cheered up when they decided they would pretend it was still happening and took a few photographs anyway. As the couple walked back into the clearing, there was a tearing sound and a large palm frond tore off one of the trees and hung dangerously above them.

We had time to kill before the reception – and wedding – so Therese bought a large cup of lemonade and Gunny drove us up to the lookout at the top of Mount Coot-tha. I was handed the lemonade but waited until Gunny had pulled out of a junction so I wouldn't spill it. He accelerated suddenly and the lemonade went all over me. My shirt was dark blue and it didn't show, but the dark patch on my grey trousers made me look as if I had lost control of my bladder. I nonchalantly paraded my accident around the lookout while Gunny marvelled at my sang-froid and was further impressed when I chatted to some French tourists in French.

We had some champagne back at Mel's place, then drove on to the reception at a community hall to find everyone was locked out and still sitting outside. The band was supposed to have been the first ones there to set up, but no one had told them that the reception had been brought forward to accommodate the wedding. Indeed, no one had told them that since they had the only key, they were supposed to let the caterer in as well. He was also waiting in his van. For their part, the band had decided that they would not need so long to set up and had delayed their arrival. Bridal party and guests waited in the hot sun.

Finally the band arrived. Willing hands helped the caterer unload his truck, then we all settled down to a well-earned beer. There were forty of us, including the band. Sadly, none of Tina's family had been able to make it from Canada.

The celebrant was late. We began to worry. Someone asked if anyone had told him that the reception had been brought forward especially for him. No one had.

He duly arrived at what he thought was the appropriate time and everyone prepared for the wedding and lined up on either side of the main door. One of the band played *Here comes the bride* on the harmonica. We all watched the door. It remained empty. Where was the bride?

"She's over there!" said someone.

We turned and saw her at a door on the other side of the hall. She went back out, we lined up at the correct door and *Here comes the bride* once more wheezed merrily across the room. Still no bride. We glanced back at the first door in case she was waiting there. Then the bridesmaid popped her head around the corner.

"Sorry, we weren't ready. Could you start again?"

Third time lucky and everyone was synchronised. Tina was given away by Andy's father, and despite having met neither of the happy couple before, I was moved by the ceremony.

With the couple finally united, we tucked into the spit roast and more beer. Then it was time for speeches. Everything was going well until the best man's speech. You see Andy had met Tina on a safari truck in Africa. He had also met Tina's friend and had got together with *her* on the trip. Later, back in London, Andy left the first girl and started going out with Tina. The girls had fallen out, but had since made up and the first girlfriend was also at the wedding.

The best man described how Andy and Tina had met. He told us how Andy had raved about a girl he had met in Africa and went on to say it was therefore not surprising that the two of them were now married. Except of course, he was talking about the ex, not the bride. Everyone pretended not to notice the mix up.

The band took the stage for another set and I joined them on the bongos. The evening deteriorated as some of the drunken relatives reckoned they were musicians and borrowed guitars.

After midnight we ended up sat outside on the kerb. Gunny and Tina took turns to sing songs to us while I nodded off, looking forward to a little sleep before the long journey up to North Queensland in the morning.

Asia
1999

I returned to the UK via Asia. It was my first experience of just how different cultures could be from one another. Every day was an adventure.

Culture shock

The service on the aircraft into Hanoi was poor. The cabin crew were slow and ran out of one of the two meal choices. After a brief overnight stop in Kuala Lumpur, I had no idea what time it was any more nor how long the flight was. The pilot had mumbled something early on, but the first I knew of our imminent arrival was when we began to lose height. The Red River meandered below us and I began to make out fields. As we flew lower, I looked at the towns and houses and wondered what it was going to be like making my way around this new country.

I had never been to East Asia and I was apprehensive about travelling there. How easy would it be? I was glad that cricketing friend Dan was meeting me and that with his position at the British Embassy, he would be able to help me find my feet.

We disembarked in the middle of the tarmac and boarded a couple of old buses. The air was thick with heat. Waiting for the bus to pull away, we watched a man being led off the plane in handcuffs surrounded by police and cameramen. The bus dropped us at a brick building that looked more like a bus station than an international airport terminal. Madness descended immediately and it was to stay like that for the next few months, only I often came to forget it was mad.

There was a frantic rush. At one end of the room was a series of booths where immigration officials sat. A few people were filling in immigration cards but no one was giving them out. Eventually I found one and went up to a booth. The woman looked at the photograph in my passport of a thick haired, bearded character. Then she looked at the clean chinned, shaven headed man standing in front of her. I grinned. She smiled and called over one of her colleagues. They both looked at the picture, then at me and we all laughed. They handed me back my passport and let me through. There was a pile of bags on the ground, I picked out my own and saw Dan just ahead standing in the doorway in a pair of shorts.

We drove into town, getting waved through toll gates because his car had diplomatic plates.

I had only been in the country a few hours before I was in a confrontation with the Vietnamese army. It was all Dan's fault. We had to go to a football match which his team of all shapes, sizes, ages and nationalities was playing against a Vietnamese side. The match was held on a pitch at an army base. The Hanoi Capitals pay 350,000 dong for the privilege. In addition, the base decided it would also charge them for parking. Dan was outraged at their barefaced cheek and had an argument with the guards at the barrier. They would not let him through unless he paid. "Right," he said. "I'll leave it here then!" stopped the car and we got out. It was parked square in front of the barrier. And off he went. You could tell he was a diplomat.

I was a little slower at leaving the car and one of the haranguing guards grabbed hold of my shirt and started complaining excitedly in Vietnamese. I decided a detailed explanation as to why I was in no position to move the car even if I wanted to was going to be neither worthwhile nor possible, so I resorted to a feeble mime of using an ignition key and gesturing over my shoulder at Dan who, disappearing into the distance, was being the perfect host.

The soldier shouted at me some more then gave up and let go. The Capitals beat the Vietnamese 2-1. The goal scorers were French and Danish, the second a lovely hooked ball into the right corner of the net.

My first impression of Vietnam was that it was mad. Looking at the way they drove, everyone was all over the road. No one looked anywhere but forwards and no one ever stopped at junctions, except just sometimes when there was a red light. Instead, they warned of their presence with their horn. Dan had got through two in the last three years and said driving in the West terrified him because everyone trusted everyone else was going to do the right thing. But the traffic in Vietnam was always moving, which may have something to do with most of it being varieties of two-wheeler, and everyone appeared to concentrate. Having said that, I had no idea what the death toll on the roads was and saw several accidents in the month I was there. It was especially exciting at night because it had to be very dark indeed before anyone was wimp enough to put their lights on and bikes were invisible until silhouetted in the lights of a huge Russian truck.

There was a big party at Dan's on that first night and a big mess the next morning. Dan phoned up the maid and by the time we came back from our day out, the house was immaculate. Four of us drove out to the cradle of Vietnamese civilisation where there was a big festival. Stalls and thousands of people wound up a forested hillside to a series of pagodas around the summit and the most boring museum I had ever seen. Some girls started to talk to me. They found it hard to believe I was not travelling with my "daaahling". We were the only foreigners for miles and whereas in Hanoi most people were used to the sight of big hairy people, many of these were country folk and had never seen anything quite so amusing. If we were foolish enough to stand still for a few seconds, a crowd would gather a few feet away and stand looking at us as if we were about to burst into song. It was my first experience of this kind of attention and I found it very odd. Apparently, just standing there was amazing. Mind you, having seen Vietnamese television, it was easy to understand why they were easy to please. I caught some Tai Chi one day: an old lady standing on a mat and doing the moves. After some time, the camera angle changed.

We went to a Wall of Death show, one of those large barrels where motorbikes ride along the wall. Our appearance managed to upstage the spectacle so much that the riders too were fascinated by us. It was a grisly accident waiting to happen and our presence seemed only to distract the riders or encourage them to greater feats of bravado. I was relieved when we left.

We sat down to fresh coconut milk straight out of the fruit with straws and gathered a crowd. When we had finished the coconuts, Dan stood up and addressed the crowd in Vietnamese.

"What is so interesting about people eating coconuts?" he demanded to the surprised audience who had not expected him to speak to them in their language. I was to find that smiling and greeting people is a good way of turning yourself from a freak into another human being.

After the flood

It was pouring with rain. The rice fields emptied and cyclists on the road cowered against the deluge. Gradually the weather began to clear and over the sea, where it was brighter, we could see the rounded limestone teeth and islands of Ha Long Bay.

It began to rain again as we boarded our little boat in Ha Long City. It chugged off at little more than a brisk walking pace. Out of the gloom emerged the grey form of an island which became green as we approached. We jumped onto a floating jetty, climbed some steps and went through a small opening.

Inside was a huge cavern that had only been discovered in 1993 by a fisherman. It had been named the Heavenly Palace Cave. A natural cathedral, it had grown pillars and shapes, stalactites and stalagmites, melting rock and cascades of calcite. It was far more beautiful than anything people could have devised. As if to demonstrate this, the Chinese had helped by decking out the cavern with coloured lights, and laid a walkway lined with cement made to imitate calcite. There was a fairy grotto which the designers had failed to improve by adding more false calcite, pebbles and a fountain. Whereas the rest had teetered on the brink of poor taste, this plunged into an abyss of kitsch.

It was still raining when we returned to the boat, but the fog had lifted so we could see the amazing shapes of the bay. There are nearly two thousand islands in an area of about fifty kilometres by thirty. We sailed through this eerie other-world, marvelling. Bushes and small trees dug their toenails in, pulling themselves away from the sheer drops behind them. The rocky islets were often long and narrow with the base of each undercut by the waves. Vegetation clung grimly to all but the lowest. In some places, the ever-moving sea had worn low arches. If the rocks had eyes, they would have been able to see their own futures in the sea stacks and lumps of rock which the waves had worn down, some into dramatic sculpted forms, before reclaiming them completely.

There were fishermen on sampans bearing low, rounded shelters. Some of the bays provided harbour to larger boats or small huts sitting on rafts. They would go into Ha Long City or Cat Ba town to sell their catch and buy supplies.

I tried to imagine this strange seascape being my home, my world. It felt as if the land had been drowned and only these peaks rose above the waters. I wondered if, for these people, the solidity of dry land was unusual.

The boat dipped and rolled as the sea became more open and we sailed around the eastern coast of Cat Ba Island. As the light began to fade, we entered a bay surrounded by islands. A few boats lay in the protected waters. Standing on the deck in the bow watching the harbour slide closer, I had never been so aware of arriving as I was then. I truly felt far removed from home and a million miles away from my old desk.

The hotel overlooked the harbour. Below it was the esplanade with clusters of spherical lights, benches and oleander bushes heavy with pink flowers. The bay was crowded with a floating village of sampans and rust buckets.

One of our party was Susanna, an Irish nurse with the International Red Cross. We chatted on the hotel's balcony. She worked in Budapest and helped former communist countries restructure their Red Cross organisations. We talked about the state of the former Yugloslavia where she spent most of her time: the well-off Slovenia; the war-ravaged states; the still totalitarian Croatia; and the ever so laid back, not-in-the-real-world Macedonians who did not really believe problems were serious, that it would all work out, and where the timing and duration of meal breaks were of more importance than the meetings themselves.

The next day Cuong, our tour guide, and I went on motorbikes through the island. It had the same steep rocky hills as the bay. Villages made the most of what little flat land there was to farm.

We climbed the highest hill. A set of steps rose quickly through the forest, lizards slipped away into the bushes as we approached. The path flattened briefly, then we had to use trees as handholds until we were scrambling using all four limbs on the branches and rugged rocks.

As we neared the summit, we heard bellowing and then a coo-ee. The latter came from an Australian. The bellow had come from an American. He talked loudly about how cheap Vietnam was for him, how much Americans would be prepared to pay for this experience, and how much Americans love to complain. He added that he was Jewish so he was even worse. His mother said you should always complain because, who knows, you might get a free meal, but if you think he's bad you should meet his three sisters, especially the oldest, Karen. She would have you swimming back to Ha Long City.

Their guide happened to mention something about peak season. The American thought he had said Pig Season and made a huge thing of it.

"I thought you meant pig. Oink oink."

Oink meant nothing to the Vietnamese, but he laboured the joke, explaining it and talking about the guide's inability to speak clear English until I wanted to push him over the edge.

Then they went down and suddenly it was quiet. The humped hills ringed a plain where there was an orchard of lychees and fields being prepared for cassava.

Later, back on the esplanade, men, women and boys in small boats shouted to me to hire them for a spin around the harbour. I refused all suggestions many times: no did not seem to be the right answer. Some gave me huge smiles as if to say "Go on, you know you want to really." I felt like I would have been making a tourist attraction of poverty, although perhaps I had already done that.

Sitting on the bench I was making myself a target for a few boat boys on foot who were being eyed jealously by those in the water. I took out my guidebook which proved to be interesting to some passersby. I was in no mood for chatting and neither were they really because what they really wanted was for me to pay them for a trip around the bay. But I was also determined not to be impolite, so although I did not attempt verbal communication, I showed them the island on a map in the book. One gaunt, rolling-eyed individual in an ex-army pith helmet pored over it for quite some time, tracing it with his finger. A student and a *xe ôm* driver joined us. The former knew a little English, but his accent was thick. In the end, I brought out my phrase book. This was a big mistake: it was even more fascinating. Rolling Eyes wanted it.

I had to wait a long time for them to be bored and wander away. Before they could return, I made my escape to a spot on the edge of town on the road to the beach. There was no one around and I took out my book and read.

Happy you come back your country lucky!

I will not be the first to remark on the friendliness of the Vietnamese and their sense of fun, nor on how, with the beautiful young women, this easily becomes flirting. Yet always lurking was the inequality between the Vietnamese and the rich tourists passing through. It was a difficult difference to overcome with small sums to us being worth so much to them. I will not be the last to be confused by cultural differences or to make stumbling friendships and leave unknown damage in my wake.

I was sitting in the park when Hiep came along selling postcards and phrasebooks. I bought a phrasebook from him, so he stopped to chat. He was twelve, although he looked younger because he was short and slight, only coming up to my ribs. His mother sold tea and cigarettes and his brother, who was 29, sold flowers.

While we were talking, a student wheeled up his bike and took over the conversation. He used unusual words, such as "abrogate" and several times described how people needed to "work buttums off". He rambled a dull monologue in a thick accent. I found myself tuning out and exchanged the odd look with Hiep who was looking even more bored than I was and also annoyed that his foreigner had been hijacked. He muttered something a couple of times and the student lightly rested a patronising hand on his shoulder to quieten him while he continued talking. After about half an hour, I told the student it was time Hiep and I went and sold some postcards.

We strolled around the lake. He told me that he had been harrassed by the police four times in the previous two years. They had confiscated all his things and made him pay 50,000 dong (about $3.50) to get it back. Most evenings he went to English lessons for two hours which cost him 200,000 a month, the equivalent of about US$15. We arranged to meet up again a couple of days later so he could show me the city.

Exploring Hanoi on my own over the next couple of days, I would spend the day being offered rides by cyclo, taxi and *xe ôm*, the moped taxi. On one occasion outside the cathedral, a little old beggar woman followed me around, tugging at my sleeve, then waited while I was accosted by first one, then a second postcard seller. The second became sullen and insistent saying that he had not sold anything all day, a common complaint, and that he was hungry and if I would just buy a book, he could go and eat something.

I went into the cathedral and sat for half an hour until it closed and I had to go back outside where my entourage was still waiting.

On the shores of the lake, a shoeshiner followed me.

"Shoeshine! Yes!" he said excitedly. "Velly good! Yes. Shoeshine. Velly velly dirty."

"No thanks."

"Shoeshine. Velly, velly dirty."

"No."

Still he insisted that they were velly, velly dirty.

"I think you'll find they're actually rather clean."

And so we continued, keeping it jocular. Each time we came to a bench, which was every few yards, he would say "Okay!" and try to guide me into it. I would dodge and we would continue until, eventually, he gave up.

I met Hiep where we had agreed. He was dressed smartly in denim jacket and jeans. We visited the Ngoc Son Jade Mountain Temple on an island in the lake where there was a large stuffed turtle. I thought it looked as though it had a smile on its face. Hiep laughed and said he had never noticed that before. I took a photograph of him standing next to a large, strange looking red horse.

We went to the history museum which had statues of grinning turtles, stone artefacts, skeletons and models of battles. One was a famous defeat of the Chinese where they had been lured up the river until the hulls of their boats were ripped open on submerged stakes. We looked in a bookshop for *Tintin* books in English but could not find any so I bought him a cassette for his English course.

Several foreigners knew him. Cannily, he seemed to make a point of getting to know them.

Finally, we went into the old city, amongst the dirty old shuttered houses and narrow streets, some with trees, balconies and busy little shop fronts. We went to the market and I bought him a football shirt and a drink to thank him for guiding me. A few people laughed at us while we were getting the shirt. I asked what they were saying.

"They say you are my father," he said.

His father had died two years before. That was when he had started to sell postcards. Before that, he had been a shoeshine boy. I felt awkward. Was he just begging? Was I just a rich westerner dishing out my largesse? I justified it by thinking of it as payment for him guiding me around the city, but he had shown me nothing I could not have found for myself. Any number of poor Vietnamese would have offered me the same service.

We would often walk in companionable silence and every now and then he would do something which reminded me that he was only a child, such as swing his arms around or be fascinated by the models of battles in the museum.

A month later, I was back in a humid Hanoi. The day I was leaving Vietnam I met Hiep again. He was pleased to see me. Perhaps people he met did not usually try to see him again. He reminded me that he was going to have to stop school because he did not have enough money to pay the 250,000 dong next month. He still needed 150,000 (about $10). The price for the course was higher than he had previously told me and I suspected he was hoping I would give him some money. I bought him lunch and he devoured a steak sandwich with chips.

Then it was time for me to go. I gave him $10 and told him it was for school. He looked embarrassed and thanked me. I told him he could learn more English and become a tour guide. He grinned, almost despite himself. Outside, I found a *xe ôm* and shook his little hand. He looked sad and wiped away a tear as I rode away.

I meant to keep in touch, to send him the odd letter or book but at some point in the following months I lost his address and all I have left is the photograph of him with the wooden horse.

In Hoi An, I spotted a sunglasses stall run by two men called Bang and Little Thanh. They made jokes as I chose a pair. Then came the price. 80,000 dong.

"That's far too expensive!"

"It is the same price for Vietnamese," they told me.

"No wonder Vietnamese don't wear sunglasses," I told them. "They can't afford them!"

"I will throw in a case for free."

"No way."

"Okay," Thanh conceded, "Vietnamese would only pay 75,000. He paused "But they would have to pay 5000 for the case." We all laughed.

Eventually we settled on 50,000, but I waited until after lunch to buy them. When I returned, they were pleased to see me and we joked some more. They said to come back the next day and take a photograph.

I returned the next day with Canadians Garth and Lynne who also decided to buy some sunglasses. They did as poor a job of haggling them down as I had done. When Garth baulked at a price, Thanh reached behind him and pulled out a fan to cool him down. Garth countered with a much lower price and Thanh laughed and started to fan himself.

I took the photograph. It shows us standing with Bang and Thanh, all of us wearing sunglasses with the tags hanging off them, and all of us grinning broadly. A couple of days later, we gave them a copy of it. Other vendors gathered around to see, so we showed them the rest of the film. Then I took out my pictures of friends, a number of whom were women. I was interrogated about my relationship with them, especially from one mischievous little woman with a twinkle in her eye.

"Fiancée?" she asked at one point.

In the end, I said I had ten fiancées and she cuffed me and laughed and wagged her finger at me. Then she said "One fiancée," and marched around, straight and full of energy. Then she said "Ten fiancées," and started hobbling, bent over. When we laughed, she did it a few more times. After that, whenever I walked past the market, I was greeted with shouts and waves.

At China Beach, a little girl approached me.

"*Voulez-vous parlez français avec moi?*" she asked in a heart-breakingly sweet voice.

So I did. And at the end, of course, she tried to sell me some of her things. I was not interested. She explained that she went to school and would I give her a present so she could buy books for school? I could not keep turning her down, which was doubtless her intention, so I took a photograph of her in exchange for 10,000 dong. Of course, a little lad selling things rushed over and wanted some too, but I walked away and told Garth I had just been a big soft bastard.

The Koho women wove beautiful fabrics from cotton and silk. There was one sheet the size of a bedspread. It was crimson with lines of a golden pattern. It had taken two months to make and the woman was asking a mere $25 before haggling even began. I almost bought it except I would need to carry it with me and did not know what I would do with it once I was home.

I also wanted to take home one of the girls. She was beautiful with big, kind brown eyes and a broad, open innocent smile. I could not help but smile at her. With a loom and her obvious skills, she could have found a whole new market, but she was from another planet, or might as well have been.

The Cao Dai religion was founded in Vietnam and is a mixture of other religions. Its gaudily coloured cathedral in Da Lat reminded me of a half-mixed pot of paint which was beginning to separate.

When I went to the toilet, a helpful little man, who seemed to work there, pointed out the urinals. I went in and began to do what I had gone in there to do. The man came in as well and stood by me. He turned on the taps which flush out the urinal, water coming out of holes in a rubber tube. As he stood there, he appeared to be looking down at my equipment. I gave him a funny look.

"You've got a good job," I said dryly.

He was folding up a piece of tissue paper. I hadn't quite finished, those last few squirts you know, when he leaned over and dabbed the end of my penis with the folded-up paper.

"Oi!" I exclaimed. He backed off rapidly. I was trying to remain calm, perhaps this was merely a strange local custom. He wasn't taking any chances however: he legged it. I looked down to do up my fly and realised the hose along the top of the urinals was spraying the water directly onto my trousers. They were soaked through. It looked as if I had had a terrible accident.

"You little bastard!" I shouted after him.

I don't know what I would have done had I caught him, but I reckon I came out of that place with a look that could have throttled at twenty paces. He was nowhere to be seen.

Doing my best to cover my wet trousers with my shirt, I found Garth. He was still in the temple and roared with laughter when I told him.

At Tam Tam's bar, the waitresses stood around with little to do, so they were very keen to collect glasses. One tried to take Garth's before he had finished it and so started a game. At any opportunity, she would take something and give us a huge shy smile. Whenever she went by I grinned at her and she would burst into a great giggling grin. Once she nudged me as she passed and at the bar, she gave me a playful kick with her foot. The humorous interaction made our evening.

A couple of nights later, we were there again. At the end of the night, she mouthed "Tomorrow" at me, between her huge, helpless smiles and when we left, I said I wanted to take a photograph of her. Her name was Yenh.

Returning to our hotel the next day, Yenh was there. She had found out where we were staying from another traveller. She handed me a note.

"To remember," she said. She said she would see us that night, climbed on the back of a motorbike, driven by an older woman and rode off. I noticed Hoa, one of the girls we joked with at the cafe next door, looking daggers. When we sat down to read the note, Phuong, the owner of the café, said with a smile "I think you have a girlfriend in Hoi An. Hoa is very angry!"

Hoa protested that she had a boyfriend in Danang.

The note said:

Dear my friend

I am 21 years old. I am very proud when I make friend with you But I am very sad when you will leave Hoi An What a pity? if I met you early, we should have a lot of chances to talk each other But at the moment I think you are my brother because now am not did take care of my family Because my mother

92

died, and my father had new wife and treat with me very indifferent so I want to have a older brother to share. When I am sad. or cheerful. About life. I had Job but not less happy because the work is very busy and leader very strict but I am still positive to work because my life. When I wish to have helping.

So can you help me? If you are pleased I will thank you very much Now I need a bicycle to go work because I don't have it. Well! What a bout your life Cant you tell me please?

Happy you come back your country lucky!

Friend girl Yenh.

I found out how much a bike would cost from Phuong. She said up to 300,000 (about US$20) for a new one, but much less for second hand. Na Na, one of the tailors we bought clothes from, doubled that. Garth and I discussed the ethics of it. It was so easy for us to do and we had made a connection with her. She had not seemed calculating, but sweet and innocent. In the end, we each wrote a note and we put about 200,000 dong in both US dollars and dong into an envelope.

At the bar that evening, Yenh watched as Garth and I played pool. I asked her if she had any brothers and sisters. She did not. She said she wanted a brother. She spoke very quietly. I asked if the man sitting in front of us was her boss. I think she misheard because she vigorously shook her head and pointed at me and said "Boyfriend." I suspected she did not understand that word in the same way as I did. When I said that I was going to Nha Trang the next day, she pouted sadly and a little crossly.

Soon before we left, I sidled over and gave her the envelope. Some of the other waitresses covered for her while she went off to open it. Coming back, she still looked pouty, but provided smiles when we left. Later that night, I found I still had my letter to Yenh in my pocket. All she had seen was the money and Garth's note. That explained her disappointed pout. I ran back to Tam Tam's. It was almost closing. One waitress was outside. I ran up.

"Yenh?" I asked, pointing inside. She nodded, then rushed upstairs ahead of me. The whole staff seemed to be in on it. I explained that I had just found the note in my pocket. She asked for my address, then I waved farewell to the crowd. There were a few words and nudges and Yenh climbed off her stool and followed me downstairs. She wished me safe travels. I kissed her hand, then she went inside and I disappeared into the night.

Like Hiep and many others I have met over the years, I still wonder what happened to her and whether she is happy.

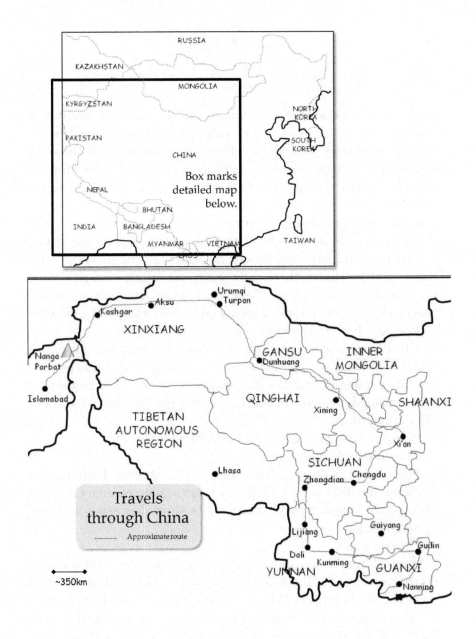

Box marks detailed map below.

Travels through China

------- Approximate route

~350km

Into China

I left the Vietnamese border officials and boarded the smart new Chinese sleeper. It was after midnight and all of us in the compartment were just dozing off when a border guard shook us awake, gave us arrivals cards to complete, then went off with them and our passports. Another man woke us a few minutes later to ask where we were from. Yet another visited with health questionnaires and customs declarations. Finally, we were woken by a man returning our passports. When I next awoke, we were on our way.

It was humid when we arrived in Nanning. The buildings were larger than in Hanoi, there were many more cars and they were segregated from the bikes. There were pedestrian overpasses and people all but ignored me. Shops were full of electronics, watches and clothes. It seemed prosperous.

I had become concerned that my visa was about to expire, so I found the police: the Public Security Bureau or PSB. I was pointed towards a young, friendly looking chap who spoke some English.

I explained my concern and he told me my visa did indeed need to be renewed.

"Could I have two months?" I asked hopefully.

"Three months," he replied.

Even better, I thought. Then came the bad news. I had to wait five days to collect it. So I explained I was leaving Nanning the next day, could I collect it then? There was a short discussion with one of his colleagues.

"No problem."

Puzzled but pleased about how easy that had been to negotiate, I booked into a hotel. It was a weary Western style hotel room, but it was to be the best room I slept in during my seven weeks in China.

After a cup of tea, I went out and bought an alarm clock. I had a laugh with the shop assistant as I tried out my Chinese. He gave me three receipts at the sales counter which I presented to the cashier at a separate desk. She stamped these and gave me two, one of which was for me, while I had to give the other back to the salesman. He then presented me with my new clock.

I went to the railway station to find out train times to Guilin. The information counter would only tell me the next train to Guilin, which was at 1530. I felt helpless without the language.

I tried the tourist information kiosk just outside the station. A speaker of English was summoned and she told me there were trains at 0830, 1000, 1500 and 1912. She did not mention the 1530. I tried the ticket office. I wrote down 10am, the next day's date and said "Guilin". He wrote down that the train went at 1105.

I clearly needed to know more Chinese. Or they needed to get their timetable sorted out.

I returned to my room and switched on the television. There was a music video in memory of the Chinese journalists killed by a NATO bomb in Belgrade. The singer sang passionately against a black background amidst piles of white flowers. The orchestra and choir gushed in the background and there were news clips of protesting Chinese, B-52 bombers, Belgrade in flames, the wreckage of the embassy and distraught relatives. Quite incongruously, this was immediately followed by the FA Cup Final and a programme about England and old paintings.

I found a channel showing the News in English. There was talk only of resolving the Kosovo conflict and nothing about what Serbia had been doing. The whole news presentation was dull. On the other hand, the female presenters on all channels were extremely attractive.

The adverts were also fascinating. They were jolly and Western in style. I managed to work out that there were pills which ate layers of fat, made you grow taller, reduced acne and one which was a cream which appeared to make you beautiful. It was made from extract of sheep placenta.

A woman kept phoning my room. I assumed it was Reception so I explained that I did not understand because I was English. After she had phoned three times I went down to talk to the receptionist. Her English for dealing with standard questions seemed competent, but the unusual was impossible for both her English and my Chinese skills. I decided *she* had not been phoning me and the strange caller persisted, despite my protestations. Eventually, I would just say I did not understand, goodbye, and hang up. Taking the phone off the hook for an hour helped too, but at 6am, she phoned again. I hung up and took it off the hook once more. I never knew what it was about, but so far, it has seemed my life has not depended on it.

Back at the PSB there was a crowd. A quiet, polite girl told me she was hoping to study at "North. London. University." Could I tell her anything about North. London. University? Was it the most excellent university in London? How many students were there? I answered her questions as best I could.

A man came out to deal with me.

"Why do you want an extension?" he asked.

I explained.

"But your visa is valid."

I didn't argue; I was satisfied, although concerned about the confusion. I took my passport and went to catch my train. It was new, clean and comfortable. I sat with three young men who were friendly and curious. We tried out my Chinese and they looked at my books.

Music played over the public address system. There were Western sounding middle-of-the-road ballads in Chinese, as well as jolly orchestrations of *Roll out the barrel* and *Highland laddie*. Staff came down the train selling noodles, duck necks, corn on the cob and even perfume. Outside, a major road was being built north of Nanning and there were rice fields, pine and banana trees.

In Guilin I took a minibus to Yangshuo.

"Y30, cheapest price!" called the barker.

I had read that Y5 was the fare. In case that was out of date, I offered Y10, then haggled poorly and paid Y20. I later met others who had paid Y5.

I sat at the back next to a couple with a small child who I greeted. Despite the parents' encouragement, he just stared at me, so I did the trick that had always worked in Vietnam: I turned my hat backwards with the neck protector covering my face and put my sunglasses on. The parents laughed, but the child burst into tears. They thought that was very funny too. The rest of the bus turned around to see what the nasty foreigner had done.

Later, a chubby girl sat between us. The father lit a cigarette and she grimaced at the smoke. Then he hawked up on the floor a couple of times. She looked disgusted.

We drove through the landscape of tall, rounded, rocky hills for an hour until we reached Yangshuo in the heart of it on the Li River. I found a hotel and immediately met some travellers.

A Norwegian told me he had come over the Karakoram Highway and had enjoyed Pakistan. I was annoyed because I had originally planned to visit Pakistan, but had been warned off by British, US and Australian government websites after the Americans had bombed Taliban bases in Pakistan.

The next day, an English girl called Fiona and I hired bikes and rode out to Moon Hill. Rice fields occupied the flat land, but they were surrounded by rounded limestone hills rising straight up like a crowd of giant grey teeth. The landscape looked quite unreal.

There were steps up Moon Hill which had a hole in the top shaped like a horizontal crescent. There were women at the bottom selling drinks and postcards. One with silver teeth, calling herself Mama Moon, suggested we go back to her house for lunch afterwards, a business we had heard about. Part way up the steps was an old man selling things. He spoke no English, but had the usual book of travellers' comments. One said: "I came here in '93 and first saw this bloke and he's still selling the same old shit."

It was a swift and sweaty climb, but even under a featureless grey sky the view was spectacular: the swarm of peaks beyond the rice fields, the brown river winding through them.

We went back to Mama Moon's house and I tried to learn some new words. I was surprised how much Chinese I was able to use, but she spoke a different dialect to the Beijing Mandarin I had learned and kept correcting me on things I was sure were right. After lunch, she led us through rice fields and neat vegetable patches. The fields were a rich green, bamboo lined the river and streams and there were buffalo swimming contentedly or being walked beside the tracks to graze.

Back at the hotel we met a Cumbrian lass called Jane and discussed Asian views of Kosovo. I had talked to the jolly Vietnamese conductor on the train to the border. He did not agree with NATO's bombing. I had asked if he knew why they were bombing. He did not. I had asked if he knew that the Serbs were forcing over a million people out of the country and murdering hundreds, possibly thousands. He did not, nor did he seem to accept it. He said that over a million Serbs had been killed in the bombing.

Jane described a lengthy discussion with some honeymooners from Harbin in northern China (there had been 43 couples on the train). They had been surprised at her audacity in travelling without a guide, It was *their* first time outside Harbin. They thought Serbia was peace-loving and knew nothing about Bosnia. They had asked if Britain and America were going to split Serbia between them, and why Tony Blair was going to give Britain to America. Also they had wondered why Princess Diana had been murdered and why she had not moved to America where she could be free.

We wondered what they must think of us and the outside world.

After wandering through souvenir stands selling identical wooden and marble carvings, Jane, Fiona and I returned to the hotel to read, write and chat, watching the rain and the low cloud pass between the limestone hulks.

We went out cycling again to the towering, bare limestone hills amongst the rice fields, villages, dirt roads, water buffalo and peasants. We were greeted and shouted at, as much mockingly as welcomingly. My first reaction was that the people were stupid, ignorant of the way the world worked. But it occurred to me that there were over a billion Chinese and much of the world *was* like this, so yes, they were right, we *were* strange.

In the English language *China Daily* there was an article on how many international laws NATO was breaking, but there was still nothing about the Serbs. Apparently the reason Kosovars were fleeing was because of the NATO bombing, which, the article implied, was making deliberate targets of refugee convoys, hospitals and embassies.

We went shopping in the afternoon. The shopkeepers would fall about laughing at our first price then go down to their "last price", which rarely was. Fiona bought a dress for Y80. They had started at Y200, she at Y60. They would say that an identical dress in a different colour would be Y60, but not the one you wanted.

We met an Irishman called Martin. He had begun his journey with his girlfriend, but on the ferry from Ireland on their first day, she had dumped him. He was furious: he had had a number of friends who had wanted to go with him. He had arrived in Yangshuo at 2am and hired a cyclo driver to take him to the hotel. The man had agreed for Y10, then simply pedalled across the road to where it was. And laughed. Martin had too.

Jane, Fiona and I took the bus back to Guilin. We found the CITS government tourist agency. Staff milled around and refused to answer or understand any of our questions. We decided this was because we had arrived during their lunch break, so settled down to wait. We watched a historic fantasy drama on television in the waiting room. Our heroes were forced to duel each other for some reason and fought up cliffs, across the sky and somersaulted huge distances. To everyone's horror, one killed the other. He was mortified. A woman thought it was funny, but an old man produced an elixir which brought him back to life. Another epic duel was in progress when a woman switched channels to a high school drama.

I tried another information office. They were very friendly and sat me down and finally produced a card of information in English which told me that the Kunming train left at 3.45. I returned to CITS where nothing continued to happen. We were just leaving when an English-speaking man Fiona had dealt with a few days before ambled in, his jacket draped nonchalantly across his shoulders. He introduced himself as Liao and told me about the Kunming trains, none of which left at 3.45. But then he told me they were impossible to book because they were full by the time they reached Guilin. There was another way however. Go to Kunming via Nanning. It took about the same time.

- Good. Could he help me with that?
- There was no problem getting a seat on the day to Nanning, but he could not book me from Nanning to Kunming from Guilin.
- Oh.
- But there was another way. He could book me a direct train but not through that office, but through...contacts. There *are* places, it was just that they were attached to tour packages. I would have to pay a commission (or a bribe, I wondered).
- Fine.

As we left, I still had little faith that I would make it to Kunming.

Our bus to Longsheng stopped almost immediately to load some furniture onto the roof, then unload it. Then we were on our way and were soon amongst tall, steep mountains swathed in cloud and draped with shawls of dense bamboo and birch forest. There were wooden houses and rushing rivers in the narrow valley bottoms. Cultivated terraces climbed up between the clouds and the trees.

At the top of a hill we stopped and the bonnet was opened. Everyone climbed out. The only sounds were burping frogs and the occasional car. A sleeper bus with reclining seats came along and we all squeezed on. Apparently ours was not going to be a quick fix.

Longsheng was a grubby, modern town along the banks of the Sang River in a pretty terraced valley with old wooden houses scattered on the hillsides. We found a restaurant and added a few more marks to the seasoned orange tablecloth. The place filled up with locals playing cards. From the room next door came bizarre chanting. I suggested they were boasting to the rest of the town that they had foreigners. Jane took this up: "One's got green eyes, one's got blue eyes, one's got brown hair, one's got blonde hair..."

We took a bus to the Dragon's Back Terraces at Huang Lao, famous for covering a large area of steep mountainsides. The bus stopped on the edge of town and everyone rushed to where people were leaning over the bridge.

"Probably someone drowning," I said wryly.

As it happened, I was right. Two men were kneeling by a figure on the bank far below.

We stopped in a town an hour from Longsheng. The engine was turned off and everyone got off the bus. Apparently we were there. We walked off and asked a farmer the way. He told us we needed to take a bus. We got back just in time to see our bus disappearing up the street. We caught up and the conductor ushered us back on. I sat at the back next to a Yao woman, one of China's many ethnic minorities and a native of the area. The sides of her hair were shaved but the rest was thickly curled into a turban.

An old woman sitting near the girls was amused by the studs in Fiona's ear. The girls decided to give her something to laugh at so pulled up their shirts to reveal their pierced navels. Much hilarity and excitement ensued as she had to show her friends. That was nothing to when they noticed that Jane had seven earrings.

We were dropped at a collection of houses by the river, over which stretched a suspension bridge. We swayed across to the houses on the other side and followed the track along the river and up the hill. It was humid and started to rain.

We climbed steadily until the path became a narrow track along the actual borders of the rice fields. A farmer confirmed our suspicions by gesturing to us that we were going the wrong way. We turned back. Another farmer squatting in a straw hat with a sheet of clear plastic over his shoulders pointed us back down as well. An old man came down the hill behind us, barefoot and carrying a staff. He pointed us down and then up. Back at the bottom after an hour of going the wrong way, the little old farmer gestured with his stick towards a well-made stone path which led through the village and straight up the hillside through the terraces. A little way up, I turned to look down. The farmer was watching. I waved and he jabbed upwards with his stick.

It had stopped raining, but that just made it even more humid. We had made it nearly halfway to the top, red-faced and streaming with sweat. We were running out of time and water and were on the lower fringes of thick cloud which obscured the upper slopes. There seemed little point in carrying on and the view down the terraced valley was still beautiful.

Our hotel had assured us that hot showers were available on the floor below our own, but the one in the public bathroom had been cold when I had tried it, so Reception had unlocked room 402 so I could use their en suite before we went out. After our day on the terraces, we all wanted showers. Jane went to 402, but the water was cold. After much trying of other rooms and general buggering about, Reception changed the gas canister and she had a hot shower.

It was my turn next. I went to 402 but the water was cold. Reception directed me to 302 instead. I had a hot shower and left the door open for Fiona, but when she went, she found 302 had been locked so she too had gone to Reception. She was then shown back to 402 where she successfully had a hot shower.

We found out it was Children's Day and were told where we could see children singing and dancing at a concert. The hall was packed and kids danced in costumes on the stage. They were mainly girls, but one routine had four lads who, it seemed, had only agreed to dance if they could wear combat gear and do moves that were more like martial arts.

Girls in the wings danced along enthusiastically with the routines on stage. Applause, if there was any, was brief, but there were others seeing the funny side of it all too. We had to restrain ourselves from hooting and cheering. A little girl in white bobbed her head from side to side and did a solo. On her second song, a chorus line in yellow danced behind her. It was great.

I woke early the next day and lay listening to the clatter and chatter of the waking town, thinking of home and the difficult travel yet to come. Jane and Fiona were going home the following week and they had turned my thoughts homeward.

I left the girls and took the bus back to Guilin. Liao was asleep when I arrived at the CITS. He called up his contact and got me on a late night train. I went out for a stroll and a woman offered to clean my shoes for Y1. After she had done it, it suddenly became Y15 because, she explained, she had used polish and wax. I protested. There were many people about who all thought the conversation was hilarious. I was careful not to lose face by becoming angry and laughed along with them. I felt outnumbered and unsure of what to do. Y15 was extortion, but I still gave Y10, feeling like a fool. She argued, supported by bystanders and other traders. I walked off, still laughing and they let me go with a smile which showed I could have got away with less. Probably Y1 in fact.

I was unhappy, but Guilin had a reputation for skinning tourists. It was hot and sweaty and I found a quiet street where a low wall provided a place to sit and read. A young lad on a bike trundled up and a woman came out of the house behind me. They both talked to me, with the lad translating. I let the lad practise his English on me then I went looking for somewhere to eat. A woman called me into her noodle house and I watched her husband whirling the dough around with his fingers.

The 'commission' on my ticket turned out to be almost twice the price of the ticket. Liao also tried to get me to pay for the extra long wait in the waiting room.

My berth was in hard sleeper. This meant that instead of a European style couchette (soft sleeper), the carriage had ten groups of six bunks, each separated by a wall but open to the corridor. It was like a dormitory. My firm bunk was comfortable enough. I awoke to a greywhite swamp of low cloud. Sixty people performed their morning ablutions using three sinks and one squat toilet which thankfully had a handle on the wall so you did not tumble into it. Some people all but showered in the sink.

The ghostly shapes of hills appeared in the thick cloud, piling up one behind the other. Limestone scenery continued to slide past all morning. We had been slowly ascending. Every available bit of flat land was cultivated with rice, maize or other crops. Buffalo ploughed the mud. Rice was picked and left in bunches in the water. Children walked in groups along tracks. I saw no motor vehicles apart from a people carrier. These were little more than an engine on wheels towing a cart where the driver and passengers sat. I had seen them in Vietnam too. The train refilled with water at a small town where people stood or squatted on other tracks watching the world and the trains go by. Even the land between the tracks and the hill in one narrow valley was sown with maize.

I spent the afternoon sleeping and reading. On emerging from some PG Wodehouse to the reality of the train, I experienced mild culture shock. One of my neighbours, who had chained his briefcase to his bunk, had earlier given me an apple. He snored all afternoon through every jolt and whistle, his hand rising and falling gently on his gut.

By the evening, people in my own carriage seemed quite used to me and it was only in the others where I was still stared at as I went to buy food.

The hills returned to normal shapes, lower with more flat land and bigger rice fields. We crossed viaducts and saw more being built. A child giggled joyously in the berth below me. The happiest thing this side of Heaven is the innocence of infancy. The apple-giver continued snoring unhealthily. A couple of men started talking to me. Not being able to communicate properly was frustrating for all of us, but there was much smiling and good will.

The next morning I was refreshed and ready to be expelled from my cocoon into Yunnan province. I said goodbye to my friends and walked up a wide boulevard lined with modern buildings. It was a fast developing city. Big office blocks of glass and marble were going up everywhere, generally in interesting shapes with rounded or pointed tops. They were being built in clusters between the boulevards, so the city still felt open. I was impressed by the number of smart shops

I passed a clothes shop playing Western pop music. One of its many shop assistants stationed himself just outside and clapped loudly in time with the music, but his face remained stern, as if he were threatening passers-by.

It was good to be in the sunshine for a while. By the river I found groups playing cards. They were mostly old men. Others watched the games over their shoulders. I tried to fathom the rules. An old crone was selling newspapers out of a bag bearing a *Playboy* bunny.

Even in the heart of this glitzy, modern city, peasant China walked in old clothes and straw hat with a wooden bar across the shoulders. They look transplanted. In contrast were the trendy young things; dubious looking youths in wide shouldered double-breasted jackets, baggy pants, white socks and slip-on shoes. Others dressed in tight-fitting sleeveless shirts on a very skinny body.

An enormous traditional design of gate had been built on a large roundabout against the Western style high rise and the huge poster of a Western woman in trendy red clothes. A tiny, elderly couple in grey overall suits hobbled around and marvelled and had their picture taken against this backdrop.

When I looked at old people I wondered at what they had been through: the warlords, the rise of the Nationalists, the Japanese invasion, the rise of Communists and the civil war, Korea and the threat of US invasion, the Great Leap Forward, the Cultural Revolution and increasing commercialism. A generation had suffered from the curse "May you live in interesting times."

I came across a block of old buildings, which seemed to have been saved from the developers. They were ramshackle brick terraces with wooden top floors and chunky roof tiles. Although they looked dilapidated, they had character.

I found narrow streets with a market and shop fronts from which goods poured onto the street. I bought freshly baked flat bread containing a sugary, honey like filling. When the man told me the price, a wet crumb flew out of his mouth and landed on the rolls which he had fortunately just wrapped in a cloth. I strolled down the lane munching. Occasionally, small school children giggled at me excitedly.

I was largely left alone on the street. Some people said hello, but often this was said only once they had walked past. Others would grin at me as if I had a piece of paper stuck to my forehead saying 'Dickhead'.

I visited the Bamboo Temple in the hills outside town surrounded by forest. Since it was first built in the thirteenth century, it had been destroyed in a fire, then rebuilt. Large warriors pulling excruciating faces and threatening to do things with their swords, bulged their eyes at visitors at the main gate.

Everything was brightly coloured: golden Buddhas, red pillars inscribed with golden characters and dragons on the tiled eaves. But what I liked most were the five hundred lifelike life-sized *louhans*, or enlightened ones. There were three layers of them lining the walls of three rooms. Wearing robes and usually shaven-headed, they

106

smiled, smirked, looked benign, talked to their neighbour or peered curiously. There were also ones who looked demonic with dark curling hair and bulging eyes. In one room they surfed down the walls on tumbling waves riding various creatures including fish, a dragon, an almost camel and almost donkeys. There was also a chap with very long white eyebrows, one looking pleased at his bare legs, one peeling back an old face to reveal a young one and one with an eye set vertically in his forehead and with a little face peering out from behind each ear.

In a quiet courtyard, a monk stepped onto his balcony and fired a ball of phlegm onto the ground.

Towns of stone

The bus to Dali travelled through dry, scrubby hills with reddish earth eroded in places and terraced in others. The flat land was mainly sown with maize. Towns and villages were clusters of mud brick houses packed together to minimise unproductive land use. Peasants moved like ants along straight dirt roads, but looked out of place when we saw them on the modern expressway. Clearly an investment for the tourist region, it went through tunnels with grand entrances into the heart of the mountain.

Dali was full of old, narrow streets, stone buildings and travellers' cafes. A man tried to shine my shoes then noticed a pouch on my camera bag had a broken zip. He said his brother could fix it for Y10. It was a fiddly job but easily done on a big, clunky sewing machine in the street under an umbrella. They were friendly.

"Where you from? Sussex? Exmoor?" asked the tailor.

At the guesthouse were two men I had met at a lunch stop earlier in the day. They were Ade, a Welshman living in Australia, and Rob from Amsterdam. We went in search of food, avoided the travellers' cafes and found a local place instead. All ingredients were in bowls on shelves, so we pointed at tomatoes and egg, broad beans, chicken and a chicken and mint soup and they cooked them for us.

Over beers in the evening, we talked about what we had got out of our time away, about being open to life's possibilities and the attitude that prevents you from slipping into a rut. Rob said he had learned that in giving you get so much in return. He described a small incident in India where he had been about to enjoy eating an orange. He had been surrounded by small children who all wanted some, so had given it all away.

It poured with rain all night. I slept badly, partially because I needed the toilet, but it was a long way to go in the rain, along the balcony, down the stairs and around the corner.

During a leisurely breakfast, we noticed one of the girls on the staff laying a tablecloth by throwing it out. She appeared to be practising. She would fold it up on itself in six inch segments then fiddle around with the completed bundle, fluff it, then fling it out. We watched her do it several times, before she saw us watching, looked shy and stopped.

The weather began to clear, but clouds still hung around the tops of the Canshang mountains. I walked along the rebuilt city wall to the south gate. Wandering further, I went among old narrow streets and came across an ornamental park with a croquet pitch. Old men and women were playing and watching. There was much heckling. One team captain, who was clearly the expert because he was the only one wearing a tracksuit, shouted commands to his doddering team mates.

I bumped into Ade and Rob and we had a kebab and potatoes on a stick fried in a wok at a stall just outside the north gate. Several squads of police marched past, singing. The sun came out as we watched men playing chess in the square.

We were having a few beers and dinner when someone suggested we go dancing at a club in town they had heard about. Other travellers had the same idea and so we hit the dance floor. There were plenty of young things grooving away, but the large dance floor was far from packed. It did not feel like China.

A group of ten girls was dancing quietly together so I went over and danced with them for a while. To my surprise they seemed impressed, or perhaps they were simply being polite. Either way, I thought it best to return to my backpacking friends. Other than that, it felt quite Western…except when the locals suddenly broke into a conga and then some line dancing.

It all stopped when they called for volunteers to play some games. A few Chinese rushed out and a tall Australian decided to go for it. I felt I had to represent my own country, so I too stepped into the unknown. Somehow we managed to work out that we had to walk down the dance floor like catwalk models. Despite getting the largest cheers for my cool strut and quick seductive flash of a bit of shoulder, I came third behind a Chinese lad and the Aussie. I was assured it must have been rigged and I should have come second. I refused to take part in the game of musical chairs that followed, but it was hilarious to watch as they circled ever slower around the diminishing number of seats, scrabbling with each other to sit before the music had even stopped.

And then the dancing began again. A song came on with obscene English lyrics. If only the demure little Chinese girls had realised what they were dancing to so daintily. By this stage, most of the locals had left.

Towards the end of the evening, some of the remaining locals returned to the floor. These included two men, one short and chubby, the other tall and thin. They were older than anyone else and danced in the only way they probably knew: holding hands and twirling each other around. Same sex physicality, arm-linking and embracing was common in China, besides, they weren't good enough dancers to be gay.

The more disturbing part came when the little chap had a rest and the tall one homed in on me as his next dance partner and kept trying to hold my hand.

When we finally called it a night, he shook everyone's hand excitedly and was pleased to point out that he was taller than most of us. We congratulated him on this achievement.

The next morning was one of slow recovery before we rented bikes and freewheeled down the long hill to visit the villages around the lake. We invaded a quiet restaurant's kitchen, once more pointing at various foods to suggest lunch. They asked us questions as to the style of cooking and we all laughed because no one knew what anyone was talking about. The result was still good.

While we were in the restaurant, a crowd went by, the women all in their bright pink traditional dress with a headdress that reminded me of feathers. A group of musicians was sitting on the street. Several were playing two stringed instruments balanced on the knee and played with a bow. There was an instrument like a guitar, a kind of xylophone and a man with cymbals. Behind them was a walled yard. Inside was a building in which we could see girls dancing in a circle. I asked an old man if it was a wedding, the only celebration for which I knew the word. He told me something, gesturing, as if it were obvious, but I was none the wiser.

The villages near the lakeshore had narrow lanes lined by buildings with plaster walls. Old men and women sat in the shade talking and observing. Usually the women were in their traditional blue dresses that looked like overalls, and the men were in their blue Mao suits.

We continued through lanes and villages until we turned back across rice fields, bright green in the sun between dry stone walls. The plain sloped gently up to the mountains which rose in a huge, hazy mass. A few people were scattered in the fields. One man was in a Mao suit, bending with a small sickle. His wife was in the next field in a conical hat, spraying the rice from a tank on her back. From time to time they would call out to each other. A horse was tethered by the track. At times the path became so narrow and bumpy we would almost plunge off it into the paddy field.

We bought tickets to Lijiang for Y30. Then the bus company phoned the hotel and told us the price had gone up to Y40 and they were now going half an hour earlier. We asked for our money back and they changed their minds about both the new price and the new departure time. In the end of course, we actually left half an hour later because they waited for there to be enough people on board.

The road quickly entered mountains. They were brown and bare, with a few rice fields far below. More mountains of cloud-topped scoured rock appeared around us.

Our journey was shorter than expected, partially due to our driver not believing in bends. He would accelerate towards them, steering very late and brake half way round, just in time to avoid leaving the road. I was glad to arrive.

We walked through Lijiang until we found ourselves quite suddenly in the touristy little streets of the old town. Taking an indirect route through the maze, we found the First Bend Inn, named after the first bend of the Yangtze on which the town sits.

Rob and I went for a walk. Passing one building we heard music, so peered in. A sign told us it was the base of the Naxi orchestra, the home of "three rarities: old music, old instruments and old musicians". And there on stage were three of the old musicians themselves in their old costumes. One straight faced man with a long beard and another younger old man played knee violins, the third, with glasses and eyes pointing in different directions, played a guitar-like instrument. Amongst them were members of the People's Liberation Army, also playing and making a show of learning from the *laoshi*, the old masters. Others stood watching, along with a reporter, TV cameraman and a photographer. The latter beckoned us to the front so we could take better photographs. Then they wanted us on stage, photographing the musicians, so we exchanged propaganda value for better photographs. We left while they were filmed looking at pictures of Chairman Zhu's recent visit.

"How was my hair?" asked Rob.

In a bar that night, we talked to two jolly Japanese with their Chinese guide. One was the retired controller of the Tokyo meat market, while the other was a professional Go player, although he insisted he wasn't any good. They had bought a bottle of 55% proof local firewater which they gave us when they left. Having tasted it, we decided it best to share it with others in the cafe.

The next morning, Rob and I hired some bikes again. The road went gradually up a valley. Dark clouds were gathering around the highest peak in front of us. We cycled on chatting until we reached the village of Shibao, a former regional capital. As soon as we entered the town the tarmac stopped and was replaced by uneven stones. The houses looked old. A two storey one appeared to be mainly a barn with a small living area on the ground floor. A few people were about, mainly sheltering from the light rain which had started to fall. The only ones who seemed to be working were old women who were carrying things or working in the fields.

On another day, Ade and I lost ourselves in the maze of the old town when it started to rain. We sheltered under over-hanging eaves by a shuttered window. After a while, an old woman came out and invited us in. We passed through a small wood-filled courtyard with a furiously barking dog and were ushered into the living room. It had a concrete floor, a television which was on, a long, low cabinet with a blue glass front, a plastic sofa and a couple of stools. A shirtless young man was sitting on the sofa reading a book. The woman bustled out a small boy. I asked the man if the child was his son. He was. That was all we got out of him. We felt unwelcome and the woman had disappeared.

The rain looked as though it had eased, so we made our excuses and left. The man brightened up and politely saw us to the gate. The rain became heavier again and, like street fighting soldiers looking for cover, we ran from house to house seeking the protection of projecting roofs.

Ade came with me for the next leg of my trip, which was to take us into the fringes of Tibet. Our bus even had computerised tickets. We wondered if life was about to become simple and organised.

Tibetan Fringe I
Searching for Shangri-La

Thousands of feet up in the eastern foothills of the Himalaya sprawls the town of Zhongdian. Because it sits on a plain, it is hard to grasp that the hills which surround it are really the peaks of 14,000 foot mountains. Many of the inhabitants are tall, their faces betraying that more angular Tibetan physiognomy, rather than the rounder one of the Han Chinese. This is Tibet in all but name. The town sits on the Yunnan Province side of the border with the Tibetan Autonomous Region. It is in a chunk of Tibet without the administrative hassles of entry of its larger cousin.

There was a Tibetan horse racing festival in Zhongdian. We had found out about it from our guide book which said it was held in the middle of June. We had climbed steadily higher as we left Kunming, travelling on the new road up into the mountains, through Dali to Lijiang where we had first asked when the festival was exactly.

The government tourist office said the big day was the 18th and it went for a week after that. Someone else we asked said it started on the 14th, while another said the 15th. We asked the cook in a restaurant who had given us some other information.

"You want to ride horses?"

"No, the horse racing festival."

"Oh. September," he said.

Lijiang sits not far from the first bend in the Yangtze River and we followed the river for a way as we took the road further north before leaving it as we went deeper into the mountains to Zhongdian. The valley sides were covered in forest, mainly spruce and fir. Things began to look Tibetan as we emerged onto a plateau. There were prayer flags over clustered houses; the clothes were different and the people in them changed too, becoming leaner, more weathered. There were yaks flicking their tails by the roadside.

113

Hills rose up on either horizon. One hill we passed was sprinkled with clumps of pink flowers. Wooden platforms for storing crops stood empty in the fields.

There were two sides to the town. The centre had wide Chinese-made streets. There was a large, efficient looking China Telecom office and a number of newly built banks with tall, grand pillars. In contrast to these signs of Communist materialism, shaven-headed, crimson-robed monks crouched on the kerb of the wide main street, watching silently.

We checked into the Tibetan Hotel at the north end of town. The lobby was a huge, colourfully ornate affair in rich gold and red. The illusion of grandeur stopped outside the lobby. Both the dorm room where we slept as well as the single rooms we saw, were plain with bare concrete floors.

We asked the hotel staff when the festival was. Ade mimed riding horses to back up my question. They replied that it was from the 16th to the 18th. It was puzzling that we never heard the same dates twice so we went into town to find out. Obviously the hotels would know. At the first, we were aided by a helpful Chinese guest who translated for us and were told it started on the 18th and went on for three days. We asked in a couple more hotels and in reply they showed us the room rates. We looked at the room rates, thanked them kindly and left.

In another, the staff rushed off to find someone who spoke English. He arrived poking a roll of money into his ear.

"Hello. Can I help you?" he smiled. We were relieved to find someone whose English was better than my Chinese.

"You've got some money in your ear," Ade pointed out helpfully.

"Hm? Money, yes."

"When is the horse-racing festival?" I asked.

He looked blank.

"*Ma*," I said, which means horse and Ade did his mime of riding horses.

"You want to ride horses?"

"No. The horse racing festival."

"You want to ride horses."

"No. We want to watch them," I explained.

"You want to buy horses?"

Ade tried a mime of photographing speeding horses.

114

"You want to photograph horses?" he tried again, hardly surprisingly.

"No. We want to watch them," I explained again then tried it in Chinese as best I could: "*Wo men yao kan ma.*"

He still looked blank. "Let's give up and find the tourist information. Where is CITS?"

"I am tourist service."

"But you can't speak English mate, your English is crap," Ade consoled him. Fortunately his English *was* too crap to understand him.

"You want to ride horses. Where?" he asked, undeterred.

"We want to watch them. Here. Zhongdian."

It was at about this point that the light dawned on our friend. A smile crept across his face as if he had finally seen a joke we had been trying to explain to him.

"Come, come," he said and beckoned us into his office. He picked up the phone and called someone, had a quick conversation and hung up. "18th, 19th and 20th," he announced.

Great. "Where is it being held?"

In reply he pointed somewhere behind him. Did he have a map? He produced one, which of course was in Chinese.

"Where are we now?" I asked to get my bearings. He looked.

"Here…no…here…" and couldn't find it.

"Where is the Tibetan Hotel?" I asked him, pointing to the north of town where I knew it was.

"No," he said and pointed to the south. He had no idea where he was. We thanked him warmly and left.

The 18th was looking more and more promising. We decided to try one more big, smart looking hotel. Four pretty receptionists stood in a line waiting for us.

"You want to ride horses?"

"No. We want to watch them."

"Ah. There are two lakes. One is eighteen kilometres away. You ride horses there."

When we returned to our hotel, we found a German sitting outside it. He too had heard the 18th, except for from our hotel, which had said the 16th. With infallible German logic, he pointed out that the 18th made more sense because that was the Friday. We had to agree.

After dinner, we went looking for somewhere which had internet. Jason, a helpful Chinese we met in a café, wrote down the Chinese for internet so that we could show it to people. A man in the street, seeing us looking for something asked us if we needed help. He told us he had internet at work because he worked for China Telecom. He led us around the back of the building, which was all locked up because it was evening, and up to his office. Ade was unable to dial in however and we thanked the man profusely so he would not be upset that we had failed to connect. We found a café which advertised internet on its door. Inside was in darkness. We called and a girl appeared so we showed her Jason's writing.

"No," she said, followed by a flurry of Chinese which could have meant "We don't have it any more," or "It's broken," or "I don't know how to work it," or even "You're both so handsome, I've gone all funny."

Now that we knew the date of the festival, we realised we had a few days to kill before it started and decided to visit the town of Deqin. On the morning when we had intended to set off, it was overcast and pouring with rain so we had a discussion about whether to go or not. Having decided to go, we found the bus was full. This gave us the chance to explore Zhongdian a little more.

We went for a walk up a small hill on the edge of town. It made us realise we were at an altitude of 3200m because we were huffing and puffing like old men. I saw a young lad who was wearing a Manchester United shirt.

"I live there," I said in Chinese, pointing to the badge on his chest. He looked blank and, assuming my Chinese had even been comprehensible, he was probably wondering why I lived on his shirt. Later, Ade bought a comb. The transaction was watched by three fascinated Tibetans who came into the shop specifically to see it.

Men sat on doorsteps in the main street with bags of ginseng. Some wrinkled women offered us dried lizards as an aphrodisiac.

"Viagra!" they exclaimed and we all laughed. Groups of girls in traditional dress followed us into shops and watched as we bought food.

We walked through town, taking a detour through some housing and found some communal toilets. There was no running water to clean them out and most of the dividing walls between the squats had been removed. There was filth everywhere. It was all we could

116

do to stay for the duration of our own relief. Soon we were out of the town and going through farmland and fields of grazing cattle and crops and up around a hill with views over the plain. There were yellow flowers in some of the fields.

As we rounded the side of the hill, we could see the monastery on the hillside facing us. There were a couple of main buildings, one of which was very much under construction and a vivid reminder that the place had been all but destroyed during the Cultural Revolution. But the larger part of the buildings were blocky, flat-roofed houses. A truckload of monks pulled up in front of us, unloaded themselves and various sacks and walked in single file down a track to a break in the wall. We followed and some signalled us to keep following. Two others beckoned from rooftops, implying we should come up. Neither could see the other, so we would have offended one of them if we did not go up. As it turned out, we lost sight of them as we went deeper into the narrow paths amongst the buildings. There were a few other tourists about, all of them Chinese. We went inside one building which looked finished on the outside. Inside however, the floorboards had not been nailed down and the wooden interior and roof ornamentation were unpainted. I liked it like that. There was a lone monk inside, intoning a mantra. He acknowledged us vaguely. On the far wall were three golden Buddhas.

We went further up the hill to the main building, past a tour group of orange coated girls from Guizhou and followed a group of men into the building. There was a large dark room with square pillars and rows of long kneelers. There were a few monks, but none praying. Up some stairs, we passed through three rooms with high ceilings. Each was colourfully painted but dark, and in each sat a huge golden Buddha with a youthful face and large eyes. Up further and an empty room looked out onto the previous rooms through an interior window. There were four prayer wheels which we rotated as we went by. In another small room, a lad was making dough while in a couple of others were altars at which some of the tourists knelt and bowed their heads.

In a final room, a monk was giving blessings. We had heard these cost Y5 but one tourist slipped the monk Y100. I would have preferred a blessing freely given or with a donation better disguised as an offering.

It was a gloomy place, a little damp but with colour emerging out of the dark. It was unlike any other religious building I had been in, although spoiled by the tour groups clomping about in much the same way as cathedrals are treated in the West. We had come in the back way and as we left down the main steps, we found a large brown building under construction with two great marble lions in the Chinese, rather than the Tibetan style, guarding the main door. The steps led down to the gaudy main gate and a host of souvenir stands where we wearily caught a bus back into town.

Tibetan Fringe II
The road to Deqin

It was a cloudy but dry morning when we caught the bus and drove out across the green plain beyond town and started climbing. It was a dirt road all the way, cut into the side of the mountains with drops ranging from the steep to the precipitous and littered with blind bends. Zhongdian was soon out of sight.

The landscape became spectacular as we reached a river of chocolate milk in a deep rocky canyon. From here, we climbed up and up, the road really clinging to the mountains which were huge lumps of bare rock plunging thousands of feet to the narrow river far below. A few houses were perched on the bare slopes and there were patches of green terraces, like bowling greens in the desert.

We crested a couple of passes. On the second, I thought we would never stop going up as we disappeared into the cloud somewhere over the four thousand metre. We emerged into purple heather and caught glimpses of snowy mountains through tears in the cloud dragging across the moorland. We stopped by some stupas for a view across a rent in the mountains that seemed to require a more impressive word to describe it than simply 'valley'.

It took us seven and a half hours to reach Deqin, or rather to within hundred yards of the bus station which we could see below us. Those last hundred yards took a further half hour. The problem was that a large yellow bulldozer was parked in the middle of the road and we needed another foot or two of space to get around it. Our driver, who had impressed us with his careful driving, went over to ask the construction workers to move it. They refused.

Our driver performed a seven point turn and went back a couple of miles out of town and turned off into a quarry. From here, a road zigzagged down and led up to Deqin from below. This would have been fine, only we came to a large truck parked right on a bend. Another truck in front of us managed to squeeze around. Again we waited while the driver assessed the situation and this time he asked everyone to get out. He would have to do a tight, steep turn to get around the truck and I suppose there was a danger the bus would tip over. He managed it and we all carried on for a few more minutes before being stopped yet again, this time by a small pile of rocks. A couple of tall, wiry Tibetans climbed out and made short work of moving the rocks and we were on our way again.

There was the bus station gate just yards away...but we could not get to it because the truck in front of us was trying to squeeze past the big yellow bulldozer which had moved and come to torment us again. When we finally arrived, I told the driver he had driven well. That at least was my intention and whatever I had said seemed to please him.

We were shown around the bus station hotel which had clean rooms but a filthy, stinking communal bathroom. If we paid a little bit more, we could have clean rooms with a filthy stinking en suite bathroom. We booked into the Deqin Hotel instead, only to discover after we had paid that they did not have any water.

We went to explore the town which was built on a hill. There were building projects under way and from the look of the hotels under construction, the tourist industry would soon be hitting town. Most of the buildings were modern with the typical white tiles and blue glass. There was a large proportion of Tibetans and we did not arouse the interest I had been expecting. We found some potatoes on a stick and a woman making crisps and we ate them while waiting for our dinner to be cooked in a small family restaurant. There was a grandmother playing with her granddaughter and she sent the girl off for some more crisps, which we tried to refuse, and some sunflower seeds which she gave us with a face that was shy, sad and timid. John went and bought some sweets which they tried to refuse but he kept insisting until they accepted. Then they went and bought us some more crisps. Dinner arrived before this could get out of hand.

The next morning was grey and there was a little rain early on. Our first job was to move hotels and we were able to get larger double rooms for the same price as the one the four of us had been sharing. We had breakfast where we had eaten the previous night then we had a game of snooker on one of the full sized tables in the hotel. Some locals watched us while we howled with laughter at how bad we were. There were more snooker tables per head of population than I had ever seen. Everyone was playing. There were tables in the market, and by the side of the road. We even saw them making one, smoothing out plaster on the table.

By lunchtime, the weather was beginning to brighten up so we decided to go for a walk, following the road out of town in the direction of Lhasa. It was a pretty good gravel road and it wound up the side of the valley on a steady gradient while the valley dropped away sharply, making it look as though we had climbed far. There were road gangs scattered along the way and most greeted us as we went by.

We walked about ten kilometres to a village at a low pass and there on the other side was the first line of the Himalaya proper, the Mei Li Snow Mountain, breaking through the cloud. The village was small and quiet and there were some new buildings even here. People sat in the shade and nodded to us. And around the bend and out of the village was the mountain of snow and rock under a tattered mantle of thick white cloud glowing in the sunlight. To the right of us was a little compound, surely too small for a monastery but with a line of seven or eight gleaming white stupas facing the valley. A little way down from the shrouded peak, a silver glacier tongued down a valley.

We walked back, the weather becoming clearer. The road gangs were back at work and surprisingly friendly and cheerful to the rich Westerners strolling amongst their hard labour. Big blue dumper trucks roared up and down with loads of gravel. Some gangs were breaking stones, others evened out the surface. The town was always a bend away and never there when we rounded it.

The next morning, our bus soon filled up; bags and people choking the aisle. We had numbered seats but decided to ignore them in case everyone else did. But one bloke was stroppy and gesticulated at Ade to move. Then he stood in the way and became angrier because Ade did not immediately leap from his seat and knock him over to get out of the way. Finally everyone was settled. It was a bigger bus and Ade and I had a pole between us that gave us a little feeling of security should the bus happen to roll. At 8.30am we pulled out, drove thirty yards down the street and stopped. Then we loaded stuff onto the roof rack and despite the bus already being full to bursting, four more people got on.

Amongst our fellow passengers was a crew of Chinese toting big cameras, presumably from the East for whom this was as much of an adventure as it was for us. They all wore special photographer waistcoats with many pockets for films, brushes and lenses. In front of us sat a little man with a taut-skinned face. He wore a suit, without a tie, and a new looking fedora. Broad brimmed hats seem common amongst the Tibetans. Ade nicknamed him Mr Gobalot because he kept spitting out of the window.

The day was clear and a wall of snowy mountains was visible over the green hills around the road. We took pictures of the plunging bare green valley. Mr Gobalot and his wife were amused. He would turn and grin and mime pointing a camera.

Next to me was a bloke sitting in the aisle on a sack. Suddenly he looked troubled and put his hand over his mouth and made movements indicating he would like to vomit out of the window. Despite there being no room to move, I was out of my seat in a jiffy and Ade had managed to worm out from behind the pole.

He wanted to stay there but we wouldn't let him. Half an hour later, he looked troubled again and lurched at our window. This time, we directed him to the poleless seat behind us, no doubt endearing us to its occupants, one of whom was a photographer. He then sat, leaning on the side of my seat with his head cradled in his arms until a stop at which point he moved down the front. He was replaced by a clean cut young chap who didn't look at all like a vomiter and fortunately lived up to his appearance.

Back in Zhongdian we went for dinner at a great little Tibetan place. One of their light bulbs needed changing, so, not trusting the wiring, we had an American called Travis change it because we told him he was tall and expendable. The mother, and cook, came in later wearing a blue bus company uniform. I stood up and saluted and they all laughed.

Ade and I went for a wander and in the market, came across a dead dog. It was lying on its back, all the fur burned off, legs in the air, stiff and smoking.

We had read with interest about what the guidebook referred to as the Chengdu backroad. This was an alternative route to the city of Chengdu which went across the mountains. Some Germans told us they had got permits for the route from the police. They had given us directions to find the police station but we got lost and asked a passing policeman. Following his directions, we came to a large compound (where they were also burning off a dog). They were a little confused by what they could understand of our request, but one kindly led us around the corner and up a road to a building with a gateway. He gestured us through and left us. We thanked him profusely and went in. There were two police jeeps and other than that we had no idea what was there but it looked like housing.

By the time we found someone else to tell us where the PSB was, it was 12.30. From our experience, lunch could have started up to an hour before and a man told us it would go on for another two. So we went away and came back later. A woman took us up to an office, told us to help ourselves to tea and went into a back room with our passports. She came back with three of them and asked what our nationality was. We told her we were British. She did not understand and nor did she understand when Ade told her he was Welsh, a word in Chinese he had made a point of learning. We knew the answer she would understand and Ade gritted his teeth as he told her he, like me, was English. We were given our Alien Travel Permits, which we were proud of and immediately used them to enable us to buy tickets on the first leg of our journey.

Back at the hotel, we got talking to a young man from Beijing who was on holiday. He was well-dressed and obviously educated and spoke reasonable English. Ade decided to engage him in a friendly discussion about Tibet. Did he think it was China? He did. Why? Because it was. It always had been and the books that said otherwise were not published in China. So Ade asked him what he had been told in school or what had he read which supported the fact that it had always been a part of China. He refused to say, reiterating his earlier answers. He became rather flustered and impatient with the questions, but he was basically saying that Tibet was China because it was. His argument, Ade told me later, was normal in his experience. Also typically, he retaliated with "What about Northern Ireland?" Although the Chinese probably had a different understanding of that line of politics, Ade said that as far as he was concerned, he felt it should be a part of Ireland and anyway, talks were in progress. And we could have further explained that Scotland and Wales are acknowledged as once having been politically separate, were still culturally separate and that independence parties are quite legal.

The trouble with all arguments like this is that they are conducted from two completely different world views and sets of information. Our Chinese friend was called away before blood was spilt, but was showing the behaviour of someone challenged on weak ground. Ade had said that all Tibetans wanted to be free of China.

"How many?" the man retaliated.

"I thought maybe he'd want names and addresses," Ade said afterwards.

Tibetan Fringe III
The horsemen of Shangri-La

We walked through the older, Tibetan part of town, then along pathways across fields with rows of crops, to where the showground fitted into a corner of the hills. Cars and trucks overflowing with people filled the road and a heavy military presence marched into the stadium amongst them, backed up by a truck with a water cannon. Under the grey sky, this looked particularly ominous.

The stadium was oval in shape and contained a track enclosing an open grassy central area. On the south side was a great concrete grandstand. Entry to this and the rest of the ground was by invitation only and a policeman barred our way. Aided by Beth, an American who spoke Mandarin, we told him we were journalists and he shrugged and let us in. On the opposite side were concrete seats which were outside the stadium fence. They were open to the elements but filled up quickly. Those without seats peered through the railings or settled on the side of a hill at the western end of the track. On the north and eastern side there were tents where visitors had set themselves up and proudly sat by their fires in full traditional costume.

They were a fierce looking people, tall and wiry and with a distinct penchant for hats including gangster fedoras, skeins of coloured wool and elaborate fur headpieces. The older men had long moustaches and beards. Some nodded in dignified greeting, others smiled broadly at us, their ferocious appearance vanishing in an instant.

Children hid behind their parents' legs then bravely rushed out to shout "Hello!" When we replied, they looked startled first before smiling and the parents grinned at us.

"Where you from? America?" asked one boy in his early teens.

"England," I replied. "Where are you from?"

"Tibet."

It was always the answer. The map may have said this was China, but no Tibetan would dream of calling it that.

The Chinese Press was there in force. This event was to show Chinese and Tibetans living in harmony. Officials claimed Zhongdian was a success story on that front. The press appeared to be pleased with the small Western presence. Television cameras seemed to be trained on us as much as on the Tibetans and the newspapermen posed with us for photographs.

"Australia, England, China: friends," said one.

The weeklong festival opened with a parade. Hundreds of dancers in bright costumes stood waiting to join the march, smoking and posing with their arms around their friends. Meanwhile, from the stand, muzak wafted out over the heads of dignitaries.

Opening the parade was a banner announcing the Shangri La Horse Racing Festival. A dozen riders galloped by on their horses. Behind them came a detachment of the army. They performed martial arts kicks and punches in perfect synchronisation, yelling with each action and slowly moving forward. Then rank by rank, they toppled forwards like felled trees onto their white-gloved hands into the mud and puddles. Next they stood and hurled themselves up almost horizontal, twisting in the air to fall flat on the ground again.

It was a spectacular show of strength, but following them were pantomime yaks: men in woolly suits skipping behind the might of the People's Liberation Army.

Monks were next. There were two wearing crested yellow hats and blowing long horns, each one supported by a young novice. The press went wild and had to be herded back from them by the police.

Then it was the turn of the dancers. There were hundreds of them. Brightly coloured, they sang as they danced, banging drums, shaking rattles and trailing scarves. The press pack looked as if it had never had so much fun as they snapped photographs, kneeling to get interesting angles and trying to get as close as possible before being guided back by the police. The muzak from the stand continued inanely. For the dignitaries, it must have all but drowned out the Tibetans' singing.

As each group of dancers passed the grandstand we expected it would march around the circuit of the stadium so that everyone

126

could see it, but instead they moved into the centre of the arena and continued dancing there. In this Communist society of equals, only the party officials and dignitaries in the grandstand appeared to be important enough. The other spectators, the people, were not this lucky and were too far away to see much from their seats on the far side of the stadium or on the hillsides.

The sky cleared and the sun started shining warmly out of a blue sky. Large red balloons hung above the borders of the arena. Beneath them the dancers sang and moved in slow circles.

They were marshalled to one side and soldiers marked out a wide lane by sitting cross-legged on the ground in two rows. This was to be a track for a display team to show off their riding skills. The photographers ignored the soldiers and stood in front of them. Only a sinister looking policeman in dark glasses attempted to keep the photographers back, but they inched forward again after he had passed.

The display team began. They rode down the lane, one at a time, hanging off one side of the horse. Then they each rode down again, performing a handstand on the saddle. This was followed by rifle firing from horseback. White scarves were laid out down the track and they leaned down and picked up as many as they could. They struggled to keep a straight line.

Two horses galloped down, a rider squatting between them with a foot in each stirrup. We realised they were veering towards the edge of the track and they were suddenly very close. We had to jump back as they came by. A few yards further on, a woman was kneeling for a better picture. She realised too late that the horses were heading straight for her and scrabbled to move out of the way. But she left it too late: a hoof caught her on the head. Inert and bleeding, she was carried off.

Lunch was called. We left the arena and mingled with the people around the stalls outside the stadium. There was candyfloss made on a hot rotating wheel worked by a foot-pedal. There were sausages, shish kebabs and fried potatoes sprinkled with dried chilli, the smell of cooking enticed us to go back for more. A small boy absent-mindedly chewed at a pig's tail. We watched him fascinated and the locals in turn watched us, laughing.

The lunch interval lasted several hours. The dancers regrouped below the grandstand. At first they stood waiting. We assumed something was going to happen. But first there were speeches. They were very long and no one seemed to be listening. The dancers sat looking bored. A line of men in pink costumes lay back on each other like tumbled dominoes and went to sleep. Others sat and chatted. It was another hour or two before any racing began.

There were only three or four riders in each race. In one, the rider and the horse seemed to have a different view on how long the race should be. Every time it passed the gate to the arena, the horse had had enough and tried to leave. The crowd whooped. In another, a woman rider had trouble controlling the horse at the start and lagged behind, only to overtake all the others to win. Once more the crowd was delighted.

That evening, the main street of the town was a mass of people. They were still dancing and singing and even the Han Chinese who had not seemed interested before watched.

An old man walked by carrying a small boy on his shoulders. Fast asleep, the child's legs buckled when his grandfather lifted him down. It had been a long, tiring day, but the festival had only just begun.

Beth, the Mandarin-speaking American, had found there would be some monks singing in the evening. We were late arriving and were puzzled to find they had waited for us. Then the monk who had spoken to Beth before gave us each a piece of paper which had some information about the prayers that would be sung.

Inside the temple, we were given a white prayer scarf which we draped over a string and a candle which we lit and we put a little money in the offerings box. Then we were shown to some benches. A taped voice gave an introduction in Chinese and then the music started.

There were about twenty monks and some donned yellow crested hats. They played a big bass drum, cymbals, long deep droning horns, and those reedy pipes. They played without apparent plan or agreement for a few minutes then stopped and removed their hats. The monk in front of me cleared his throat and started the guttural droning I associate with Tibetan monks. This quickly became a more normal deep chant and was joined by the others. It was deep and slow but gradually rose in pitch. It was mesmerising, filling the darkness. And they would start again, always that one monk's guttural rolling, chucklechant. My mind wandered and then

I would open my eyes to the gloom, the pillars, the hanging drapes and the faces of the monks lit by a single candle.

They finished off with the music again, then the lights came on and a man in a wide brimmed trilby walked amongst us and handed out what seemed to be tickets for Y25. Beth and the Malay Chinese with us protested. We had not been told we had to pay. But this is just like a park or a museum, they said. But in that case you should advertise the price when you go in, Beth pointed out. He had no answer to this.

There were two guys in hats. It was not clear who they were. We asked where the money was going. Monks' salaries. Could we put it in the collection box then? Some monks said yes, the one who seemed to be arranging things said no, that was just for the upkeep of the temple. But he was probably compromised by these mysterious men in hats. In the end, they agreed to letting us put the money in the box and watched as we did so. Some travellers refused to pay. We were harangued on the door by one of the hatmen who insisted on talking to Ade because he was a man despite it being Beth who was talking to him. It was a nasty atmosphere. We were embarrassed. At least some of the monks looked it too, although it was unclear whether it was we or the men in hats who were embarrassing them.

We left the temple in the dark, unlit streets of the old town. Beth talked to two monks who left when we did, apologising for making a fuss and explaining. They said not to worry. Those men were from the department of Tourism and Culture and insisted on the money. If it were down to them, then people would pay what they could afford. That made us feel better.

But we were still left with a bad feeling and an impression of the Chinese twisting a culture to its own advantage, perverting it with something very un-Buddhist. It was not that we objected to paying, just the underhand method. We felt cheated and they had looked and acted like gangsters. It was an unpleasant way to end our Zhongdian experience.

Off-roading, West Coast of the South Island, New Zealand.

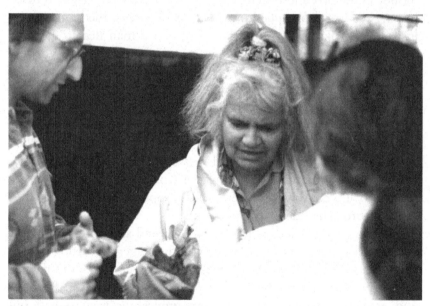

Maureen Watson with friends in Canberra.

The Twelve Apostles, Great Ocean Road, Australia.

With Bang and Thanh the sunglasses salesmen, Hoi An, Vietnam.

Typically unrealistic scenery near Yangshuo, China.

Dancers wait to perform at the Zhongdian horse racing festival, China.

Aerial display team: the People's Liberation Army at the Zhongdian horse racing festival, China.

Morning mist rises on the way to Kanding, China.

Stopping for a chat on the bridge at Luding, China.

Spice sellers in Kashgar, Xinjiang Uyghur Autonomous Region, China.

Waiting for trucks at the landslide. Kunjerab Pass, Karakoram Highway.

Reading with a backdrop of mountains designed by a child, Passu, Pakistan.

The Monastery in the ancient city of Petra, Jordan.

Treading in the footsteps of TE Lawrence in Wadi Rum, Jordan.

The sunlit, sharp lines of Portugal.

Ripples in the Atacama Desert, near San Pedro de Atacama, Chile, at the start of the crossing of the Bolivian Andes.

Altiplano rock, Bolivian Andes.

The final destination of the Torres del Paine walk were the Cuernos del Paine, the Horns of Paine.

Day 2 of the Cerro Catedral walk in Argentina and Liz pauses on the way down, high above Lago Jakob.

Boardwalks, bogs and bush, Hump Ridge Track, Southland, New Zealand.

Tors and tarn on the Hump Ridge, Southland, New Zealand.

Martian landscape, Namibia.

Our home and transport in Namibia, returning from Palmweg.

Tibetan Fringe IV
The Chengdu backroad

It was 7.30 in the morning and the bus out of Zhongdian was filling up with some odd characters. We recognised a few of the Tibetans who had sat around on the streets reaching into little sacks to offer us ginseng. There was the usual amount of milling around. One particularly spaced-out individual was occupying my seat. His bloodshot eyes stared blankly from under a mane of long black hair. On previous buses, we had been told off for not taking the seat numbers on our tickets, so we asked him to move. He showed little inclination, preferring to look dangerously unpredictable instead.

"Let him sit there," I suggested to Ade. Then, with a suddenness that was startling, he moved calmly across the aisle.

People struggled on and off with bags. Someone going in one direction would be sure to meet someone else coming the other way. Each would both push into the same gap and shuffle, barge and after a minute or two force their way past.

"My sixth sense is tingling like mad," said Ade, concerned about the dubious appearance and unknown customs of our travelling companions. I thought he was overreacting, but still smiled at everyone.

There were few women on the bus, but two were Chinese and were hard to miss. They fussed over their makeup and hair and changed seats several times. We were about half an hour late leaving, but it was only then that we noticed we were missing a window. Where there should have been two sliding panes of glass covering three rows of seats, we shared only one with John and Wendy in front and the Chinese women behind. It was only big enough to protect one row. The other pane was presumably lying in pieces half way down a mountain.

As we set off, slowly rising out of the plain and into the mountains again, a chilling wind rushed in at us. We were all wearing several layers but the Chinese women had only thin, tight fitting sweaters. They begged Ade for the window. He gave them half. They pulled it further. He pulled it back. They pulled it back again, accompanying it with a gush of frenzied Chinese. Ade did not tend to bother with knowing the language; he just talked English and let the tone of voice get the message across.

"Yeah but I'm cold as well. All right, you can have a bit more. Not that bloody much! Give me some to bloody lean on! Oi!"

We were wedged firmly into our seats. They were designed for short Chinese with no bottom, not long, wide-arsed foreigners. So we sat there with our knees tucked under our armpits. John and Wendy were having other problems. Right in front of them was the tank for the bus's cooling system and water kept splashing out from the badly bunged hole in the top as we bumped along the road.

As the valleys began to drop away more, the surrounding hills quickly turned into mountains. The gravel road was cut into their side. This should have meant that we could hug the rock face, but the driver chose the middle and often drifted over to the edge, doubtless for the sake of visibility, which left our tyres mere inches away from thousands of feet of tumbling death.

We climbed slowly and as we crested the first pass, an ear-piercing whoop began from the back of the bus and echoed around all the Tibetans as they gave thanks for our safe arrival at the top. Prayer flags fluttered a welcome at the summit. On the other side, the world changed. Across the valley above the tree-covered slopes, rose sheer, jagged grey crags. The bus stopped. An old man rushed across from a tent. He had a grey beard and a large furry hat. Grinning ecstatically, he waved around prayer scarves and held up little sheets of thin coloured paper with prayers written on them in tiny Tibetan script. We handed him some money and he thrust more prayers at us.

These were to be tossed out of the windows so that the wind could carry them to Heaven. We noticed one of the sheets was blank. We wrote 'Safe travel' on it. The next pass was laden with rhododendron bushes, as well as the usual prayer flags. There was a repeat of the mini-carnival and we threw the prayers from the window while our fellow passengers cheered encouragement. Mountain passes would never be the same again.

Meanwhile, one of the girls behind us began to stroke Ade's hair and talk to him. When she realised only I could speak any Chinese, she quickly began to share her attentions. She tugged our noses and I responded with *"Hen da! Hen hao!* Very big! Very good!" She ruffled our hair and said things from which I understood "wife" and "girlfriend". I would respond in Chinese and English and when she realised Ade and I were making fun of her, as she quite clearly was of us, she would pout. She was amazed at our hair, so Ade and I pulled down our collars and displayed the top of our hairy chests. She gasped in horrified fascination.

As her flirting increased, some of the Tibetan men around started making gestures regarding our future prospects. She was not doing anything for her reputation, but did not seem to mind. I realised this could quite easily go too far. She asked if we had wives or children. We said we each had two wives, because you could in Britain (pout, slap) and I got out my photos from home and selected a number of wives and children to prove it. The photos were quickly handed around half the bus and everyone was impressed.

We stopped for water at a stream to replenish the water tank at the front of the bus. Wendy and John got out of their seats as a seemingly endless succession of buckets was sloshed down a funnel made from the top of a water bottle. The pouring began neatly, but as the pourer's arm became tired, it became sloppier and correspondingly wetter at the front. The man filling seemed to be one of the passengers. Another passenger, well dressed with the swept-back hair and demeanour of a man with authority, kept the grateful driver chain-smoking with a constant supply of cigarettes.

There was much singing of Tibetan songs from around the bus. We were persuaded to add a chorus of the Beatles' *Yellow Submarine* to the general hubbub. One young fellow had an electronic keyboard. He made it play the same hateful little tune over and over again.

Late in the day, we glimpsed a valley of green patchwork maybe four thousand feet below and half an hour later we had zigzagged down into it. Great blocky houses like small fortresses were scattered along the valley. They each had a flat roof with a low parapet and usually a higher platform in one corner. Sheaves of wheat straddled the parapet. Windows and doors were shuttered and ornately carved. Peasants were working in the fields like a scene out of a history book, cutting golden wheat with small sickles.

The Sichuan border was at a small town with a wooden barrier across the road. We all got out and a policeman searched the bus, but not our bags. While we stood around, the lad with the electronic keyboard thoughtfully let it play that same jingle over and over again to entertain us. Meanwhile, we wondered what the policeman was looking for. Perhaps it was drugs; Yunnan province is on the edge of the Golden Triangle bordering Vietnam, Laos and Myanmar, but it would have been quite easy to smuggle anything through, or simply to avoid the checkpoint altogether and take to the hills.

After nearly 12 hours travel, we pulled into the bus station at Xiangcheng. A woman approached us and told us she had a guesthouse nearby. It contained a couple of dormitories, crowded with narrow cots and no toilet or washing facilities. She suggested we use the bus station's rather unpleasant toilets and pointed out a temperamental tap in the courtyard. The courtyard also contained piles of junk and a truck that was mysteriously too large to have fitted through the gateway.

We walked into town to find something to eat. People were out and about, strolling or sitting and they stared at us as if the circus was in town. The inside of the restaurant we chose was large, but one side had been separated off with some folding screens. A party was underway for the first birthday of a little boy. The men were around one table, chanting, raising toasts and being rowdy. The women and children were at the next table and were much quieter. They asked for a photograph of us with mother and child and we were happy to oblige. We joined in singing happy birthday but managed to toast with tea. It was not the time to become involved in a suicidal drinking game with the Chinese.

I woke early. The plan was to get up in time to be at the ticket office for when it opened at six. I crept out of bed to go to the bus station for a toilet, only to find that the guesthouse courtyard was locked. I raised a member of the family to get it opened, but my hopes of relief were dashed when I found that the gates to the bus station were also chained together. It was still dark and there was no one around, so I found a dark spot to squat down in against a wall in a narrow lane. It was far more pleasant than the filthy, stinking bus station toilets anyway.

It was a much better bus too. For a start, it had a karaoke DVD player that was immediately put into action. We were drowned in a treacle of tuneless ballads and dreamy slow-motion lush fields, mountains and fluttering prayer flags. The other passengers sang along. This was followed by a series of rather staged comedy acts in front of a live audience of suited Chinese. The situations included young lovers with a disapproving father, a robot woman to do all the cleaning who was operated with a TV remote control and a couple of blokes who did impersonations of musical instruments, all of which were doubtless very amusing.

The landscape had become flatter and less dramatic than the day before. The houses had changed with it and were shorter with grey layers of larger stone divided by much smaller ones.

We drove on through rolling moorland, dropping off a couple of men in the middle of nowhere. They were excited to be home and disappeared over a hill. At other points there were black tents and grazing yaks scattered near the roads and women came out to meet their returning menfolk.

The hills became steeper and were scattered with pine trees. This gave way to a wide undulating plain of boulders. The rock emerging though the thin soil was showing cracks and disintegrating creating a landscape formed by the rapid extremes of heat and cold. In turn, this gave way to wide moorland with heather and wildflowers. China at fifteen thousand feet looked like Scotland at three thousand. Eventually we came out on a grassy plain bounded by hills. On the edge of the hills was the town of Litang.

Walking down the main street, we were clearly the focus of attention. There were hardly any Chinese and the Tibetans were a wild looking lot. They wore long green coats over one shoulder like a cape and belted them in at the waist. Many wore their hair long and loose under high-crowned, broad-brimmed felt hats. Their faces were hard, weathered, creased, frowning and rough-toothed. Long knives hung at their belts in gold or silver scabbards and calf-length black boots were on their feet. These guys made Spaghetti Western extras look like the Queen Mother.

A crowd gathered as we checked into our hotel. We had lunch across the road. The cook was a young, surly-looking Chinese in a suit and tie. His jacket sleeves were rolled up and he wore an apron over his paunch. Despite throwing his cigarette butts on the floor, the food he created was good and served with all the ginger tea we could drink, which helps with the altitude.

Ade and I took a stroll up the hill into the Tibetan town on the edge of the Chinese white-tiled one. We armed ourselves with stones in case some of the furious dogs we could hear and sometimes saw, turned out not to be chained up. Four little boys tagged along with us and asked for money. One put his hand into Ade's pocket so Ade took it out and smacked it. Another, seeing the rock in my hand, offered me another to add to my collection. The houses were yet another design; still blocky, but made of a brown rock. Drying dung lined the walls.

On the edge of town some women and children sat and chatted and looked as if they were having a picnic. They smiled at us. On the hilltop above the town were a stupa and two sleeping monks. Some snotty-nosed children followed us up the hill, asking for money and trying to get into our photos. The two boys vigorously shook my hand. One had a damp hand and I tried not to think why this should be. Further away, surrounded by a long wall, was the monastery with gold glittering from its roofs.

As we approached, we could see it was solid and fort-like. Steps rose up to a huge porch area where black drapes hung in front of great red pillars. The walls were colourfully painted with images of the monastery, the wheel of life and the Buddha. A monk poked his head out of the door and beckoned us into the prayer hall.

Long kneelers filled the square room amongst square pillars. A small cabin stood on one side near a row of Buddhas and other deities. A few monks were chanting and two more came over to talk to us. There was a photograph of the Dalai Lama. Ade tried to explain that he had once shaken his hand. The walls were glossily painted with hundreds of intricate scenes of pink Buddhas, blue devils and at least one many-armed god having sex with a clinging woman.

We walked through more streets. A couple of monks stopped to chat and to peer through our cameras. A buffalo strolled in front of a monument that was swathed in prayer-covered cloth. An old man sat outside his door, absent-mindedly spinning a prayer wheel on a stick. Women carried baskets on their backs filled with firewood. Others sat talking. A horse was tethered at the roadside. In the market, slabs of meat hung from hooks and wild looking young men played pool in the open air.

When John and Wendy returned to the hotel, a local followed them into their room and sat on the bed, watching them. The only way they could get him to leave was to go out again and give him the slip.

The karaoke down the hotel corridor had started by the time we took to our beds for an early night. I went to sleep immediately and heard neither the music nor the drunken wanderings of another hotel guest trying to persuade his friends to let him into his room. We woke at 3.30am. The night porter was unwilling to come out from under his blankets on the sofa in reception to unlock the door, but gestured towards another door. But through it the gate to the street was still locked, so we had to go back and wake him again anyway.

In the street a couple of distant pools of light thrown from buildings hovered in the blackness. Dogs barked at us, unseen and menacing. Five Tibetans were waiting outside the bus station. They stopped chatting and turned to watch us. Some trucks were parked across the road. Whenever anyone walked by, the dogs chained to them went into a frenzy. There seemed to be many groups of people coming out of the darkness on the edge of town, so the dogs were rarely quiet. I was glad we had decided not to stay in the bus station's hotel.

The bus arrived on time and was already full, apart from, miraculously, our reserved seats. It was another vehicle held together by optimism and we noted that our bus of the first day had actually been quite roomy. To fit, we had to dislocate our hips and knees, clench our buttocks and carry our arms in our laps. There followed much disorganised organising and the usual shouting, pushing and general disagreements. A sick man was gently helped into the seats in front of us. He did not look well enough to travel. There was a glow over the horizon when we left.

The sun came up as we drove into hills covered with golden-green grass. The woman in front moved her child out of the way and vomited out the window. Then we were on the tops and I gasped. Cloud was rising out of the valleys, lit bright white by the sun behind it. It was like a vision of heaven. The air was refreshing and clean, the hills were softly curved and a silver mist rose out of the ground.

We dropped out of the hills and into a series of hairpin bends. We came upon an army convoy carrying logs. We managed to overtake some before we were brought to a halt. A civilian truck had broken down right across one of the bends and blocked the road in both directions. Eight army drivers piled inside the breakdown's bonnet to offer advice and spoil the broth.

We stood around waiting for them to fix it.

"Why don't they just roll the truck back down the hill a few yards? It would make enough room to get past," Ade wondered. But the tinkering continued and we looked around for someone in charge of this rabble. They all looked terribly young. Further up the road, two were mucking about pushing each other and giggling like little kids. Finally a puffed-up little officer appeared and laid into his men impatiently. He stuck his face into the melee around the bonnet and we continued to roll our eyes. It was beginning to seem that a secret weapon against Chinese invasion would simply be a truck across the middle of the road. That would hold up the advance long enough for the boy scouts to arrive and sort them out.

A soldier went running up the road and came back with a pickaxe. Rolling the truck backwards was still beyond them, but they were going to do some digging. Along each side of the road was a drainage ditch. They were going to fill in the one on the inside of the bend to give them the extra yard which would enable them to get around. With one soldier digging and the rest watching, the ditch was soon filled in. Our bus was first in line and we inched around. There was not much space, but we made it and drove on down the hill. It had all taken an hour.

We crawled around the sides of steep mountains and crept up passes like a sack of potatoes dragged by a tortoise. We passed a truck which had rolled off the road and been caught amongst the trees some time before.

We stopped for lunch at a small town in pouring rain. There were a couple of new passengers and sorting them out took an extra half hour. The driver had a problem with one and after some violent shoving, the passenger in question took all his bags and got out of the bus. And then got back in again.

We drove out through a long forested valley, which gave way to Derbyshire on a larger scale. The Tibetan blockhouses were grand affairs made of limestone. We came across a bus and a truck that had hit head on, fortunately with little damage. We stopped for half an hour to enable everyone to go and stare at it. Another bus came along, gave us its four passengers and set about preparing to tow the other. I wondered at the magical form of organisation that existed here.

We drove on amongst mountains and moors draped in mist. We were stopped by an army breakdown. The breakdown itself was not what blocked the road; it was the second army truck that had stopped alongside for a look and a chat.

We dragged frustratingly up more hills, grinding and toiling until at last we came to prayer flags and a sign announcing a pass at 4298m. From here we descended into a long, wide valley lit by the afternoon sun. The military convoy stretched down the road that doubled back along the valley sides. Far away to the left, tall, ice-scaled summits rose higher like a set of giant fangs. Mist floated around below the clear sky, but as the afternoon wore on, more cloud moved in and the mountains were obscured. Finally we entered a deep gorge containing a muddy torrent and found Kanding fitted inside it, dwarfed by swampy peaks.

We bought our tickets out for the next day. I thought the clerk said that the sleeper bus for Chengdu went at 11 o'clock.

"*Wangshang* or *zuoshang*?" I asked, "Morning or evening?"

"*Zhongwu*," was the reply. I didn't know what that meant, so I asked my question again, several times, hoping for either morning or evening to be the reply. The clerk was getting frustrated and buried her head in her arm at my stupidity. Then fortunately I stumbled across *zhongwu* in my phrasebook. Midday.

Ade and I arrived early at the bus station the next morning and were the only ones on the bus other than the driver and his wife. We saw John and Wendy looking around for us.

"Over 'ere!" I shouted. The two Chinese joined in laughing and called out, trying to imitate me. There were two layers of bunks on board with just about enough room to sit up.

We set off at a brisk speed. We later calculated it as averaging thirty kilometres per hour which says a lot for how fast our previous buses must have been going. We stopped in Luding in a car park with no toilets. We did as the locals do and found a place to go by some trees, behind trucks, overlooking the river, then we set off again. After fifty metres, we stopped by a number of mechanics who removed a tyre and took an hour to mend it. Setting off again we reached the car park where we had stopped earlier and pulled into the bus station that turned out to be opposite.

"We'll probably stop here again for a toilet break," said Ade. Imagine our hilarity when this turned out to be true. We asked how long we were going to be there this time. Until 9pm, came the answer. It was 2.30pm.

Wendy went out for a walk and found real toilets in the bus station. While she was out, three sixteen year old schoolgirls stopped her to practise their English. She brought them back to help us find out what the latest delay was all about. We were told it was quite normal. We were waiting for other buses to arrive so we could cross the notoriously dangerous Erlanshan Pass together, even though this would mean crossing it at night, which surely would not help.

The girls were intelligent, pretty and very sweet and offered to show us the town's famous bridge. This was a scene of a battle during the Long March where the Nationalist Kuomingtang had attempted to block the path of the Communists. It was a chain suspension bridge over the fast flowing brown water. The Nationalists removed all the planks and lay in wait on the other side. Twenty-two of the Communists, armed with grenades, crossed the bridge's chain skeleton under what was presumably a hail of gunfire. Somehow, most of them made it over and even more implausibly managed to overcome the Nationalists.

Interestingly, the planks had been removed again, for repair this time, but this did not stop some brave souls from crossing its one hundred and fifty metre width by walking along the chains. Two had even stopped part way and were having a yarn. Mind you, no one was shooting at them, which I suppose made it easier.

The girls insisted we have dinner with them, so we went along to Ren Rong Rong's house. The other two were Pan Li Yun, who had just got top marks in an English exam and Wang Na Na.

The flat was modest but comfortable and Rong Rong's parents, who had been warned of our arrival, were very hospitable. Her mother worked as an accountant and her father was a manager in a factory and had recently completed a degree. First we had sweet dumplings filled with sugared minced nuts that tasted mainly of sweetness, which we all lied about enjoying. This was followed by fried grated potato and good vegetable noodle soup.

We discovered that they went to school from 7am until 4.45pm and had an hour and a half for lunch. They went to school every day apart from Sunday afternoon. They had homework on Sunday afternoon and each evening. Their main hobby seemed to be watching television, but it was surprising they found time for that. I produced my photographs. They remarked on the number of women friends I have, doubtless misunderstanding their status.

153

I asked if they had boyfriends. They all giggled. They told us it is not allowed to have boyfriends until you were 17. At college it is "allowed but not supported" because it would interfere with study and besides, they added, "we have too many children." Quite what did they understood by boyfriend? In fact, what kind of an idea about Western morality had we just given them by telling them that in the West some twelve year olds have boyfriends and girlfriends? After photographs with the whole family, they escorted us back to the bus in time to leave at 9pm. We actually left at 10.15pm.

We drove into the mountains. After an hour we stopped behind a long line of trucks and buses. Ominously, they had the appearance of being parked, rather than in a queue. We had heard about a four hour wait caused by a one lane road. Perhaps this was the cause.

We slept.

In the small hours, trucks started coming the other way. We assumed this meant that we would be on our way soon. One truck stopped right by the bus and belched out thick exhaust fumes that quickly found their way inside. It got thicker and thicker. Beside me Ade, who is asthmatic, started to cough. He sounded very unwell and the truck continued to pour out its evil fumes. Then, just as Ade was about to rush out in search of cleaner air, it moved on. I opened my window and the mountain breeze washed over us.

The flow of traffic stopped after an hour or so. It was nearing 5am. Nothing else happened. Our drivers stirred but were just turning over in their sleep. Why didn't we set off? What were the other trucks doing? Light began to show behind the dark outlines of mountains. The valley emerged below us as a lake of cloud. Two or three trucks and a bus overtook us. We puzzled over what our drivers were waiting for and began to think we would never leave. Our windows fogged up.

"When we get into Chengdu, I'm just going to jump in a taxi and head for the hotel," said Ade.

"They might not be using taxis any more in 2010," I said.

There was some silence before Ade wailed "I'll miss the Millennium! 'Where were you for the Millennium?' I don't know, I couldn't see out the window."

"I'll miss my thirties!" John realised. We consoled him.

We lapsed back into silence during which he obviously fell to musing.

"I've always wanted to grow my hair."

"By the time we get out of here my beard will be trailing across the floor," Ade replied.

"By the time we get out of here, *Wendy* will have a beard," I added.

"Kevin," said John, "let me have a look at your Bible."

"It's a shame it's not a Gideons," I said. "They have that section: for those in sorrow, for those who are lonely, for those stuck in a bus on a mountain in China..."

A trickle of early morning urinators from our bus turned into a flood and our drivers were woken and started the engine. It was 6.05am. It was great to be off at last. Then the driver cut the engine. A bus that had overtaken us was stopped a hundred yards up the road. I couldn't see why. Traffic was still parked up in front and around the bend. We waited.

At 6.45am we moved off again and jerked up the road, stopping every few minutes. We could never see why. Over-loaded trucks bearing a forest of logs rolled and heaved in the badly pot-holed road, digging the holes ever deeper. We crawled over the pass in low cloud at about 7.30am. Just over the other side, a truck had rolled onto its roof. A recovery crane waited patiently as the endless convoy dribbled by.

As we hair-pinned down the hill, we managed to overtake other buses and the army trucks. Above us were sheer rock faces, liberally cloaked in thick deciduous forest, bright green in the mist. Suddenly, the rattling of the unsurfaced road stopped as we drove onto tarmac. It was wonderful. Not long afterwards, we stopped for breakfast where a bridge spanned the river near a large building. It was 10am.

The Chinese gathered around a couple of taps and set about cleaning themselves fastidiously. I went to the toilets in a small concrete shed over the road. Men were pissing up against the outside wall. On the left hand end of the block was the Ladies' and the Gents' was on the right. In the middle section, two long, grubby pink pigs lay on the floor with their noses against the gate. There were three holes in the floor for the men, separated by the usual low partitions. The man at the far end was having a relaxed smoke and was in no hurry to leave. The holes gave onto the steep bank of the river. An eye-searing smell rose up in fumes through them, while shit and piss dripped down their rims.

Outside, the passengers continued to scrub themselves and other buses were arriving all the time. There was a commotion. A woman had gone around the side of the building past two miserable looking chained up dogs. One had bitten her on the leg. A man took it around the back and beat it, before returning it to its shelter. She was taken away and brought back an hour or so later, bandaged.

There was a roadblock on the bridge, manned by policemen. They eyed me suspiciously as I wandered over, so rather stupidly I tried to look like I was sussing the gorge out for a commando attack. I asked the driver when we would be moving again. Two o'clock he said. We could not believe it. Or rather we could, all too easily.

A young man started talking to me. He turned out to work for the police and had been visiting his sick father. He explained that "The. Delay. Is. Because. The. Road. Is. Under. Construction", so traffic took it in turns to go in each direction. He said it was one day at a time, but that sounded too stupid to be true. I asked the policeman why they didn't allow a few bits of traffic through in each direction. He smiled at me. Ade appeared and swore and made exasperated noises. "Your. Friend. Is. Humorous," said the policeman.

The army arrived and was waved through. An officer who had been travelling on our bus slipped some cash to the driver of a Japanese-made jeep who in turn had probably slipped the police some money and got a lift. The rest of us had to wait. Suddenly there was a flurry of engines starting. Everyone dashed for the buses which jockeyed for position then we were off, across the bridge.

The stretch of road being built went on for miles. We drove by wooden cabins where little children and wispy-bearded old men looked at us with mild interest. Out of the mountains now, we continued along the river through ugly grey industrial towns set in a brown wasteland where the air was thick with pollution from tall, filthy chimneys. I marvelled to think that people lived in this.

Eventually we came out onto good road again. We were relieved. It would be like this all the way to Chengdu now. Only 147km. On a good road, that could be less than three hours. Maybe even two.

We hit more road building.

The whole of the main road from Tibet to Chengdu seemed to have been dug up so that it was little more that a dirt track. In places there was one lane of concrete highway which traffic in both directions wanted to use. Naturally, this caused traffic jams. We would simply stop for ten minutes or half an hour.

156

At one point there was a gap which only one vehicle could get through in each direction. We were closer and the truck coming the other way just needed to slow down for half a second and we would be through and he could go after. But that would have been too simple. He speeded up and we both got there at the same time. It was a stand-off. Neither side moved. Our driver cut the engine. Cars and trucks drove up alongside so there was really no way out. Someone got off our bus and went to relieve himself by the side of the road. We waited.

I don't know how the stalemate was broken, but the four of us gestured in a Mediterranean manner at the truck driver as he went by. It wasn't the last time that sort of thing happened, but in this way we bumped our way onwards. I noticed that to our right there was a brand new tarmac highway, surfaced in both directions.

"Look!" I pointed at it like it was a mirage of a lost city. Some children were walking down it. "There are no cars on it! They must be saving it so it doesn't wear out."

We went through a town and stopped for a few minutes while we dropped off one of the drivers. A little further on, we stopped again. The driver got out and retrieved a large inner tube from a man in a shop and handed over some money.

It was getting dark. With ninety kilometres to go, I dozed off. When I awoke, we were mercifully only a few kilometres from our destination. It was pouring with rain, but we were in Chengdu. The bus windows were steamed up. I rubbed them and looked out at the city. Traffic, buildings, streets, lights. It had taken us 36 hours to travel about 350km.

The next day I was in a department store coming down an escalator when I saw a Tibetan woman standing at the top. She had been marooned there when her husband went down. He was at the bottom encouraging her to come down, to step onto that strange moving stair. It was the closest she was ever going to come to my world and I had just had a glimpse of hers. As I passed her, we smiled at each other.

In the market

The Chengdu street was busy with shops, stalls and people. Despite the humidity, meat hung on racks. Shirtless men pounded dried chillies in wooden bowls, fruit and vegetables were piled high and people bought and bargained. We ducked into backstreets which had yet to see the wrecking ball. These too were alive with business.

I haggled for a painting in an art gallery which was later to cost me more to frame than it did to buy. A trader offered us a thangka, a Tibetan painting of Bhudda, for Y50.

Ade offered Y10.

The trader laughed, but dropped to Y30.

Ade offered Y15.

No, said the trader.

Ade walked away – and got it for Y15.

An old man who spoke some English had watched this exchange and followed us to the next stall out of amusement. The next stallholder also had thangkas, but we could see they had been printed because there was still the printer's colour guide on the page edge. The stallholder insisted they were not printed. We insisted they were. The old man watching us chuckled merrily.

Ade looked over some sculptures at the next stall.

"Moulded. Look," he said, pointing at some mould marks.

"You clever," said our old man.

The stallholder pointed at another item. "Ming dynasty," he said.

Ade looked at our old man.

"More like Mau dynasty," he said. The old man sniggered.

Ade picked up another piece and showed it to the old man.

"Would *you* buy this?" he asked him.

"No," he said.

"Why not?"

"Maybe it is fake," he replied.

"*May*be?" grinned Ade.

The old man who had doubtless seen many things he could not laugh at, laughed once more at this modern game of tourism.

Across the desert…

I only passed through the ancient capital of China to see the warriors. Xi'an was hot and dry and I jumped on a local minibus to take me out of the city to see them. But first, it set to roaming the streets, trawling for more passengers, the driver's assistant shouting the destination out of the door until we had enough to make the trip worthwhile. In Hubao, everyone else left the bus and only I was led to another to be taken the last few miles…but not before we had spent twenty minutes doing a circuit of town trying to find some more passengers.

The warriors are thought to guard an Emperor's tomb and it is suspected that there could be more waiting to be discovered in the surrounding countryside. A great deal of money and care has gone into these warriors since they were found by peasants digging a well. Great air-conditioned hangars have been built over them and they have been the subjects of much research. Masses of information has been dredged from the site, not merely on warfare and weapons of the era, but about art, dyes, society and textiles.

I expected a sea of thousands of warriors, but many had yet to be excavated, while others lay as half rubble, melted into the earth, or stood as if wading through chest high mud. Each one was different: their faces, height, hair, clothes. Originally each had been painted and armed. Swords were excavated still sharp.

The walkway was high enough above the soldiers for a grand view, but too high to see detail. For this, individual statues had been mounted in glass cases. Captions offered descriptions of their faces. The general, for example, was apparently "determined and resolute", although I thought his face displayed more of an impish sense of humour. The officer who supposedly looked "decisive" actually looked weak and vacillating and it was the "stern and valiant" foot soldier who looked as though he would be the most reliable in a crisis.

I walked the gauntlet of the vendors outside. One brandished a boxed set of moulded metal warriors (doubtless made in China).

"Two dollar!" he said. A price in dollars was a reminder that I was now amongst package tourism rather than backpacker tourism.

"*Bu yao*. Don't want," I said which was taken as a haggling ploy.

"One dollar!"

"*Bu yao*."

"Five yuan," and without any effort I had accidentally haggled him down to 20% of his first price. The next two were women with marble circles in a box for 20 yuan. It was the first time I had heard the currency called yuan, rather than the more colloquial *kuai*.

My bus back took half the time it had taken me to arrive. I met up with Ade for a last meal before we went our separate ways, he east to Mongolia, me west on the Silk Road.

I spent the afternoon before my train left looking around Xi'an itself. The massive walls and gateways looked new. What was more interesting was the contrast between the wide grey main streets, scorching in the sun and the quieter net of back streets with little shops, resting under the trees inside the walls. People were sitting or squatting, chatting or watching and rarely bothered by any traffic.

The next morning on the train, I lounged on my bunk in hard sleeper for a while as the other passengers went into the usual routine of getting up early, fussing around, waking me up, then going back to bed and going to sleep once they were quite sure I was awake and not going to sleep again. The music on the PA began as annoyingly loud, jolly synthesised pap but improved into a more western style.

The land through which we were travelling was loess plateau; the hard packed dust of long ago glacial deposits I had first heard about in a geography lesson years before. Then it had sounded like a distant place I would never visit, but there I was winding through its pale, deep, compressed dirt cut through with steep gullies. Behind, higher levels rose into hills riven with erosion channels. These became higher still and suddenly we rounded a bend and there were mountains behind them with a remnant of snow around their highest peaks.

As the train snaked through these hills and curved around bends, I was able to look along its whole length. We wound on through valleys of rich looking cropland until the vegetation all but disappeared and it was really beginning to look like desert. Up the valley sides and into low hills it was bare. There were small villages with dried mud walls. The hills ran off into the distance, rocky parallel ranges becoming higher.

I was awake to see the sun rise. It came up from behind a few far hills and all before it was a broad, grassless plain. I was heading for the oasis town of Dunhuang, two and half hours by minibus from the station at Liuyuan. We drove out through desert. Low black gravel hills piled up on either side of us, but the road curved away from them, leaving a sandy coloured plain of stones. At one point there were lumps of mud wall, the remnants of the Han Great Wall dating from about 200BC. Tussocks of grass appeared, then trees backed by high dunes.

Dunhuang was a very Chinese town with typical white tiled buildings and blue glass windows, but the streets were often tree-lined and the heat gave it a Middle Eastern feel, the Han Chinese indolent in the shade. I reviewed my plans over breakfast. A local policeman came over to chat to his friend who ran the café and served me my breakfast in as graceful a display of waiting on as I have seen anywhere. He balanced the tray on one hand with splayed fingers and placed cutlery and dishes delicately in front of me, giving me a quick grin as he did so. The proprietor's son made squeaking noises with his hands by rubbing them together. I have been doing this for years, to the weariness of my friends, so I did it back to him and we all exchanged smiles.

In the late afternoon, when the heat had subsided a little, I cycled out to the dunes. A cloud of dust hung high above me in the sky. It must have been almost stationary, but it seemed to be moving forward, reaching out overhead. Only the front layer of dunes was visible. To my disbelief, they were walled in and there was a charge to enter the desert. As visibility had almost gone by this time, I went back around the fields on the edge of town where irrigation channels fed fields of maize, fruit trees and wheat. The wall of sand hung in the sky over the dunes, moving no further, but I could feel sand between my teeth.

The night market was filled with lanterns, glowing barbecues and the smell and smoke of cooking meat. Most of the stall holders were Uighur, the Muslim natives of Western China. I had a kebab, nearly losing the roof of my mouth thanks to the copious amounts of dried chilli tossed over the barbecuing meat and bread by the grinning cook.

161

Back in the hotel, two rather dubious looking Chinese men pushed past me in the corridor. I decided to explore through the doors behind them. On the stairs going up to the next floor were large photographs of naked Western women admiring themselves. I put two and two together and suddenly understood why there were a large number of steamy looking women in thin dressing gowns occupying the room next door to mine.

The next morning, I caught a bus into the desert to the Mogao Caves. There are over seven hundred carved into the soft rock, over four hundred of which are temples. I was led by the slowest walking, softest talking guide in the world, but the caves were amazing. Most of the murals and ceilings were sixth and seventh century Tang. They are called the Thousand Buddha Caves because each contains hundreds and hundreds of tiny paintings of Buddha, looking like a collection of identical cigarette cards. Murals would variously depict stories about Buddha impervious to attacks from demons or scenes from everyday life. One story had Buddha and his three brothers coming across a starving tigress and her cubs. Buddha waited for his brothers to leave then took off his clothes and offered himself as food to save the lives of the cubs. The tigress was too weak to kill him, so Buddha climbed up a rock, cut his throat with some sharp bamboo and fell off, whereupon he was eaten and saved all the tigers.

Many statues were seventeenth century Qin. They usually had Buddha flanked by his oldest and youngest disciples who were usually larger than life size. One huge reclining Buddha had seventy two disciples crowding behind him along his body. Then there were two enormous Buddhas, one twenty-eight, the other thirty-four metres high. The bulk of the body was carved out of the cliff face then clay was moulded over this, perfectly capturing the folds in his robes.

I had been in two minds about whether to stay another night, but the rain which had begun to fall decided me. On my way back to the hotel, I bumped into two New Zealanders, Liz and Fiona, who I had met briefly a week earlier in Zhongdian, and Karl, an Australian. We were heading the same way. I was to spend the next two weeks and more with them. Liz was short with curly brown hair and glasses. Fe was taller and a dark blonde. Karl was tall and slim with straight brown hair and a permanent growth of several days' beard.

On the bus back through the Gobi Desert to Liuyuan, I chatted and joked with Wang Li. He worked part time for the China Travel Service. He commented on Westerners' big noses and feeling the cold. I said I didn't feel the cold because I could wrap my big nose around myself. At the station, he tried, without success to book us sleepers, but there were none, so we resigned ourselves to a night in hard seat class.

We spent the hours waiting for the train getting to know each other. We shone a torch in Fiona's eyes and interrogated her about her two most recent relationships which had both been with men called Dave. We all enjoyed that and decided we would all divulge intimate details over the next few days. As we sat, a cleaner came over and said something to us at length. Karl stood up and waggled his tongue around in his mouth making a gibberish noise. He told us later that this was what he did when locals insisted on telling him things he quite obviously would not understand. Most English speakers in an equivalent situation would either have thumped him or simply talked slower and louder. This poor woman laughed. Karl reckoned this had broken the ice, but I thought she was simply embarrassed.

Karl had been travelling for three years on this trip and had been all over the world. One of the reasons why he had decided to get away was the pressure of several court cases in which he had been involved. Over dinner in a local restaurant, he told us about them. One was an ex-girlfriend who had decided to appropriate half his belongings and two were strange cults who had tried to take him and the Victorian police for libel. He had won them all, defending himself.

As the train arrived, faces gawped at us through the windows as if we were the circus or newly landed Martians.

Once on the train, conversation moved on to how Karl had been almost torn limb from limb in India when he had accidentally incited a mob. This had been years before when he had left behind his wild youth in Melbourne to travel. Once in India, he had decided to be like the saddhus and had left his belongings in a locker and wandered the country. There had been a misunderstanding with a real saddhu and some passers-by took the saddhu's side. He was hauled out of the mob by the local police for his own safety and put in the cells for the night. From there it was easy to move onto talking about personal philosophies of life. Karl

163

had managed to both lose and find himself in India, but from that high point, our conversation managed to slip right down to that other travellers' favourite, the bowels.

Having exhausted that theme, we each found a hard two seat bench to sleep on. The three seat benches were already taken but several Chinese insisted we take their seats and would not take no for an answer. It was yet another of the conflicting traits of the Chinese: one moment they were staring at you as if you were some kind of joke and the next they were giving up their own night's comfort for the poor pampered Westerners.

This poor pampered Westerner managed to get some sleep, alternating between lying on my side with my legs tucked up and sitting along it with legs stretched out, waking every hour to change my position like a carefully cooked piece of meat. We woke to more desert and boarded a bus at Daheyan to take us to Turpan, sixty kilometres away. The bus had no roof rack and I spent the next two hours with my pack on my lap and my foot squashed into a gap between someone else's bag and my neighbour's leg. Fortunately there was scenery to distract me. High rugged mountains sprinkled with snow lined each horizon and a desolate grey stony plain spread out from our tattered road to meet them. There was no sign of vegetation, not a blade of grass. It was wild, dramatic and empty.

Within minutes of arriving, we had options for tours to the local sites. These came firstly from a Uighur motor-cyclist from John's Café, the chain of backpacker cafes that haunt the Silk Road, and secondly from a porter in our hotel called Momin. The latter had a refreshing sense of humour and a brother with a taxi who would give us a tour for a good price and split over two days so we would not have to rush.

In the mood for breakfast, we walked under trellises draped with vines to John's café and disappointment. The staff were wheeler dealer types who would not leave us alone, told us it took three days to get to Kashgar (it doesn't) and we would be far better off doing it in a van with them for Y1000 each. When we pointed out it was only Y1250 to fly, the price dropped immediately to Y500. Karl made us uncomfortable by teasing our host with all the eastern salesmen's favourite lines such as "For you, special price" and, fortunately, our host kept smiling. Karl also made a larger than necessary fuss about the high price of tea which most places provide free. We decided we would have no further dealings with

164

the oily, dubious individuals at John's and signed on with Momin and his brother Hamet instead.

Our first stop was Grape Valley. We walked under vines dripping with grapes. The lush green was a stark contrast to the steep, sand coloured rocky hills on either side. The six hundred year old Emin minaret and adjoining mosque were more interesting, although it had been rebuilt in its dried mud bricks several times as it kept falling down. The mosque was one large, plain hall surrounded by a kind of cloister with a small royal reception room at the rear.

Momin asked us to visit a gift shop where a friend of his worked so she could impress her manager with some foreigners. We agreed, although everything was rather pricey, so there was little chance of us buying anything. As we walked in, the staff leapt up and ran behind their counters. The women were mostly dressed in attractive diaphanous pale blue dresses. As I looked at the goodies in the first counter, I smiled at the rather lovely young lady behind it. She coyly dropped her head and got the giggles. This led me to do it again and her identical reactions only encouraged me further. Fiona and Liz rolled their eyes, but I kept catching the poor girl's eyes from all over the shop and when we left I waved at her. She smiled shyly and all the other girls in the shop smiled knowingly. Her behaviour seemed old-fashioned, innocent and immature. Mine of course was only possible because her father and brothers were not there.

Our last and best stop of the day was the ruined city of Jiaohe, built on a leaf shaped island of rock about a kilometre long with green irrigated valleys on either side. The buildings had been carved straight out of a soft rock. Larger structures like the grand temple had used mud blocks. Only the dry atmosphere had kept the place from crumbling completely to dust. I tried to imagine the streets alive with people or Genghis Khan charging through to destroy it.

We talked to Momin about Islam and his beliefs. He knew he should not drink alcohol, he said, but he would only do a few years in Limbo for it and seemed to think it would be worth it. That could be a good advertising slogan: so good you'd do time in Limbo for it.

We had dinner in a Uighur restaurant. Karl was vegetarian and in a part of the world where they have a habit of putting bits of sheep in everything, this meant restaurants could be an adventure. I went into the kitchen to see what they might cook us and concoct a menu. I had become pretty good at this in Mandarin, but these people spoke only Uighur and Karl was not convinced that they had understood that he did not eat meat, so went into the kitchen to explain it himself. In his three years of travelling, he had developed an epic language of mime. From where we sat, we could see him in the kitchen. With flailing arms, flaring nostrils and strange braying noises, he transformed himself into a werebeast with curling horns then made emphatic gestures with his arms and pointed at his mouth and shook his head. We shifted around in our seats, wondering quite what response he was receiving from the now doubtless confused cook and his family, but he came back reassured. Mind you, I thought I had ordered several meat dishes and one vegetarian, but what we got was one bowl of noodles with a few bits of vegetable in it. I would not have been at all surprised if it had been cooked in a sheepy stock. We told him he was a liability.

The next morning, we got talking to an affable bearded Englishman called John who was from Ely. During the conversation, it transpired that Karl had heard of people being given seven day transit visas on the Pakistan border. This excited me. Not only would this avoid a dull week-long bus and train trek back east to Beijing to fly home, but I could do the fabled Karakoram Highway and fly home from Islamabad instead. John and the girls were similarly inspired, so we all became excited about the prospect together as we sat on the roof outside our room eating melon and bread for breakfast.

The second half of our tour took us out into the Flaming Mountains where we decided to conquer a great sandy hill. It was a tough climb with the temperature somewhere in the forties. The sand gave way under our feet and I had to keep stopping to catch my breath. Momin had never climbed it either, but was more used to the heat.

At the top, he made a line of stones. There were three for him, Karl and me and two smaller ones for the girls. The girls objected to being represented by smaller stones, but he just grinned at them. The top was a narrow ridge. On our left it dropped away to a valley on the other side of which were coloured bands like an orange brown rainbow spread across the ground, carved by hundreds of gullies in a series of steps. On our right was another valley with a small river tucked into a crease amongst sand coloured rocky hills. A line of tracks tip-toed across them; Momin said they were wolf.

Beyond was irrigated green and, in the distance, mountains topped with snow. I felt a long way from anywhere.

The final stop was another ruined city, Gaochang, an ancient ghostly metropolis fading into the arid scrubland.

We treated the boys to lunch back at the Uighur restaurant and had a much better meal than the night before because Momin ordered it: rice with yellow and orange carrot through it and a hunk of mutton, all washed down with gallons of tea.

We had a lazy afternoon in the hotel and I dreamed of the Karakoram. Then as evening came on, we wandered out to the street market. It was always hard to know what time it was in Turkestan. Officially everything still worked on Beijing time, but as this meant the sun setting at 10.30pm, most people operated on unofficial Xinjiang time which was two hours behind Beijing.

We found a small concrete stadium where kids were playing with racquets and a shuttlecock. We sat down and watched them. One was a little tearaway, bursting with energy, mischief and a machine gun laugh. He could have been from any housing estate in Britain. They fought over whose go it was next then invited us to play. The tearaway would shake his fists and roar victoriously whenever he felt he had scored a point over one of us, even when, quite frankly, it would have gone miles out of any badminton court I knew. So when it came to my go, I shook my fist and roared victoriously back at him, which he thought was hilarious. Another kid climbed on my back while I sat watching, so I ran off around the stadium with him, galloping, jumping and whirling him around, so he giggled, but was also relieved to get off again.

A young Chinese woman had been sitting nearby watching us and she finally summoned up the courage to talk to us and then ask if she could have a photo taken with the girls. We took the picture, then there was some confusion when we tried to get her address. Finally, when she followed us out, I realised she wanted her picture taken by one of the photographers in the square. These pose people by the statue of the three grape maidens who look like entrants to a wet tee-shirt competition. So they posed again and made her day and we all said *zaijian* and headed for the night market.

We saw someone with a corn on the cob that looked very tasty, but we could not see anyone selling them.

"I'll ask someone!" said Karl.

"Oh no!" we said.

He accosted a man walking past and went into an elaborate mime of eating a corn on the cob. You could see his teeth biting off individual pieces of corn at lightning speed. It reminded me of a Bugs Bunny cartoon where he eats a corn cob to the sound effects of a type writer. The passer-by roared with laughter at this unexpected piece of street theatre and we found somewhere selling fruit beer and pancakes instead.

We were joined on the bus back to the station by a German called Peter. I had first met him back in Dali. He was a tall, gangly bloke with long hair, a big nose, long wispy beard and hands and feet like shovels. Karl called him the Preying Mantis and if the Chinese thought we looked odd, Peter took the biscuit. We got dinner at a restaurant near the station, sitting outside of which we had a view of the town. It was an uninspiring place, but the Bank of China was a splendid example of Chinese white tiled, blue-windowed architecture.

Peter did not have a reserved seat on the train, so had to join the orderly queues on the platform, marshalled by railway staff as if the passengers were primary school children. We waited further up because we had tickets. Both the eastbound and westbound trains rolled in, wonderfully accompanied by a Strauss waltz over the public address system. Railway staff lined the platform and stood between the tracks by the water hoses. As the train passed them, they stood to attention, then turned to face it.

This train would take us to Aksu. Although the line had been newly laid all the way to Kashgar, it would not be opened to passenger traffic for another few months. Soon we were back into the desert again: sand and rocks and bands of colour. But what surprised us were the green hills we went into, steep and covered in short grass. They were softly rounded in the late, yellowy sun and then a ridge of snow-capped mountains slid from behind them while the line snaked around for no apparent reason other than to prolong the lovely views.

As we sat on our bunks, a little girl with her mother stopped to look at us. She was very young.

"*Meiguo*?" she asked her mother.

We told her we weren't American. She studied Liz who was closest to her a little longer, then gestured to her mother that she had a big nose. We burst out laughing and, relieved, the locals joined in.

168

By the time the sun rose again, we were out of the hills and back into arid wasteland. We arrived in Aksu around breakfast time. The town itself was a mile or two up the road, but a satellite settlement had grown up around the railway's temporary terminus, a gold rush town with buildings a combination of tent and shed.

We boarded a bus. The driver told us it cost Y47 to Kashgar and drove us the few minutes to the bus station in Aksu. I went to buy our tickets and from the ensuing experience, advised travellers I knew to be following us to buy their tickets on the bus. The woman in the ticket office insisted on charging foreigners' prices, which were double. These are not supposed to exist anymore, but the news has yet to filter through in some places, even though this was a government run operation. I argued as best I could and offered her the money for the Chinese price, but she just tossed it back at me. She did not care whether I spent the money or not, she would get paid anyway. I had no choice but to pay, so I just told her what she was doing was illegal and called her a pirate. But that was in English. I ruefully told the driver we had had to pay foreigners' prices and he just laughed.

Despite the view of distant mountains, it was a mean little town. It was nothing more than a couple of wide main streets, lined with a grey one storey terrace of shops. There were a few larger buildings or shabby blocks of flats in the back streets, the ubiquitous big Dong Feng trucks and a few street stalls. We were relieved to leave the miserable, soulless, dusty place and return to the desert, at last on the road to Kashgar.

We followed parallel ridges of steep but low mountains all the rest of the way. They were north of us on our right, while to the left was desert, covered in tufts of rough grass, through which ran the new railway line. Somewhere over the horizon began the grey sands and bewildering storms of the Taklamakan.

We stopped for dinner at a small Uighur settlement where there were several restaurants. None of us was hungry and we just bought some melons. A group of Uighur men in beards and hats squatted by the roadside and some likely looking lads asked to have their picture taken. Two looked Mediterranean. Looking around us, it was difficult to believe we were still in China. They wrote down their address and I sent them that photograph, but have no idea if it made it to that small town in the desert. Would China Post have known what to do with the address they had written in Arabic which I taped to the envelope? I hope it did.

While we stood waiting by our bus, another arrived. The café owners prodded us and gestured for us to board our bus, presumably so as to show there was space at the café for the newly arrived passengers. There was no need, as there was plenty of room for everybody, so we stood our ground. Karl, as usual was playfully aggressive, but in a way that I thought could easily have been misunderstood. A lad crossly gestured to me to board.

"Up your arse," I explained with a smile, as if I was telling him what a lovely evening it was. They lost interest for a while. "Let's get on now," I said.

"No, not yet," said Karl.

"But if we leave it, they might start trying to get us on just as we actually *want* to get on and then it'll look like we're doing just what they want us to do."

"Good point." We got on.

The man next to me was a Mr Ma. Unusually, he had a Chinese father and a Uighur mother. He owned a shop in Korla and was on his way to Kashgar to buy Pakistani milk to turn into butter for his shop. I think. Born only a few weeks after me, he was married with a five year old son. I produced my photos which he and the few other passengers enjoyed.

The landscape stayed consistent throughout, which was more than could be said for the road. There were a couple of hours where it was completely dug up with only dirt roads at the mercy of flash floods to see traffic through the road works. I was beginning to think that Chinese road builders were only allowed to have a tarmac ripper for a limited amount of time, so they just dug up everything in one go, rather than only when they needed to.

Once it got dark, an unknown passenger towards the back, made shadow animals on the wall. Liz, thinking it was me, responded. It kept us amused and we arrived in Kashgar just as we were getting fed up with the journey.

Kashgar. Famous oasis. That place on the map in the middle of nowhere. I forget how many years I had wanted to get there. Out of our window in one direction were mountains with snow, while in the other, there were bare desert hills. Below us were the town's concrete buildings and clusters of dried mud brick houses.

The bazaar was one of the parts of town with flat-roofed mud buildings. Some were larger and plastered. A teahouse had a second storey, fronted by a balcony of arches that looked out onto a small square. Most of the traffic was pedestrian with bicycles, motorbikes and donkey carts far outnumbering cars.

Telephone and power lines hung between poles as if they were waiting for washing day. Crafts crowded together with each shop's wares appearing to be identical to their neighbour's. There were shops selling musical instruments or aluminium buckets, pots and churns. Knives, teapots, wooden items or plastic bowls poured onto the street beyond wooden shutters raised during the day as a shade from the burning sun. Honey melons and water melons were sold off the backs of carts. There were kebab stalls with skewers of mutton over a constantly fanned smoking barbecue. And there was bread; round and flat, the first real bread we had seen in Asia.

There was a great variety of races at this central Asian crossroads. Hair was usually dark, but there was brown and even blond. Eyes were blue as well as brown and skin was usually olive but varied from white to a weathered brown looking like the soft desert rock itself, eroded into gullies. There were old men with turbans and big, full, white beards. Some had little white chin beards, shaven heads under a white skullcap and a lined face decorated with bristling eyebrows. Some wore long coats and furry hats, in spite of the heat. These people would be Uighur, Kazak, Uzbek, Kyrgyz, Afghans and others. There were few Han Chinese.

Hats were extremely common. Often it would be a four-sided green Uighur hat, but flat caps and Mau caps were also to be seen. Women were usually dressed traditionally: a long dress, belted, often a scarf. Many older women had a brown woollen scarf which some drooped over their faces, but I wondered if it was to protect their faces from the sun as much as anything, because many did not cover themselves.

Younger women wore make up: red lips and pencilled eyebrows drawn sometimes so that they met in the middle. A few had placed dots above their nose, one above and one below the eyebrow. Some wore eyeliner. Young girls were dressed exactly like the adults and looked like little women. The little boys had their hair cropped or shaven. It was the same on the smallest girls too.

171

Men, women and children went about their business. Many of the men stood in groups, chatting. Some with venerable beards leaned around a donkey cart, discussing something with relaxed animation. A man sat lounged across the counter of his stall selling beads and charms. Fresh meat hung in long joints in the shade, which was a few degrees cooler than the dry 40°C heat.

We walked through evening back streets and found children playing. They skipped after us, pulled faces and laughed with us, displaying a friendliness and innocence often missing at home. A man came up to us as we ate that night. He produced a knife and tried to sell it to me.

"I don't think they'd let me through customs with that," I explained. Next, he produced one the size of a small sword.

The next day we searched for the bus to the village of Muq where we had heard there was a market. We tramped the old streets once more. Karl had a bowl of ice mixed with yoghurt and honey, I photographed a man reading and surrounded by colourful carpets. And I talked to a spice seller by using signs and the odd word. He told me he was a Muslim and had four children, three of whom were married. He asked me what I thought of Kashgar. I had discovered that numbers in Uighur were similar to Turkish, so I tried another Turkish word.

"*Guzel*," I said. Beautiful.

"*Guzel*," he smiled and nodded.

We continued our search for bus 15. We passed a pile of melons spread across the side of the road, big, green and firm. We passed groups of people sitting under shades, eating ice and honey and watching television. Karl decided to ask one group where to find the bus. He went and stood in front of the small semi-circle and began his act. He scanned the horizon with his hand shielding his eyes, he looked in various directions, he turned a steering wheel and did several other actions that lost me, let alone his audience who were looking either confused or impatient to get back to their television programme, while we shuffled in embarrassment behind them.

Finally, I tried saying Bus 15 in some of my Turkish: "*Otobus on besh?*" Several men immediately turned and pointed up a nearby street.

The bus drove along straight roads lined with poplars. We passed mud-walled houses, wheat being winnowed and donkey

172

carts. A woman got on and was talked to by three men. At least one had been drinking. Liz and Fiona told me later that one had been trying to set fire to her hair with his cigarette lighter and tried to trip her up as she left. It was very strange.

The market was small with the usual assortment of interesting old men in well-worn coats and hats. Fruit and vegetables of wonderful quality were displayed on blankets in colourful profusion. Brightly coloured sheets of material hung gleaming in the sunlight, billowing gently in the breeze. One man beckoned me over to sit on a low stool where his wares were displayed on a blanket. He mimed taking a pulse to show he was selling medicines. These westerners were much better at sign language than the Han Chinese. Maybe it came from trading with such an ethnic mix. I inspected his goods and was delighted to find some Cordyceps Deer Tail Penis Pills. He said they were for kidneys. I took his word for it.

Liz and Fiona decided to buy an ice lolly each. We had already attracted some kids just by standing still for a few minutes, but this gathered a much larger crowd. And of course, once others saw a crowd gathering, more joined it to see what was so interesting. The girls disappeared from view.

Back in Kashgar, Karl and I were on our way back from a pot of tea at the tea-house on the square. We chose a honey melon from a barrow. The seller asked for Y15. Three, we responded, which to foreigners at least was a typical price.

"No, 15," the man said.

At that, Karl took out a 50 note and demanded they take that. "No no no no no!" said another seller crossly. Karl then turned around, pointed to his rear and invited them, in English "Why don't you take me up the arse while you're at it?" I pulled him away before he got a melon knife for his pains.

"I really can't understand how you've survived so long," I said.

Another day trip took us, on bicycles this time, along poplar lined roads. We stopped to watch women and children drying apricots on large sheets by the side of the road. A couple of boys ran over and gave us a handful. We had a look around the Appak Hojam Tomb, a tiled building with a minaret. It contained a hall of seventy-two coffins of all sizes, from babies to grown men. We ate a picnic in the garden, eating bread and fruit and nuts while Chinese tourists stopped to talk to us. Afterwards we watched a woman spinning silk out of fishy smelling cocoons.

On the way back, we stopped to look at some carpets. One of the sellers, assuming Fiona was my wife, told me she was an angel come down from heaven. She was blonde you see.

A small dust storm gusted in, reminding us we were in the middle of a desert. Several awnings flapped madly in the sudden wind, our bikes were knocked over and we had to shield our eyes from the dust. It was over in a few minutes.

The next day was Sunday. It was hot and we walked across town to where the famous Sunday market spread out by the river, a town of its own as tens of thousands of people flocked in from all over the region. The animal market was packed with sheep, cattle, donkeys and horses. A nervous horse kicked an old German who happened to walk behind him. There were masses of people. Men and boys, coaxing, prodding, feeling. A grizzled old man sat next to a thoughtful young boy on a wagon. A man trotted up and down showing off horses and sitting upright like some proud warrior chieftain. Another turned donkey carts on a sixpence, presumably to display the animal's agility. Sheep were lined up, side by side and nose to nose, to make the best use of space while a young lad crouched by them with a fly swat.

In the produce market, fruit and vegetables were piled up. My favourite was a row of carts each carrying a mountain of fine looking bright white onions. A group of street barbers were gathered in one lane. They were busy scraping cut-throat razors over the heads of unflinching leather skinned men with patriarchal beards. All the women seemed to be in the cloth market. They held up coloured sheets to an experienced eye and exchanged opinions with their friends.

There were many hat stalls, mainly selling the standard green Uighur hat. One man started at 30 and dropped to 15, then wouldn't budge. I walked away and the man opposite excitedly called me over, presumably to beat 15 but then started at 50. I bought one from the first man. Then there were stalls of pens, bike parts, plastics, pots, wood, clothes, rubbish. At this crossroads of Asia, you could apparently sell anything.

...over the mountains...

Apart from a few Pakistanis, the bus was filled with backpackers. Once we had loaded up the roof and sat down, we were told that we would have to change buses. Our new bus, which arrived surprisingly quickly, was smaller but somehow we all still fitted in. The engine started, the bus jolted forward. Our journey into spectacular scenery and visa uncertainty had begun. A few minutes later we stopped so the driver could have a chat with someone. But then we were off again, once more embarking on our epic voyage...only to stop again after a few minutes, this time for petrol.

Our next stop was not for a few hours and was at a village for lunch. When I tried to buy some water, the large, hearty shopkeeper shook my hand with his big paw and wanted ten yuan. I offered five, which was already over the going rate for rich tourists but I thought we were a long way from anywhere so he probably deserved it. At this he slapped his forehead. I only had another one in my pocket so he grudgingly took that, shaking my hand again. I knew he had still made a tidy profit.

Then we were driving south through sand dunes. Reaching mountains, we entered a wide valley with sides of steep, bare rock. The bottom was filled with stones and the river was narrow but fast-flowing. A pair of camels stood in the middle of the river bed. The boulder debris was evidence of a wilder appearance during the spring melt. The rocks turned red and the sides gradually narrowed until we were in a gorge. This widened again and a seven thousand metre peak became visible on our left. Its appearance belied its height because it was wide and rounded with a great deal of snow. A lake appeared, glittering in the sun, with snowy mountains on one side and high dunes spreading their arms around the other. Sand blew across the ground.

Soon after, we came to another lake, backed by dark, snow-capped peaks. The land sloped a few hundred yards down to the water's edge. Seeing us stop for some road works, some of the inhabitants of a small stone-built village ran over to us, or rode out on horses and camels. They were Kyrgyz and were selling cloth and jewellery. Bearded John from Ely who had joined us on the journey, bought a yak bone, carved in the shape of a yak. A little man in riding boots, a long coat, white skullcap and a drooping moustache on a face like a ploughed field peered through a traveller's camera.

Evening was coming on and the late sun gave a richer colour to the rocks. We drove within a few miles of Tajikistan over a rolling plain of small stones while mountains gradually rose up around us. The plain became greener and cultivation signalled that we were nearing Tashkurgan, a mainly Tajik town and the last settlement of any note inside China.

The friendly owner of the Ice Mountain Hotel was delighted when most of the bus decided to stay with him and he showed us a restaurant. I was feeling very tired, probably because in one day we had climbed from 1400m to 3800m. With so many of us in the restaurant, service was slow, but we passed the time with chatter and persuading the waiters that a single teapot was going to struggle to serve the needs of twelve people. Our simple dish of fried noodles and vegetables took over an hour to prepare and was barely warm.

In the early morning, I went out for a walk. The sun was just lighting the highest peaks a dramatic orange against the clear sky. As it climbed, the light poured down their sides and into the valley. The local policeman was Chinese and ran a small shop where I bought some bread, steamed dumplings and boiled eggs to take back to the others for breakfast. We had plenty of time to eat it, because we had to wait around for the bus for over an hour.

The next wait was at Customs, assuming something was about to happen and wondering why nothing actually did. It wasn't as if they were busy. Eventually, they let us into the building, our bags going through an x-ray machine which no one was monitoring and then we went through immigration, where exit stamps were added to our visas. All the officials were Han and I wondered if they trusted anyone else with their Muslim borders.

We sat outside again, waiting for the next thing to happen and unsure what it might be. A bus company official inspected all our passports to make sure they had been stamped. Several, including mine, were very faint because they had run out of ink for the stamp and he wandered away with them in a manner of officious concern until we chased after him and showed him where they were.

The sun rose higher and hotter. I inspected our companions: Germans, New Zealanders, Australians, Japanese, French Canadian. I had been impressed by John's small backpack, but there was a travel veteran called Janet who had merely a large belt pouch.

Finally, with the mandatory pointless period of waiting around complete, we were able to set off. As we left the compound, a policeman boarded and inspected all our passports. He too struggled to find some visas, flicking through in a growing panic. Karl momentarily made him excited to think he had found an irregularity by deliberately showing him his previous Chinese visa which of course was out of date. A hundred yards down the road, we were stopped at another checkpoint. Three policemen came on board, fighting to get through the door at the same time in a way we had seen a number of times in China. They came down the bus checking our passports again in what was either a job creation scheme or something to alleviate the boredom of this mountainous border post. I noted the now familiar excitement when the policeman failed to find the exit stamp in my passport and calmly pointed it out to him.

At last, the barrier was lifted and we were away, still several hours inside China, but officially out of it. We paused for an open air toilet stop on a broad meadowland scattered with flowers and bordered by mountains. Telegraph poles marched alongside us down the straight road. Then we started to climb up to the Khunjerab pass. The mountains were rounded and there was snow. We were given a final check by the Chinese Frontier Defence: a policeman in slippers who shambled out of a green caravan.

There was no giant sign welcoming us to Pakistan, but just over the 4730m summit, there were signs telling us to drive on the left and another bearing the logo of the World Wildlife Fund which announced we were entering the Khunjerab National Park where hunting was prohibited.

Just inside the border were a hut and a barrier. A moustached Pakistani soldier emerged, dressed in a British style uniform of large beret, a cosy grey jumper and green trousers. He boarded the bus to poke half-heartedly at a couple of bags then raised the barrier.

The road descended. An icefall had blocked it and a way had been bulldozed through but was not wide enough for the bus which had to take a detour track above the slip while we watched from the roadside. Small, hard white flakes of snow ran with the wind. Below

177

the obstruction, a convoy of trucks was backed up down the hill. They would take a run up at the dirt road detour, dust and black exhaust billowing behind them. They did this at the same time as other trucks were coming down the hill, causing a blockage. Another truck decided he would have a go as well presumably feeling that a new way would open up magically in front of him instead of just completely snarling up the road. A Pakistani and a German joined forces to remonstrate with him and finally common sense prevailed at least long enough for our bus to make it down. The others are probably still there to this day.

Descending further into a narrow gorge, we came to a checkpoint manned by the Karakoram Security Force. They wore camouflage smocks, seemed relaxed, professional and generally looked like they could have knocked over the Chinese Frontier Defence by coughing apologetically. A tall shyly friendly soldier with a big moustache shook my hand warmly. We trooped inside a hut where a burly, grey-bearded sergeant who looked as if he could send an invading army fleeing over the nearest hill by raising an eyebrow, had us write our details in a large book.

Then we were away again, winding through a narrow chasm beside a churning river. Rock rose up sheer around us, reaching straight up to snowy peaks. Scree chutes poured out of steep valleys and we emerged at the small town of Sost. At the customs and immigration post, three men sat outside at rough desks for those with visas, while the five of us without were taken inside where we were given a magical seven day pass without any fuss. We told them we were looking forward to some Pakistani food. They laughed and wished us well.

Karl directed us to a money changer he had persuaded to offer a better rate than any others in town. However, when we arrived, encouraged by another dealer, he tried to go back on the deal, saying that Karl had only changed a small amount, which I knew was a lie. We stood firm and he gave in, but he was unhappy about it.

We packed onto a small minibus. It was difficult to see much of the view other than the grey river which looked like mushroom soup, so the driver stopped so we could get out and look. Amazing mountains rose up pinnacle upon jagged pinnacle. Snow was scattered amongst their myriad peaks and specks of cloud hung above them in an otherwise clear, deep blue sky. It was breathtakingly beautiful.

We were let off at the Batura Inn on the northern edge of the village of Passu. Those same peaks rose up behind it across the wide riverbed where channels of water made their way amongst the stone shoals. The village was a scattering of low stone houses amongst fields. There were some little shops selling crisps, drinks, Mars bars, biscuits and processed cheese which we found sadly exciting as if we had been away from such Western trifles for very long. Really, they were just rumours of home.

We walked through the village, marvelling that we were in Pakistan and amongst this incredible scenery. It was a particular thrill for those of us who had not expected to come this way and had managed to pick up transit visas. The local women were attractive with coffee brown skin and eyes of green, grey, blue and brown. Children giggled and said hello. Two little boys started dancing for us, pulling strange faces and were not to be deterred from showing off by thwacks from their big sisters who were taking advantage while they still could.

I was ill in the night. To say the toilet was an en suite would give a false impression of our lodgings, which were primitive. We were in a stone hut with a hard trodden earth floor on wire frame beds. The toilet was a hole in the floor of the adjoining room with a sink on the wall. There was no light, so my head torch came in handy when I needed both hands for other things.

Liz brought me a flower the next morning to cheer me up and provide an alternative perfume to the room. I was too weak to join the others who were going to walk up past one of the local glaciers and I decided to go on the thirty-six hour fast which Karl recommended. I sat and read in the sun by the river for a while, then went for a walk. Near Passu, I talked to one of the villagers. He was an unemployed graduate in Commerce. He told me that the village of ninety households and a thousand people had produced doctors and bankers and other successes, but he had yet to get his break. Unemployment was worse every year.

I was trying to make it to the tongue of the Passu Glacier, but the rough uphill track looked like it would be too much for me in my weakened state. Instead, I found a rock in the shade by a pleasant trickling stream and sat there to read.

Everyone returned hot and thirsty from the walk. While waiting for dinner, Liz, Fiona and I sat on the river bank, watching as the tops of the mountains caught the last direct rays of the sun. Once more we marvelled at our surroundings. It was breath-taking, it was unreal, it was a bonus for the end of my trip to be amongst such towering beauty.

We waited for a bus the next morning, saying goodbye to Karl and replacing him with John. We passed the time watching a driver clean his jeep. He had been hired by a young American who was travelling with a cook and four porters. They had piled into the jeep with all their bags and driven off. I do not know why they needed four porters, other than to carry the things the porters themselves needed. When the driver came back, he drove it into a large puddle and proceeded to wash it, scooping up water with a cut-off plastic bottle, hurling it underneath and wiping with a rag or his hand. Then he drove it out of the puddle so that he could lie under and scrub away at it. Then he drove it back into the puddle and seemingly started all over again. He was obsessive, but it did gleam in the sun.

We persuaded a minibus not to go up the road to Sost, but back the other way instead. In one village, we saw a polite sign outside a building explaining that the backpackers' hostel was closing to keep the village unspoiled. We left the bus at Ganesh from where the town of Karimabad was a mile or so off the highway up a hill road. We were just starting up it when a tourist bus stopped. There was only the driver and one other man on board and they offered us a lift up to the town. It turned out that the bus was going back to Rawalpindi empty the next day. For a payment that was little more than the scheduled buses, he would give us a lift. This would be much simpler and more comfortable and would avoid us having to change at Gilgit, so we agreed. They also showed us a good hotel. The Golden Refuge was clean and roomy and had a superb view across the Hunza Valley to where a hanging valley came down from a snowy peak. It was all working out beautifully.

Karimabad is a major tourist destination, although tradesmen told us that times had been hard since the escalation of fighting over Kashmir. A steep, narrow dusty road climbed up the hillside towards a small fort perched above the town. Shops were selling handicrafts, jewellery, brass plates, clothes, hats and rugs. The other buildings seemed to be restaurants.

It was hot, but not humid and we found some shade, away from the shops, in the residential part of town on a dusty path under a mulberry tree. A woman greeted us and thought it was funny that we could not understand each other. In fact, she seemed to think that everything was funny. She fetched us a tray of mulberries. Some children came and stood by us. The girls were beautiful with brown hair, olive skin and brown eyes. They shyly told Fe and Liz their names and after a short conference, agreed to have their photograph taken. We talked to a serious fourteen year old boy about cricket. It amazed me that on the other side of the mountains was a land where the idea of cricket was a completely alien concept.

We continued up the path and through the village. Houses were set a little way up the hill from the road. They were stone with flat roofed and ladders from one level to another. Families sat in the shade, the children usually calling out to us from a repertoire of "Hallo!", "How. Are. *You!*", "Goodbye!", "*One* photo!" or "*One* pen!" Some of them wore black eyeliner to stop evil spirits entering through their eyes. At one place we offered some sweets to two boys who were passing. A few minutes later they returned with a handful of apricots.

This is yet another place that has been called Shangri La and it seemed to fit it well. The valley was green with terraces rising above the river. Behind the terraces of wheat and apricots and the poplars and the stone houses, the mountains reared up, the highest with snow, one a slim pinnacle called the Lady's Finger.

We were just starting dinner when a man came over to talk to us. He introduced himself as Hyamon. He would also be on the bus the next day because he was a guide with the company who had hired it. He told us that there would be a couple of other guides too. He made further arrangements for meeting us. We felt more confident that the ride was real and later we joined him and Riyaz the driver for tea. But first, it was John's turn to be put under the interrogation spotlight, with which he complied, quietly and intimately as befitted an English country gentleman with a story to tell.

We had breakfast gazing at the mountains across the valley. I went to do some shopping, but did not do very well because I misunderstood the local situation. For months I had been haggling, but in Karimabad, there was no haggling. Goods were already a fair price and being new to the country, I did not yet know what a fair price. In my ignorance, I took this refusal to haggle as the result of being spoiled by busloads of rich tourists. An indication of the type of customer they had was the *shatoosh* that one shopkeeper showed me. It was a shawl spun from feathers, so soft and delicate it could be pulled through a ring an inch in diameter. He said it would normally sell for $2200 but that I could have it for $1800.

We met our companions at the bus. Amit was a lively, jokey fellow, whereas quiet Afad was only a trainee. We stopped for lunch at a café by the side of a stream running off the glacier which piled down Rakaposhi. It stood nearly eighteen thousand feet higher than us, but with nothing to show scale, it really did not look very high. We peered through binoculars at grey crevasses and seracs which seemed like mere corrugations but were probably about sixty feet high.

Afternoon tea was at a caravanserai with Bedfords trucks lined up outside. They were decorated in the most colourful styles. Chains and other jingling ornaments hung from them to give a noise of movement harking back to swaying camels and rocking carriages. I could not help but compare the rainbow line of trucks with three shining red, yellow and green big rigs I had seen parked at a truck stop in the Arizona desert over two years before. A latticed roof provided some shade from the fiery heat where drivers slept on benches with their arms across eyes, or sat drinking tea, speckled by the light knifing through the holes in the roof. The tea came sweet and milky, which I found undrinkable after the refreshing green tea of China.

The high mountains retreated from view for a while. There was no longer any snow, just bare dirt and dust. There were frequent signs of rockfalls: boulders in the valley and piles by the side of the road. Along the hillsides or the edge of the valley could sometimes be seen the old jeep track. This was used before the highway went through, but in those days the two hour journey from Hunza to Gilgit, used to take eighteen. These tracks had been used long before there were jeeps as it had been one branch of the Silk Road. It had seen much political intrigue between Russia and Britain when Victoria ruled half the world. Mixed up with that was the competition between the local tribes who no one could tame but themselves. There were no settlements along the highway itself: the tribes lived in valleys behind the hills. There it was more fertile and timber was a major local product. Although within the borders of

Pakistan, the tribes were all but autonomous and ran their own affairs with their own laws. Many carried guns as a matter of course and relations between them could still be strained.

Further south, we came to an epic location. We had been following the Karakoram range and this was joined from the west by the Hindu Raj mountains, bringing with it the mighty Indus River which was to stay with us for the rest of the journey. On the east, the Himalayas appeared, rearing rocky and snowy behind the lower mountains. We were travelling in a desert of bare earth and hills. The Indus gouged through it, churning brown and fast and tumbled into rapids by thousands of submerged boulders.

It was unbearably hot in the valley where the rocks had absorbed the heat and were now radiating it as the afternoon wore on. We passed by the white bulk of Nangaparbat, at 26,660 feet, the world's ninth highest mountain. As the evening arrived, the wind picked up and the air became dusty. Men on the road walked with faces covered. Trees on the hilltops showed where the surrounding valleys received some rain when the valley in which we were driving received none.

We stopped for dinner at the Afghan Hotel. Some men were praying on a mat in the corner, the rest sat at tables. Hyamon said that some were probably extremely wealthy, owning large tracts of land and forest. They had come there to do business. Liz and Fe were the only women in what was definitely men's territory. Hyamon said that he thought the British occupation had been a good thing because it brought infrastructure and stability.

"If it hadn't been for them, we would still be cannibals," he added, which I felt was something of an exaggeration, but I decided not to spoil the compliment by mentioning the plundering East India Company.

We drove on into the night. Hyamon spent some time talking to Liz. I later learned he had been telling her how beautiful she was and how he meant that from his heart and he would like to go dancing with her. Once she was asleep, he had turned his attention to Fe, but they had only talked about their travel plans into central Asia and how he could help them once we were in Islamabad. I made sure they knew I was awake, as moral support for Fe and a vague deterrent to Hyamon, although he was never anything but polite. When we arrived at our hotel for the night, he did suggest they go for a walk down to the Indus, but Fe declined saying she

183

was too tired. As both girls said later, it was a tricky situation. He was always polite and a rebuff appropriate in the West would have felt impolite, so they ended up being polite back which could have been seen as encouraging.

The hotel was rather smart and Hyamon negotiated us a single room rate. He understood the difference between backpackers and the tour parties he normally guided. During the night, I felt something crawling on my legs and swatted it. When I peered into the sheet sleeping bag with my torch, all I could find were what seemed to be a couple of little legs. In the morning, I tipped up the bag and a rather battered centipede rolled out.

We left early. Everything was much greener and it was cooler with grey cloud cover, occasionally broken by sun. We stopped at a little place for breakfast, serving the usual sickly tea plus chapatti, ghee, macan and lentils. Hyamon said he was enjoying showing us the kind of places Pakistanis would normally stop, rather than where he would usually stop with his tourists.

Next door to the café was a gun shop. The owner showed me a 1917 Lee Enfield rifle and a newer Pakistani copy. I knew automatic weapons were illegal, but asked if he had any Kalashnikovs. The shopkeeper pushed a panel at the back of a cupboard and pulled out one of several for me to look at. Chinese made, it would cost about 14,000 rupees (£170). An automatic pistol would have cost a mere R3000 (£36).

We drove through a green terraced valley with rice fields and eventually came to a bridge marking the end of the Karakoram Highway. The road was busier on the other side. We went through more towns, ramshackle, busy little places with open fronted shops and men sitting amongst their fruit and hanging meat. There were no women around. Men did all the shopping, although I saw one couple on the edge of a town. When we made a brief toilet stop at one place, some of the men stared at the girls.

We passed clusters of beehives and shepherds with small flocks of goats. We crossed a pass of about eighteen hundred metres where it was a little cooler and it drizzled. A man went by leading two camels, which on this side of the mountains had only one hump. There were crops of tobacco and maize as well as tea, apparently a successful new experiment. On the road were colourful trucks and buses with open, curved sides, packed full of people.

We arrived at the M2 motorway, part of the old Calcutta to Kabul Mogul Highway. The plains around us shimmered in the wet heat. There were two lanes of steady traffic travelling at around forty miles per hour in each direction and people and other vehicles wandered across it. We dropped off Amit at a bus station from where he was going to pay a quick visit to Lahore to see his sister on a visit from Toronto.

Saddar Bazaar was in the centre of Rawalpindi, the older brother of the new capital of Islamabad. Our friends took us to the Pakistan Airlines office where John and I found availability on a flight to Manchester leaving the next day. I was very excited. Hyamon bargained us a good rate at a hotel with air-conditioning and en suite and left us, to meet him later. He promised to bring gin.

We went out to buy air tickets and change money. The humidity was intense after the dryness of the mountains. John and I both bought our tickets to Manchester while the girls bought ones to Kazakhstan in two days' time. I went to the Telecommunications office from where I called home. It was Saturday and Dad answered.

"Peel some extra potatoes for dinner tomorrow," I said. "I'll be home at lunchtime."

"Will you really? Where are you?"

I walked back to the hotel, passing lads at cricket practice and eagles sitting on parapets of buildings. I danced around the hotel room with excitement, making the girls jealous that I was going to be eating pork and roast potatoes. They had several more months of mutton ahead of them.

I went out to buy some snacks and drinks from a little shop nearby. I smiled at a mother and daughter. The daughter got the giggles.

"Salaam alekum," I said and the mother asked if I spoke Urdu and the daughter asked me in English where I was from. Upstairs in the hotel, a lad in a flowing robe accosted me.

"Are you Bri'ish? Yeah, so am I. It's bloody amazing 'ere innit?"

As dusk came on, I looked out over the city. It was hard to believe that this was my last evening away from home. A man and his son were praying on a roof below us. Two other men joined them and they sat chatting.

Hyamon collected us in his car complete with the gin. We had tonic and poured the gin into a water bottle and served ourselves G and Ts as we cruised around the night streets of Rawalpindi, windows down to the thick night air. He showed us the walled house where Bhutto had lived and the park opposite where he was eventually hung. We drove into Rajah Bazaar, the old part of town. The place was alive, seething. Men in white *shalwar qamiz* were everywhere and once more, there were no women. There were small open fronted shops, three hundred year old buildings which probably looked shabby in daylight but looked grand by night. There were cars and pedestrians and bicycles and horse drawn *tongas*, there were smells and noise. The only light was what spilled out of shops. Hyamon would point things out and when John clung to the door and gazed out entranced, groaning "Oh! Oh! Yes! Wonnnderful!" he was speaking for us all. We went for a tonga ride, the horse trotting though the seething Asian night with us, right in the middle of this living city which positively oozed human energy.

We were pulling into a side street when a van reversed into us. Hyamon got out for the inevitable animated discussion. A crowd gathered. John and I stood by as moral support. The argument was in Urdu and Pashto, but from the body language, Hyamon seemed to have the advantage and certainly the moral high ground. Towards the end he gestured at us and I heard "foreigners". It turned out he had said he had a car load of foreigners who could testify and he had also called on family connections, including a senior police officer. The other driver caved in and gave him some money for the damage, which was minor. Hyamon was pleased.

We went to a restaurant for a local style barbecue. It was open air and there were many families. Hyamon was jolly and excited. He told me about his girlfriend, but said it was not serious and he had lots of foreign girlfriends, one of whom he stayed with in Japan. I shuddered to think of the potential cultural confusions. He seemed to consider himself a bit of a charmer and with his Imran Khan looks, I could see how he could be. But at least he was talking to us all tonight, not just the girls.

He took us to a carpet exhibition in one of the big hotels where he said we would get a fair deal from the trader who was a friend of his called Suleiman. The carpets were gorgeous, each one more beautiful than anything we had seen in Kashgar. Most were Afghan and made with longer lasting vegetable dyes that he said were not made any more. Suleiman would unroll the carpets with a flick of the wrist and they would land on the floor with a healthy sounding wump. Among them were three beautiful shimmering silk ones which were an orgasm for bare feet but a cold shower for the wallet.

Liz bought two carpets at a price that was as good as any she had been offered before and John allowed himself to be talked into a gilim blanket, woven by hand rather than on a loom. An Afghan called Shahji wrapped them up in sacking which he stitched together quickly and efficiently, making a neat little parcel with a handle. He had smuggled many of these out of Afghanistan himself and he showed me photographs of him on snowy mountainsides, a carpet rolled and wrapped over his back, a Kalashnikov in his hand. Hyamon said the gun was not so much for use as to look like everyone else, but it could be for protection if he strayed into sensitive areas. I showed him the bearded photo of me in my passport.

"The same!" he laughed.

Hyamon dropped us off back at the hotel. It had been a great evening and a fitting end to my trip. He was still trying to suggest to the girls that they call him the next day so he could show them around. They were unsure whether the gentleman host or the charmer playboy would be on offer without their English escort and never called him. They also lost his address which meant I could never write and thank him for his hospitality.

John and I got up at 4.30am. It was pouring with rain. We hugged the girls goodbye, heaved our packs onto our backs and took the lift downstairs to find a cab to the airport. And home.

...to home

My last haggle was a dismal failure. I went to find a cab to take us to the airport. It was soon after 5am and it was pouring with rain.

"One hundred," said the taxi driver.

"Sixty," I replied.

"No. Hundred. It is government standard price to the airport."

"There is no government standard price. Seventy."

"No," he said emphatically and then did what he wasn't supposed to do: he walked away. I had heard that fifty to seventy was the going rate, although they might charge a foreigner a hundred. I looked around. There was no other traffic in sight, let alone another taxi. He had me over a barrel.

A few minutes later, we coasted into a garage to refill on petrol. He couldn't have cut it any finer. He was empty. He got us safely to the airport, through the masses of people to the dullest, most sterile departure lounge I have ever been in.

The Pakistani next to John had never flown before. He covered his eyes as we took off. John gently coaxed him to look out at the wonders beneath us, the Northwest Frontier and the rugged brown mountains of Afghanistan.

Eight hours later and I had my first sight of England through the clouds. Our Pakistani friend was going to live in Britain. He stared transfixed at the new, alien world outside: the hills and the green and the neat little towns on the edge of Manchester. Then we were really low, the airport was rushing beneath and before I could fully realise what was happening, I was home again.

I needed to get my passport stamped so that I could prove I had returned that day and could claim back some duty on goods I had shipped from Australia. The immigration officer made a fuss: it wasn't normal to stamp EU passports, he said. But could he do it for me, it was worth £190 in duty to me? But it held up the line, he said. There was only one person holding up the line, I thought. He laboriously stamped it anyway and wrote "On request" over the stamp. Welcome home, I thought.

There was an immensity of baggage. Huge suitcases, packing cases, boxes of fruit (often split), cricket bats, items of small wooden furniture. Our bags took nearly an hour to appear. Finally I emerged in the arrivals hall and into a mass of Pakistanis not unlike the one I had left in Islamabad. I hugged Mum and Dad. They looked older, thinner. I carried my bags to the car. It was warm, close. We drove through a verdant summer Cheshire, all so familiar.

Had I been away at all? Had it been two years, two months and two days since I had last been to that house, to my old room? There was a pile of things in my room: boxes, books, clothes. I pulled out the few interesting things from my pack. The Uighur hat, the weathered clothes. I didn't really know what to do with myself. What to do first? Too many stories to tell and some already half told through email. Two thousand photographs to look at. For several nights I was to doze off with jet lag looking at slides. After less than a day I was thinking how good it would be to move on again.

While being at home again felt normal, it was the differences I noticed. After three months in Asia, it was great to eat toast and to be able to drink water from the tap. And it was good to be able to chat to people in shops and to understand overheard conversations. The Macclesfield accent sounded funny and everything seemed so expensive when prices were converted into Australian dollars.

When you are away, you realise that the world is much bigger, that the strange other worlds on this earth really do exist outside the television or National Geographic magazine. But now I was home again, this once more became a strange thought. Surely Britain is all there is and the rest only exists while I am there?

The travels were not over. A few days later I was driving down to the South West. I had arrived home into a glorious summer. When they actually happen, British summers are wonderful. It was to be a journey of ten days and more than 1100 miles; a rhapsody of southern England.

I drove to the Devon village of Dunsford with its thatched cottages and hanging baskets in shimmering heat. It was the start of the annual Mystics and Magicians cricket tour; a group of friends who gather for a week-long tour each year. Few knew I was back because I wanted to surprise them. There were hugs and jokes. We played a match on the Sunday with the village church and forested hillsides as backdrop.

It was three years since I had last run around in whites and my muscles strained and bruised themselves in protest, so it was useful that I had planned to visit my brother in Sussex for a few days. The drive took me through hot sunshine and the rolling patchwork of southern England: hedgerows; stone farmhouses in valleys; the spire of Salisbury cathedral rising above the surrounding hills; Stonehenge looking like it had been erected only the week before. I looked at the great stones and at the crowds, then I walked up a track between two fields and gazing at this country of mine, I felt a connection which had been missing through the adventure.

My brother lived in a small village near Lewes. I strolled across the fields to the next village to sit in the little old oak-beamed church. I picked blackberries off hedges, played with the cats, sat in the front garden, listened to horses' hooves clopping down the lane in front of the house and supped local beer in the village pub.

I visited friends in Hampshire. We sat in the garden eating tasty home-grown salad and chicken cooked in tarragon and garlic.

Back in Devon there were narrow, winding lanes with high hedgerows or overarching trees. There were cool clear streams, hazy ranges of hills and glimpses of Dartmoor. There was the smell of flowers in the morning and long summer evenings sitting out the back of country pubs with a pint of creamy ale. There were the comforting, peaceful sounds of cricket in the heart of England and finally, there were old friends who I could risk boring with my tales of soaring mountains, wide, scorched deserts and lush tropics.

Closer to home
2000 – 2003

Much of this time was spent travelling for business around Britain, but also in Europe. Fifteen months after first meeting her in Zhongdian, Liz and I became a couple. Our first overseas adventure together was to New York to visit her brother where the December skies were blue and the air was crisp. Prague and Portugal followed, and so did a visit to Jordan. We arrived on the day the world changed.

Ron

I first met Ron in early 1986. Less than three feet tall and green, he was to be my constant travel companion for years. I named him after a salesman who was visiting where I worked when I returned with him from the camping shop. His namesake was dubious looking with a moustache. He bore no resemblance at all to my Ron, so the appeal can only have been the alliteration of Ron the Rucksack.

I love carrying my world on my back. A tent and sleeping bag can disappear inside leaving no trace of my presence. You can lean on a rucksack or sleep against it. Packing them is an art. I know where things go and where to get at things quickly: raincoat and waterbottle are always in one of the side pockets, diary and book are in the lid pocket.

Ron was a Karrimor Jaguar 75 litre. I bought him before I went to Australia. Since then, he has become stained and travel worn. Some of those stains tell a story. I accidentally tipped lemon oil from a sardine can on him in Quebec City. A seagull dropped a gift while I was waiting on the quay in Ullapool for a ferry to Barra in the Western Isles. And a small dog cocked his leg on him in a French street in Arles.

The rest of his look is an accumulation of the world from travelling on the exposed roofs and grimy bellies of buses, or a long marinade of sweat from walking many hours in the sun with him on my back.

In a few places he is split and starting to wear. Concerned about his long term viability, I bought a younger model. Ron 2 is also a Karrimor Jaguar but can extend to a larger capacity and has more straps, buckles and padding. I used to be embarrassed carrying the new Ron: he looked so new, I didn't appear to have been anywhere. Even now, he still looks fresh but his trips have largely been brief and better protected from the elements. After all, he has a fitted rain cover which Ron never had.

Ron 2 has not been to as many places as Ron, but he has walked, hiked and tramped through the mountains of South America and New Zealand in a way Ron never did. As I write, he sits on a shelf lined with various bags in the garage in Auckland. Ron, on the other hand, is in retirement in Macclesfield, waiting for a time when his seasoned expertise will be called on once more.

Driving down Watling Street

Before the legions came they walked that track,
trading, visiting and making war.
Now that land is hidden beneath tarmac and towns.
But if it moved me to be driving on that ancient way,
perhaps some anonymous ancestor
might have turned to his companion in wonder saying:
"Imagine. One day, this will be the A5 through Milton Keynes."

Sunday lunch

Another walled Portuguese town of white plaster. The restaurant was filled with families eating Sunday lunch together. The waiter showed us to our table, pleasingly speaking to us in Portuguese. It was good to be part of this view of family life and not to be noticed as tourists.

My menu Portuguese had become quite passable and we looked at what was on offer. There was the usual pan fried chicken and pork which we had been eating with chips in most places we found, but there were also some new things to eat. This seemed like the perfect opportunity. I found a lamb stew which I thought would be interesting.

"…and that one is roast something sheep. That'll be roast lamb or mutton," I said knowledgeably.

The waiter came over, still speaking to us in Portuguese. We placed our order. Suddenly he straightened up, wide-eyed and exclaimed in English: "You want sheep's *head?!*"

"Er no," said Liz. "The chicken please."

Fever

We became lost in Evora's narrow streets and, struggling to find somewhere to stay, settled for the YHA hostel. It cost the same as the pensions we had been staying in elsewhere in Portugal, but we had to sleep apart. The rooms smelled of people and the showers were cold, but at least we had somewhere to sleep.

I lay awake until some time after my two German room mates had returned from their night out. Even then, I slept so badly I was aware of every hour, as the two nearest churches chimed one after the other. It was a long night. At some point, I teetered out of my high top bunk to perform some loud, echoing, explosive diarrhoea in the en suite bathroom. I returned to bed, still feeling uncomfortable, but getting up was such a palaver I hung on as long as I could until my second bout. My self-consciousness at the sound of my bowels diminished when I noticed one of the Germans slept with ear plugs and that when *he* got up in the night, he not only left the door open but also performed a loud comedy bottom quack. When morning came, I was exhausted and glad to get up.

Our first job was to find somewhere else to stay. We moved to a small hotel in a seventeenth century merchant's house. The friendly owner showed us how to drive the car there, tracing a line on the map like the way out of a maze in a puzzle book.

I was feeling ropey and the room was not ready for us, so we sat in the square by the columns of the old Roman temple which had survived because it had been walled in for hundreds of years. Then, still feeling unwell, I sat in a chair in the entrance lobby while Liz went to buy some fruit and vegetables.

When the room became available, I went to bed. I slept off and on, aching all over in a fluey kind of way. I had occasional diarrhoea, nibbled unenthusiastically on food, read a little and felt guilty that Liz was being forced to sit around instead of exploring. At least it was a grey day.

In the evening, I had a change of scene, sitting in the lounge by the old fireplace before I hobbled back to bed. Liz tried a relaxation technique on me that I had done on her once. I had her imagine herself on a beach in New Zealand's Abel Tasman National Park with the gentle sun on her and the waves breaking. Her version was to imagine my flesh was slowly melting into the ground. I said that was a horrible image; I had a picture of my flesh dissolving into the soil, leaving behind only my bleached skeleton. So she suggested lying on the beach and evaporating or dissolving into the sand to leave just a damp patch. I didn't like that one either.

I had another rough night, tossing, turning and groaning. During my dreams we had amassed a huge pile of accumulated agreements as a result of which we knew there were some things we did not want to agree to, but we had a starting point to work from.

Going to sleep and dreaming again, this pile became a huge tangle. I followed threads, lifting loops to go underneath and sometimes doing much threading through to untangle only the smallest piece. When I woke next, I had resolved a large chunk of it.

Sleeping once more, I tried to pick off the easy problems, pulling out particular things that were small and together and made sense. When I woke up, I was aware that this dreaming process was getting me closer to being well again. I had another dose of dreams and there was just one theme left to deal with.

In a half awake state, I tried to explain to Liz that I had been thinking through the little chores, the little jobs – I could not find the words. She retorted that wasn't being very restful. She tried again to get me to relax as I was restless. None of it would work.

At last I had to get up and go to the toilet just outside our room. I broke out in a cold sweat. I felt awful. I thought I was getting worse again. I could feel the beginnings of muscle cramps in my hands which I had had once before from dehydration. I was concerned that I had to get back to the bedroom before I seized up and they had to break the door down. I got back, had a drink and collapsed into bed exhausted. I also realised I was feeling much better. The fever must have broken. I slept better.

The next day we went to the fascinatingly gruesome chapel of bones. This giant memento mori had limb bones piled so that the joints formed the face of the wall. Patterns were made by skulls or pieces of cranium in lines and arches. Pillars had bones cemented into them and a desiccated corpse hung from one wall. I wondered if someone had told *him* to relax while his flesh dissolved into the ground.

War and empires

We were in the Roman amphitheatre in Amman in Jordan when we heard that a plane had crashed into the World Trade Center. My first thought was that they meant a light aircraft and that it was an accident. We went with our Peace Corps friend to their base where the scale of what had happened soon became apparent. The young Americans were glued to the television and emailing home.

No one was sure what would happen next, but they felt there would be a US military incursion into the Middle East. They just hoped they remembered the Peace Corps before all hell broke loose.

We took a shared taxi down the Desert Highway to Petra. There were three other passengers, a local and a couple who were a Jewish-American girl and a Palestinian living in Jericho. She had been working in Yemen and was enjoying the relative freedom of Jordan, but I still thought their mild canoodling in the car was inappropriate.

We stopped off at Al Shawbak castle, one of the Crusader forts, later taken over by Saladin. There was no one about apart from a couple of workmen restoring walls with new stone and another man who turned out to be a guide. "The village below us is empty now. They have all moved to the next village. Why? Because the houses were antique and these are more modern."

In the mid-afternoon, we crested a rise and behind the sand coloured hills were lines of rugged red rock. Petra.

We were up early the next morning, assisted by the 5am call to prayer from at least three muezzin around the valley, one of which sounded as though he was perched on our window sill.

We spent two days exploring the city. The way into Petra began down a wadi, past cube shaped tombs, the Djinn blocks, scattered by the path and a grander tomb surmounted by four obelisks carved into the rock. Local Bedouin tried to persuade us to ride horses the eight hundred metres to the entrance of the Siq, a chasm twelve hundred metres long. At the base of either wall was a channel which once contained terracotta pipes of which only a few remained.

199

There were also remnants of the original paving on the ground. The walls rose sheer, twisting around. Occasionally it was so narrow, the light was blocked out. In most places rock faces hung overhead, catching the sun. It was a perfect way to enter a lost city.

After winding down this rock passage for a quarter of an hour, it opened into a wide junction in the ravine. Right opposite was the spectacular tomb known as the Treasury. Normally ancient buildings like this are reduced to a few feet of walls, but it had been carved out of the cliff face and was protected by the surrounding mountain from the elements. It was classical in design with pillars and a triangular portico split by an urn rumoured to contain pirates' treasure which had provided the name to the building. There were bullet holes in it from optimists hoping to shatter it and let out the treasure. Inside was a big, cool, empty space.

We continued between the rock walls. There were tombs at ground level and some up steps. We paused by the theatre, its semi-circular rows of seats had been cut by the Romans straight out of the rock and through some of the older architecture. We detoured from the colonnaded street of the old city centre up one of the hills to the side. These were covered in rubble from the city which had been destroyed by earthquakes.

A Byzantine church on the hill, containing wonderful mosaics, was being restored by a friendly Jordanian, under the auspices of an American agency. He was concerned about his "doctor" who was currently in the US. He had not heard from him since the 9/11 attacks a few days before. He thought "the third war" might be coming. He sat up on the back wall behind the altar and drank Pepsi and ate a falafel roll and invited us to climb up too for a better view down the mosaics which ran the length of the north and south apses. One had animals and people. The other was themed around the four seasons.

At the end of the city centre, past the massive walled remains of the Temple to Dushaneh, a woman approached Liz.

"Are you English?" she asked.

"No," Liz replied.

"Neither am I."

She was Bronwyn from Ireland. With her grey hair, crucifix and long black skirt, I wondered if she might be a nun. She said she had been on the Petra By Night walk the previous day and had got into trouble. She had wanted to say a prayer for peace, but the Italians in the group had not understood. Then she had corrected the guide a couple of times, which, not surprisingly, had annoyed him. She asked if she could walk with us up to the tomb known as the Monastery. As we went, I happened to mention that there were eight hundred steps.

"Fucking hell," said Bronwyn.

Not a nun then.

"Sorry," she added.

It was only then that I noticed she smelled of alcohol. She stopped to light up a cigarette. She continued to dawdle and we left her behind as we went higher into the rocks on the stone stairway.

We came out onto a wide flat space on one side of which was the Monastery, built in the third century BC, a tomb similar to the Treasury, but much larger. It became larger still when someone provided scale by standing in the doorway. Inside was huge, empty and refreshingly cool and the ceiling displayed the coloured patterns of the sandstone.

A little further on, we were able to look across rugged mountains leading away to a hazy plain, across sheer drops into wild valleys. In the distance was a white tomb on the summit of Jebel Haroun. It marked the supposed resting place of Moses' brother Aaron.

We climbed the steep stone stairway above the theatre to the High Place of Sacrifice to sit and gaze at the mountains and the city. On the way down, we came across an English couple. He had a baby strapped to his back and was arguing with his wife about how well Eddie was shaded. He had popped up onto the top but went back down disappointed.

"There's nothing there. I thought there'd be something like the Monastery."

"Was there a view?" she asked.

"A bit of one," he replied. "But not worth the walk up by any stretch of the imagination."

Crass bastard, I thought.

We found the way up to the crusader fort, on a rock above the city centre, looking over the remains of the temples and public buildings below and some of the tombs at the other end of the valley. So many empires had occupied this city, the Nabataeans, the Romans, Byzantines and Crusaders. We climbed down to the still paved main street.

Men with camels, mules and horses all offered us "taxi, taxi, air conditioned". Bedouin women were selling silver bangles, bead necklaces, clay camels and little boxes.

"Have-a-look. Have-a-look. Cheap price."

No one was looking or buying. And there were few tourists. The intifada in Israel had put off many. With the attacks in the US, I did not think business was going to pick up any time soon. I estimated that there were only a few hundred in the city where normally there would have been thousands.

Only foreigners were on the minibus to Wadi Rum. The radio was playing the BBC Arab Service of which we tantalisingly understood only names: George Bush, America, Osama Bin Laden, Afghanistan, Georges Chirac…What was happening in the world?

Once on the Desert Highway, there were hills on the left and rock formations hazily a little way below us on the right. I must admit to occasional paranoia, such as when a group of figures appeared ahead on the roadside, but they turned out to the schoolboys from a village just off the road.

The village of Rum sat between two great hills of rock, one of which was Jordan's highest point at over 1700 metres. We were met by the tour guide's brother and sat in a woollen tent open on one side for shade, eating breakfast and waiting for our tour guide to arrive from Aquaba. Two of our companions were Kevin and Katarina from Ottawa and Stuttgart. They had just been in Beirut. They said that when people had heard about the 9/11 attacks, they had danced in the street and invited them to join them in their homes.

Zahedan arrived. He was tall, wore a long white robe and the Bedouin headscarf and walked in an upright, uncaring, regal way as if nothing really interested him and everything could wait. He took us to his house where we sat around some more. He failed to get his internet connected, I showed him how to clean his computer mouse and we had a pot of tea.

A driver took us on the tour. We piled into the flatbed of a Toyota Landcruiser, drove up the road, round the corner then parked by his house. He went inside while we sat, heating up in the sun. It had been bearable while we were moving because it had created a breeze. He came back with a teapot and some cups and we were off again, out of the dusty streets of breezeblock houses with four wheel drives and camels outside and off into the desert on old tracks and making new ones.

We spent five hours bouncing around in the back of the truck. We visited sites, such as a concrete cistern fed by a hose down the rocks called Lawrence's Spring and a stone wall up against a rock called Lawrence's house and a couple of rock bridges, but mainly they were places from which to look at the amazing landscape. Sometimes we would bang on the cab roof and the driver would stop. It was wonderful. Some of the rock was sandy coloured, another type redder. And there were two colours of sand to match the rock it came from.

We had lunch at a natural rock bridge. Every time we stopped, the driver would tinker with the engine which did not inspire confidence. We ate, he tinkered, prayed and then starting making a pot of tea. He got a fire going from dead scraps, sitting cross-legged by it and grunting softly as if with effort, but it took no effort. When it was almost boiling, he poured half a cup into a cup of tea leaves and sugar and let it steep for a while as it continued boiling. It tasted fine in the end. He also gave us pieces of cheese which was dry, crunchy and salty.

At 3.30pm, we arrived at the camp: a brown woollen Bedouin tent, fenced with windbreaks, set against a big lump of rock. There he left us to ourselves for a few hours. It was hot and we flaked out for a while then read in the shade. I had one of those moments when I stopped and thought about where I was.

I was sitting in the shade of a rock in the Negev Desert. It was late afternoon and I was being washed by a warm breeze that was cooler than the sun beyond the shadow. Flies annoyed us, buzzing in our faces and around our ears. I looked at the rippled redbrown sand, dotted with rough tussocks of a low desert bush spreading away from the rock where I sat. The semi-circle of horizon had sheer rock walls, variously riven into towers and fortresses with heaps of dark grey rubble at their feet. Directly in front of me was a formation that looked like a block of milk chocolate built in terraces which was beginning to melt. Four-wheel drive tracks forked across the sand and the shadows were just starting to lengthen.

We climbed on top of our own shady lump of melted chocolate to watch the sunset, the rock changing colour and texture as the sun went down and the sky turned a deeper and darker blue.

Back in the camp, a lad had brought our dinner, a chicken stew. He sat silent as we ate and talked. We went out to look at the stars. It had been years since I had seen that many. We all decided to sleep outside. It took me a while to go to sleep because if I closed my eyes I could no longer see the stars. I woke again at 5am and watched as they faded.

We took a packed bus to Aquaba and watched the sun set over Israel on the opposite side of the Red Sea and a crescent moon appear above the crescent moon on a mosque.

The hotel was full of about ninety British soldiers on rest and recuperation from exercises. They were polite and well behaved, although I had expected less from a bunch of tattooed, shaven headed, highly trained thugs. I was a little proud of them none the less. After all, they were prepared to do things that I was not.

In the hotel basement was a television and a selection of DVDs. Several soldiers had already chosen to watch *Lawrence of Arabia*. They laughed at the army jokes about saluting officers. Anthony Quinn invited Omar Sharif and Peter O'Toole to Wadi Rum. It felt surreal to be sitting with the British Army in Aquaba, watching hordes of Bedouin descend on Aquaba and rout the Turks.

We took an early bus to Karak. It followed the Dead Sea Highway, a quiet road that ran alongside the Israeli border, past occasional towers looking over an emptiness that looked emptier because of the occasional signs of people in the lookout towers. Signs told us not to take pictures. The mountains of the Sinai began not far away and mountains began to rise to the east as well. Some of the land became irrigated. We arrived at the southern end of the Dead Sea where the Arab Potash Company was extracting salts from wide, shallow evaporation pans. Then we turned right to climb steeply up to Karak. More signs ordered us not to take photographs. Karak was at an altitude of nine hundred metres but the Dead Sea was four hundred and fifty metres *below* sea level, so it was a bit of a climb.

The giant crusader castle was a silhouette in the sun. There were ramps and giant chambers, stable blocks and crumbling walls. The knights of the west were long gone. We could not stay either: service disruptions had brought our flight forward a day. We flew home from the Holy Land on a guided missile.

South America
2004

In 2004 Liz and I moved to New Zealand. Moving countries is a great opportunity to do a bit of travelling and it also provides a transition between different ways of life. We chose South America for our transition. It was not a trip of anecdotes, about which we felt a little cheated, but it was a trip of incredible landscapes.

Travels through South America

~ 500km

Climbing the cathedral

We were about to set off when the howling and yelps of what sounded like a pack of wolves rose up from amongst the trees above us. Liz looked as disturbed as I felt and Warren, an Australian we had met in Bariloche, looked puzzled. We had not heard warnings about wolves and it worried us until we reached the trailhead and saw an advert for something involving sled dogs.

We quickly gained height, then followed a contour amongst dense bushes with yellow flowers and stands of bamboo until we entered a burnt wood of ghost white trees. Some undulations led us, after a couple of hours, along the Arroyo Van Titter that bubbled up below the southern flank of Cerro Catedral. We were in lenga forest proper now, walking up hill through corridors of bamboo and the occasional scotch thistle, neither of which I had expected to see in Argentina.

The undergrowth thinned and we paused for a light lunch and to refill our bottles and drink our fill of the wonderful water. Nearby was the Refugio Piedritas, a basic log cabin built under a huge boulder.

The way became steeper and the trees shorter and we could see the jagged sandy coloured edge of the Cordon Catedral above scree. I did not realise at the time that we would be climbing to the same height. This was fortunate because the afternoon was hot and by this stage I was plodding, concentrating on each step or trying to think of other things. At last I could see the Refugio Frey above me. I climbed the last boulder slope and over the stream and was up in the cirque.

Laguna Toncek lay blue before me on a green plain at 1760 metres. Around and above it, it looked as though someone had built several huge gothic cathedrals: it was all towers, spires and statues on pinnacles. Climbers were busy scaling one particular tower slab above the Refugio.

By now we were ravenous and we set up the tent a few yards from the lake shore and put on some fresh pasta and tomato sauce to cook.

We slept for nine or ten hours and woke refreshed. As we set off around the lake, we realised the lack of vegetation to provide scale, meant it was further than we thought to the boulder slope on the far side. We found our path by occasional red marker dots and we had to use both hands and feet to scramble up. Streams tumbled over the rocks and we filled our bottles with the delicious cold water.

At the top was Lago Schmoll, a much smaller lake hidden in another cirque. We tried to see where the path went, looking for a way up this other boulder slope. I saw the next red dot first.

"Where?" asked the others. I chuckled to myself before giving them what I felt was a ridiculous first clue.

"Do you see that boulder?" In fact, not only did they both look at the boulder I meant, but they also saw the red dot.

There was more use of hands on the next stretch as we pulled our way past tumbled rock, looking down on the cirque and the upper valley, clearly seeing the different depths of Schmoll where the silt collected from the stream flowing in. It was hard to see where the water came from. There was some icy snow on the slopes but not a great deal, so perhaps it was dew. Behind us were the jagged, shattered ridges of Catedral. We were now at the Cancha de Futbol, the football pitch. At 2100 metres it was hardly a good place to play football, but a flattish space where two ridges joined. Then again, we had already noticed that in South America, if there was a flat space, there would be a football pitch on it. We looked down into the forested Rucaco Valley. Beyond were more ridges and nearby, several snow-capped peaks and beyond those, lakes lay in the hazy distance.

We started down the steep slope, picking our way carefully amongst boulders. Liz, who dislikes downhills at the best of times, did not like this one at all. As it descended, it became more like scree, sandy in colour, that would give as you walked on it. This made scree-skiing possible. Before we reached this however, we heard voices from above and two lean, dreadlocked, bearded men in packs came running down.

"Some monkeys are coming," I said. As they passed Warren, one tripped and tumbled over, gashing his leg. Then he was up and running again. His friend, a little slower, skidded and almost fell a couple of times and soon we could see little of them for dust. I pondered how the Tumbling Scree Monkeys would be a good name for a band.

Scrub grew on the lower sections and the rocks were larger as we followed a route through them and into more lenga forest. We stopped on the edge of a meadow for lunch of cheese, tomato and lettuce sandwiches, reminding ourselves we were supposed to be roughing it, then continued along the valley floor, sometimes on the grass but mainly in the trees where there was little undergrowth and just a few purple flowers. We refilled our water in the stream and admired a little waterfall. We looked back at our route into the valley. The slope appeared to be far too steep to have walked down.

We started to climb again, up an exposed, dusty, scrubby, stone-filled path that wound up the other side of the valley. Weary, we arrived at a terrace where the ground was now a stony grey. As we approached, we could see from the progress of another couple in the distance that the next stretch was further than it looked. I managed it by not looking to see how far away the horizon still was. Near the ridge, when I was most tired, I needed to use my hands as well which distracted me from my fatigue and thirst.

At the top of this next ridge however, we looked across lines of mountains. At our feet, a scree slope even steeper than the morning's plunged to the valley floor. Any steeper, I decided, and all the scree would have been at the bottom. It was a wide, forested U-shaped valley, bare rock rising from the forest. To the left, dark rock towers emerged from a snowy ridge above the deep green of Lago Jakob. The valley ran off to the right to be joined by several tributaries, some widened ravines, others merely deeper hollows where shorter valleys came in. It was all quite magical and spoiled only by the thought of having to go down.

The descent proved to be much tougher than the first because the rock was too irregular in size to do much scree-skiing. To add to Liz's downhill antipathy was that she was tired, hungry and bothered by flies. I kept stopping to wait for her, which I found more tiring than just keeping on a downward momentum and I was beginning to get grumpy too. At the bottom, we hopped across boggy ground and stepping stones to reach the campsite behind Refugio Jakob four hundred metres below the ridge. Both Liz and Warren went for a dip in the lake, as they had also done the day before. It was cold. They warmed up on a kind of risotto with rice, chicken soup, chickpeas and some fried onion and green pepper.

The next day we headed down the valley, following the Arroyo Casa de Piedra, the House of Stone stream. To our right, it cut a sharp gorge and dropped over a waterfall. The crossing point was just yards from a waterfall. It was a single cable stretched loosely across the water. Despite the wire appearing to promise a difficult crossing, if you ignored the nearby steep drop, the stepping stones were easy. We dropped down over the lip of the valley where the trees were taller and there were thickets of bamboo. Flowers were yellow and orange and violet. It was like walking through a garden. We left the lenga trees and came out into what the guidebook said were "mogotes, calafate bushes and ñirres – typical dryland vegetation". We could see the surrounding mountains and the trees climbing the lower slopes. It was a lovely walk and we developed a brisk pace.

Crossing a rickety suspension bridge, which would have been much more worrying had it been suspended over a chasm instead of a shallow stream, we refilled our water bottles and had lunch. Here the stream was wider, as was the valley. Several times we climbed hills as the river dropped away below, but these spurs in the valley sides had the good manners to even out as our head of steam died at their summit. Then we joined a four wheel drive track and watched the miniature explosions our boots made in the fine dust.

The trail ended at a tumbledown farm house outside which was a sign advertising drinks. An old man sat in the garden with his single tooth for company and asked us a few questions in incomprehensible one-toothed Spanish. We continued until we reached a gravel road. There was no shade and it went on for five miles of eternity as the afternoon sun beat down on us.

We emerged onto the main lake shore road at Barrio Casa de Piedra. Miraculously there was a shop selling cold Quilmes beer and we collapsed at a table outside with our glasses of beer and a bag of potato crisps. Covered in a paste of dust, sweat and sunblock, we looked back up at the mountains we had crossed and felt smug and healthy. We smiled at each other, raised a toast and drank the best glass of beer in the world.

Journey into the imagination

The road to Argentina was a good, tarmac road. We turned off it to take the dirt road that led to Bolivia.

We bumped through yellow tussock lit golden by the morning sun and scattered with occasional green. Licancubur is a classic volcano shape and we skirted around its bare gravel flanks to reach a desolate border post. A guard in a neatly pressed uniform sat beneath Bolivia's red, yellow and green flag that looked like a flag out of a make believe country in a Tintin book, and stamped 30 days into our entry visa. Liz found what turned out to be a popular place for a rest stop behind a rusting wreck of a bus.

The Laguna Blanca, named for the borax which froths on the shore, reflected the bare red brown hills under a clear blue sky. There, we transferred into a Landcruiser. Our guide and driver was Ambrosio. Also in our jeep were Arnaut and Katrien, two Flems recently graduated from university; Enrico, a wiry and perky Italian from Milan; and Gorka, a Basque who would write his nationality as Euskadi. Had he let his beard grow, he would have made a good conquistador with his Robert de Niro smile. He mumbled Spanish in a thick accent that confused even Ambrosio.

Over a rise, and once part of the same lake, was the emerald coloured Laguna Verde in a setting of white stones. Driving on, we had a surreal experience of bathing in a thermal pool inside a wire fence by an adobe hut in a wasteland where flamingos stalked.

We drove into vast bowls under a blue dome of sky, ringed with brown mountains and volcanoes, often dusted with the familiar mix of powder paint colours. Inside one bowl was a collection of Dali-esque rocks, moulded and sculpted by wind and sand.

We climbed higher to Sol de Mañana at over five thousand metres where the atmospheric pressure was like someone squeezing my temples. It was another planet: red hills framed a landscape of bubbling mud pits and fumaroles roaring out steam that billowed across green, yellow and grey ground which looked like painted papier-mâché.

At the Laguna Colorada we walked along the grey gravel shore backed by distant grey mountains. Flamingos were dotted across the lake, sieving the water through the tops of their beaks. The wind blew strongly and we pulled our hats over our ears for protection.

We spent the night at a nearby refugio, a basic row of dormitories and a toilet block containing shoulder high cubicles with curtains on wires for doors. But they were real toilets, flushed with water from a barrel.

Gorka dressed up in his cycling gear and went off for a ride. Dinner was a soup followed by spaghetti which Enrico dolled out like an Italian mama, urging us to eat more.

Bedtime was not entirely successful. The beds were short, sagging and uncomfortable and had extremely noisy springs so that the slightest movement was accompanied by their tortured screeching. The effects of altitude and coca tea had me getting up an hour after getting into bed. I was still awake an hour later and needed to go again but resisted the urge and drifted off. I woke at 4am and had to go. Accompanied by the bed banshees, I sneaked from the room and went outside. Wearing only underpants and T-shirt it was chilly, but I was mesmerised by the sky. Maybe I had seen that many stars before in the desert in Jordan or Australia, but I did not remember it. The only time I have been closer to stars has been in an airliner. There were millions in the clear air; so many that it seemed that, had there been any more, the sky would have been completely white.

Perhaps I managed two or three hours sleep. Most of us slept badly but Arnaut talked in his sleep in a mixture of Spanish and English saying things along the lines of "Señoras, we're coming." We were up just before sunrise and the tussock was backlit against the desert while the hill behind the refugio glowed orange.

We were on our way again by 7am, skirting the Laguna Colorada and its silhouetted flamingos and crossing into another volcano-ringed plain. We continued through valleys strewn with boulders thrown out by eruptions. There were humps of them and low, exposed outcrops that looked like stone walls. This landscape merged into one that was more like a desert and the surrounding mountains disappeared for a short time as we climbed higher again. We came upon another lake where flamingos perched on the end of their reflections. Behind was a gravel sloped plateau that stood apart from the other mountains and looked as though it could have once been a fortress. As we continued around three of its sides, the impression grew that it was an ancient city that had been obliterated in some cataclysmic event.

Over a pass, snow-topped mountains herded smaller cousins. There was another lake and the ruin of a borax collecting operation. A rhea and her three large chicks ran quickly across the scrub.

The landscape changed again. One view in particular appeared like a painting of a fantasy world. The ground was covered in green tufts of grass, but curving through it was a great trench made up of a brown rock cliff on the left and a sloping bank on the right. This led back into mountains. One on the left had a clear snowline and to its right was a volcano, dark grey, scarred with a strip of paler grey like a white streak in someone's hair.

We entered a valley of rounded mountains, but these too were volcanoes and boulders littered their green slopes. Then out into browner country where the rock showed through like a giant dusty patio. It was really beginning to feel like we were driving through someone's imagination.

We drove into a world of rock. First came curiously shaped brown clumps, then grey outcrops like ruined castles. These became stripes of brown ridges, sometimes broken, always eroded fantastically by the wind and all tending down a long slope to a greenish plain. We looked back at white topped peaks. I was sure I had seen a column of smoke coming from one mountain a few miles back. Ahead of us, a piling storm cloud was spreading across the sky like spilled ink, flashing occasional lightning and rumbling ominously. Tendrils of cloud reached out over the land ahead of it but it seemed to collapse on itself only for another to begin to grow to our right.

We drove down the valley, past a volcano whose top had been blown open leaving avalanches of rubble and lava visible in the shape of the contours below its broken crater. The track turned from dust to stone and became much bumpier. We reached the valley floor, a marshy green plain where llama grazed and groups of small houses were tucked into hollows. As we followed the valley around, it narrowed to the width of a football pitch with sloping sides topped by little cliffs. A narrow stream ran through it and more llama and a few sheep grazed while young ones played.

There were small cropped areas of green cereal fenced off on the slopes and dry stone walls separated other cultivated plots from the grazing, sometimes on quite steep sections. A concrete irrigation channel ran along by the road and eventually we came to the town of San Augustin, a motley collection of thatched adobe, stone and plaster along dusty streets. We parked in front of the town hall by the bandstand and the little church. There was a pretty garden in the small piazza and one street over was the valley which was filled with a series of walled plots thick with vegetables and cereals. Above the far side, grey clouds were threatening. A group of women laughed as they worked in a nearby garden. Two men walked down the street, a sheep trotting along behind and running to keep up when they called for it like a dog.

The valley changed its character with the steep but low sides looking like they had been melted and poked into strange shapes and patterns. The valley walls became higher and wider apart until they must have been a hundred foot high cliffs. We drove away from them and the clouds that were building over the valley. The land was wider and flatter and became a mud coloured dusty plain and on it was the township of Julaca.

Deserted but for ten families, I could only assume they worked on the railway that ran down one side of the main street. This was about as wide as a football pitch and because we were in South America, it contained a set of goal posts. A water tower stood in the street with a pipe for the steam engines. It looked like the set of a Spaghetti Western. A couple of dogs wandered about and a small scruffy child talked to Enrico and Gorka. It was a strange place, a barely populated backwater somewhere beyond nowhere.

We drove across a causeway raised above the mud and around the muddy fringes of the great salt lake, the Salar de Uyuni. We passed through a sorry little town. Signs a few miles out advertised it with a bed, knife and fork, tap, red cross and telephone.

We spent the night in the jeep company's own hostel. Much smarter than the previous night, it had firm, comfortable beds. Enrico hung a washing line the length of our room for his little white briefs and socks. The place was full of other truckloads of tourists and we ate dinner in one canteen, each group at its own table and served by our drivers. We slept much better.

Within a few minutes of leaving the hostel we were at a pivot barrier and a sign on a stone that pointed to Uyuni. It pointed up another causeway that led out into the vastness of the Salar de

215

Uyuni and petered out. It is at least a third of the size of Belgium and twice the size of Utah's Great Salt Lake.

Leaving the causeway like a pier in the ocean behind us, we drove out onto the gleaming whiteness of salt which can be up to 125 metres in depth. Across much of it was a reflective film of water which gave the impression that we were driving across the sky. We steered towards an island, Isla de Incahaus, and drove up onto its shore as if we were grounding a speedboat. The island was made up of sharp volcanic rock and was thick with tall, bristled cacti. They grew one centimetre a year. Liz posed for a photograph by one twelve metres tall. If she grew at that rate, she would not even be a foot tall.

Back out into the mirror of whiteness, we skimmed through a dream in a world of sky with clouds above and below us and distant floating islands.

We had lunch at a former hotel that had been built entirely out of salt but was now just a shop and snack bar. We sat outside on table and chairs of salt to eat. I picked up a hard boiled egg and asked Ambrosio if there was any salt.

Much of the sky was blue with fluffy white clouds, except for where a huge storm was brewing and had turned a section of the sky black. This monster seemed to pause before the Salar, afraid to step out onto the strange white floor.

Passing a few salt workers scraping piles together, we drove up onto the mud shore and a small dirty village where Ambrosio hosed down the car and removed the tarpaulins he had tied across the underside to protect it from the salt.

Through a sprinkling of rain along a dirt road on a plain bordered by hills, we came at last to the train cemetery outside Uyuni. Three lines of rusting and partly dismantled steam trains stood shunted together on rails amongst rubbish and bits of coal facing an empty horizon of grey cloud. Large black flies with red wings buzzed by us like aliens. A complex formula attributed to Einstein had been daubed in neat white paint on the boiler of one locomotive. It was as if the metaphorical end of the line had been made into a reality. But we had just a little further to go.

We drove into Uyuni itself, through scrub bearing a rich crop of torn plastic bags, passing from the dreamscape into reality once more. Uyuni itself was a busy town with wide streets. The town was littered with the usual wandering dogs and there was a power cut in the afternoon. We had our final dinner together at a pizza place, where we tried llama which was dry and salty but not unlike beef.

Many of the women were dressed traditionally in wide skirts, shawls and hats, usually a bowler hat but sometimes a straw hat, trilby or Stetson. Some looked as though they ought to be wearing gun belts too. It was women who sat in the market surrounded by fruit, vegetables or parts of animal. It was also usually women who sat in the little shops which were tiny cubes packed with boxes, jars and other goods.

We were woken by the Bolivian army's worst bugler in the barracks next door. This was followed by energetic chanting and a marching band which, despite playing an annoyingly catchy tune, still sounded like an over-enthusiastic school second orchestra.

We walked through a bustling market which filled the main street. There were pens and pencils, clothes, household items, stereos and even computers. I had no idea who was going to buy any of it, but people looked confident that somebody would and the stall holders chatted happily amongst themselves.

We investigated buses to Potosí and found out that all of them left at 10am. Ours was half full of foreigners and to our surprise, left on the stroke of ten o'clock. It was a dramatic journey through the mountains. Despite the welcome return of trees, these mountains were like shards of flint in their sharpness and steepness, sometimes showing off their tilted strata. We followed a river bed for a way and went through a gorge that would have been a major tourist draw in many countries.

We stopped in a village at around lunchtime, a poor, dirty looking place full of people in filthy clothes and where the dirt road became muddier. But beyond the houses and immediate fields were a river and beautiful mountains. This effect of being idyllic from a distance was enhanced by the willows and poplars that often grew around small settlements.

An old woman got on the bus somewhere. Arnaut was going to offer her his seat but Katrien said she smelled really bad and did not let him. The woman sat on the floor. Gorka gave up his seat for another. A young girl coughed up studiously into a plastic bag on the back seat behind us.

We left Gorka in Potosí and continued to Sucre, the official capital. Bus hawkers called out the destination in set chants which we collected as we travelled: "La. Paz. La. Paz. La. Paz." Next came "Potto-*see*! Potto-*see*!", "Sooc-ray! Sooc-ray!" or "Villazonvillazon!", the second with a rising intonation.

Sucre was three hours on a paved road followed by seven on a dirt one. We crossed a plain bordered by great spines of tilted rock. It was green and agricultural with many villages and a few scattered trees. Then suddenly we were on the edge of a deep, steep valley at the bottom of which curved a wide brown river bed of silt with a stream flowing through it. We wound down to the bottom, passing a strange brick castellated gatehouse which guarded one end of a wooden suspension bridge.

Sucre sits at a mere 2790 metres. The architecture in the centre of town was very Spanish. It would have been easy to think we were in Spain were it not for the Quecha women in their shawls and conical hats. Kids would ask if I wanted my boots shined, men would wander up and offer us native textiles. The buildings were all white. The cathedral was grand and stood next to the government building in the main square. This was filled with tall, shady trees and scattered amongst them, statues of various national heroes in uniform. The church of San Miguel dated from 1626. It was a calm, restful place with an intricate Moorish ceiling. A woman was sobbing out a story to a calmly spoken man near the front.

The streets were alive with water bombs. Quecha women sat filling up balloons with water until they were the size of small balls. When the schools came out, there were running street battles. Young lads bought them then launched them at friends, strangers and girls. The results were sometimes giggles, sometimes stern looks. There were also water pistols shaped like automatic rifles.

We found the Park Bolivar which seemed to be where the richer people went. There we saw a monument funded by fining bakers for selling underweight bread and wondered if a similar system could work for Bolivia's worst street cleaner. He was rather picky, deciding which rubbish he was going to sweep up, leaving behind more than he tidied.

We caught the Dino-truck covered in paintings of dinosaurs to a cement quarry on a hill outside town. Dinosaur footprints had been found there, but many were destroyed as quarrying continued. The latest set had been saved thanks to the rock being no good for cement and it had been made a national monument and a money spinner in its own right. The layers of rock have been pushed up to the vertical. Millions of years ago, Sucre had been a lake and the quarry a beach where dinosaurs would come to drink. Explanations were short or non-existent and I was left wanting to know more. Apparently the footprints had been fossilised by volcanic ash but did this apply to each layer? And did that mean that there had been an eruption after they had gone to drink because no footprints led away from the water.

But that aside, it was amazing. Here two beasts had lumbered down one behind the other; there a larger carnivore had run diagonally down to the water. Running across the beach were a raptor's tracks, the longest single set in the world. One animal seemed to have a strange way of walking. It would move its back legs up to its front before moving its front legs forward again. The back legs were 80cm in diameter. There were also fossilised lumps of algae and ripples on the sand. Because there were tufts of grass clinging to the rock, it looked an aerial view of the beach and I imagined that if we just turned out heads, maybe we would see some giant animals quietly drinking.

We returned to Potosí and stayed at a seventeenth century guest house originally built as a lodge for travelling monks. It was built around a courtyard with a tree in the middle. I thought it was a yew tree, in which case it was probably at least as old as the building.

Potosí was once the fourth largest city in the world. It was hard to believe that as it sprawled at the feet of the reason for its erstwhile wealth: Cerro Rico. Once a volcano, this mountain had become an amazing tangled maze of mines that had sought out silver and other minerals for the last 450 years. They were still pulling out some silver but mostly quartz, zinc, asbestos, wolfram, pyrites, copper and many others.

Its slopes were brown and grey, littered with the vomit from the mines and it was up this moonscape of bare rock and rubble in orange, brown and grey that we climbed, not feeling too perky after stomach trouble and accompanying lack of sleep.

Almost anyone who drove for a living was on strike against diesel price hikes that day and the centre of town was blockaded. Our guide, Robert, had kitted us up in bright yellow overalls, boots and a helmet which bore a Davey lamp. This was preferred to electric light because the colour of the flame would change when noxious gases were present.

We felt like spacemen as we walked a few blocks to where a jeep was waiting. Then being hustled into the back of it felt like we were in a spy film and this only intensified as we drove up a road and turned into a street only to find it blocked by a couple of buses so spun around and tried another route. We ducked down narrow alleys and up steep streets, finding our way through a miners' neighbourhood. From the edge of this, we had to walk down to the gates to the mountain area which was blocked by three big trucks.

We took a miners' taxi up to a kiosk and bought some gifts for the miners we were to meet: a bottle of 96% proof *"alcohol potable"*, a bag of coca leaves which dull hunger and gave energy, two packets of biscuits, several concentrated chews, three packets of cigarettes which were a special combination of tobacco, menthol and eucalyptus, a stick of dynamite, a fuse and a detonator, plus a chemical in little balls which the miners add to dynamite which apparently made its effect similar to TNT.

Robert had worked as a miner from when he was twelve until he was eighteen. That had been two years before. He prepared our lamps while we chewed some of the coca. These also assisted with altitude. We were at 4426m at the mouth of a mine owned by the cooperative called La Grita de Piedra – the scream of stone. I was apprehensive about what it would be like inside the mine. Neither the name of the mine, nor the fact that the stone arch entranceway was smeared with blood from a sacrificed llama was helping.

Into the bowels of the earth we went, stepping over a pipe feeding a pneumatic drill. Of about six hundred mines, this was one of the few to have one. This cooperative employed seventy miners.

The tunnel was large enough to walk through and we soon came to a miner. He was 52 and had probably been a miner for decades. He was hitting a chisel with a two kilogramme lump hammer. He offered it to me and I started to swing it against the chisel.

"You can go now," I said. "I'll look after this."

Apart from the fact that my arms were getting sore after barely a minute, it was also mind-bogglingly dull work. I seemed to be getting nowhere, but given time, it would do. After about two and a half hours, the chisel would make a twenty-five inch hole in which some dynamite would be rammed, the detonator set and then they would retreat to a safe distance and wait. He was going to do about four holes that day. We had already heard some dull thuds. Drums in the deep.

"Miners' music. Rock music," chuckled Robert, probably for the thousandth time.

Climbing up levels was a challenge. Robert made it look easy whereas Liz struggled with her shorter arms and legs. I was somewhere in between, but I could not have done it without Robert who would have thrown himself over chasms to let us walk across him if necessary. Where our boots slipped on the rocks and the dust, he firmly planted his foot for us to stand on, or we could lean on his shoulder or his hand for support. The first climb was aided by a few stones piled onto one another leading up to a hole that we then pulled ourselves through. There was another with a couple of timbers across it several feet apart. We used these to climb up as best we could. Then walking along a bit of a passage we came to a hole in the floor leading to pitch blackness. Across the middle was another piece of timber to stand on. Where that hole went, we had no way of knowing. It was disconcerting to step over it, while finding handholds in the bare rock walls.

We baulked at the fourth level up of at least eight levels in that mine alone. The three we had climbed had not been as bad as we had expected but we were both feeling spooked and my arms felt weaker than normal after the previous night of nearly being ill.

We could hear the miner above us, a groan accompanying each hammer blow. Robert called Jose down to see us. He was twenty-nine but looked older as he grinned manically at us. He showed us how much of the tunnel he had blown open in the previous year, a zigzag shape upwards to avoid cave-ins. He received his gift of dynamite like it was the Christmas present he had always wanted before worming his way back up to his post, his light disappearing as I wished him "Buena fortuna."

We met other miners. At least one was doing evening classes. Robert told us about some friends whose parents were paying for them to go to college. They had not been all that keen on study until Robert took them down the mine to show them the alternative. Miners made between 500 and 700 bolivianos a month. That was £35 to £50. Those who were not members of the cooperative received half the value of what they extracted while the younger assistants received a flat rate of between B25 and B30 a day. All of them had to buy their own kit. Most had a helmet, but some had only a wad of cloth wound around their head under a cap.

Christ, the Father Miner, is worshipped outside the mine, but inside the Quecha miners have their own gods. We were introduced to Uncle George. When the Spanish first forced the locals down the mine, they did not like them worshipping their own gods, so they told them that the devil would get them if they did not work hard enough. Over the centuries, from being a threat, this new god or Dios became more of a friend whose union with the earth mother Pachamama produced the minerals. They found Dios hard to pronounce and it became Tio - uncle. All mines now have a statue of this well endowed chap carved out of the mud and every Friday they offer him coca leaves, cigarettes and alcohol. We had a taste of the 96 proof and I believe I still had some lips left afterwards. The rest they drink watered down or mix in with Coca-cola. Robert told us that there were many lawyers in town – and we did see many firms. He explained that the miners got drunk and had arguments.

After more dull thuds, shouts in the darkness and broken ladder rungs over gaps of nothingness, we emerged into the bright sunlight. I could see why the natives had worshipped the sun.

The main squares were always places to go and chat. Potosí's in particular was always full of people sitting, talking, friendly. We came upon some activity in the square with people in costume milling about. Then the church doors opened and out came four caskets carried on poles by groups of men. They bore the names of mining companies. Then a brass band started up, with a drum beating time. The dancers formed up and the procession set off, girls in orange waving handkerchiefs, followed by men in white wearing stylised conquistador helmets and spurs which jingled. Then there were some little girls, one dancing much more prettily than the others and men in white carrying baskets of plastic grapes, followed by a band playing a different tune. The bands were similar in style, a tune repeated over and over. They had trumpets and trombones and the music was brash, confident, carefree and big.

Faces amongst the crowds varied. There were many native Quecha and Amarya speakers in Bolivia. Sometimes they looked Far Eastern with almond shaped eyes and brown skin. European faces were few. Many girls dressed in a Far Eastern way too with long, straight dark hair, tight tops, flared trousers and chunky heels.

The police were everywhere, always doing very little in their clean, neatly pressed uniforms. Several guarded each bank, usually standing outside in flak jackets holding pump action shotguns.

Two policewomen were chatting as they crossed a road when they were almost run down by a quad bike carrying four people, including two girls on the mud guards. They watched it go up the hill as if pondering whether a law had been broken and they should do something about it. As they were lost in shared thought, they were almost run down by a motorbike carrying two people. They stood looking after that as well as if saying "Now *that* should be illegal. No one has any respect for us any more."

We took the night bus to Tupiza, arriving after 4am at the bustling terminal. We walked through empty streets where the shutters were down on the shops and a lone dog barked. On a corner was a group of people singing around a guitar. It was much better and folkier than the accordion pap with cheers and screaming girls that we were subjected to on most of the buses. A groggy porter with dishevelled hair let us into the hotel and by the time we awoke, the town was unrecognisable. Goods spilled out of windows and doorways, people milled about in the sunshine and everyone was smiling and cheerful.

Tupiza was the starting point of the Aramayo Company Payroll robbed by Butch Cassidy and the Sundance Kid in November 1908. They escaped back towards Uyuni where they came up against a four man posse in San Vincente. Here apparently they killed themselves rather than be taken alive, but there are still rumours that they escaped.

We spent a couple of days exploring the area. We walked to a canyon where the mountainsides looked like chocolate chip cookie mix. These had been cut into gullies which created deep corrugations. Cacti and low scrub grew where it could. Some school children accompanied us part of the way back and chatted to us. Juan, for example, liked maths.

We hired a friendly local driver called Xavier and drove out beside the muddy brown Rio Tupiza, swollen by the night's rain, to where it met the red coloured Rio Doro. In the valley bottom, maize, onions and other vegetables under willows contrasted richly with the bare red rock. Another canyon was called El cañon de la duende, its name alluding to a goblin which lived there and stole away children who wasted all their time playing with toys. We had lunch at a slow curve in the river where, from the steep hillsides above, a flock of goats came bleating down. The two women with them stayed sat up on the bluff.

We saw where a level of strata had been tipped vertical and the softer rocks around it eroded to leave a thick high wall standing in sections. A gap that had been seemingly blown apart was known as the Devil's Gate and on the other side did indeed lie Hell – a rubbish dump. Another geological oddity was the Valle de los Machos, named for a group of phallic pinnacles that looked more like strange alien statues with angled foreheads and bulbous eyes.

Our final destination was a saddle at 3750m which overlooked valleys of eroded badlands. A rainstorm was clearing and the sun shone between the clearing clouds. The deeply eroded land gave a beautiful interplay of light and shade on the reds, yellows and browns of the rocks.

The town was quiet again as we made our way in the small hours to the bus station. An old ramshackle bus that shook loose every bone in the body juddered us south to the border. The kids who loaded luggage huddled together under a blanket on the co-driver's seat and the crewman who took the ticket money lay on the gearbox with his head on the boys' chests. Once it was light enough, the child on the seat across the aisle stared through the front windscreen or at me when I grinned at him. When we were in sight of Villazon, he started singing and even gave me a bit of a smile.

The rising sun revealed a high desert with short grass and bushes. Villazon became visible in a shallow valley, a frontier town of dust, buses, snack kiosks and stray dogs.

We walked to a bridge over a valley which marked the border. The Bolivian official looked at my passport, said "Britanico," then asked if I was a "Yanqui". I looked suitably appalled and was directed to the window on the Argentine side. There, a European looking man, called Ciccione according to his badge, looked dubiously at my passport photograph and stamped us through. Customs had only to find out I was English to stop searching my bag, but outside a big blue sign announced that Las Malvinas belonged to Argentina. Welcome.

Mixed grill

What were we thinking? We had only gone out for a light snack. That cafe selling slices of pizza and a couple of empanadas looked perfect, but we just kept going because someone had told us about a good place and we were distracted by a pleasant looking restaurant. We could read some of the menu, but what was this parillada for two people? We went in and asked: a bit of rump steak, some rib, some pork and some other words I didn't understand.

"Oh it's a mixed grill," I said to Liz.

A little Spanish is a dangerous thing.

To keep us going, they gave us some bread and a tasty marinated eggplant dish. Our salad (served first) was good too and Liz said she was satisfied with those. Then the waiter brought out the mixed grill, gently crackling on a metal tray above some coals. The look on the waiter's face as he put it down was ambiguous. It could have been "that's more than you thought it would be isn't it?" or alternatively "Eat that sucker!"

The hot plate did indeed contain some steak, pork and rib. There was also rather a lot of kidney (several cows' worth), intestines, a big round blood pudding and a strange sausage filled with some glistening pink material. I tried everything. We ate all the meat, I had all the blood pudding, which was more like boudin and quite tasty, and I even managed my half of that pink thing. I was very full.

Even after we had asked for the bill and the plates had been cleared, the waiter left the still sizzling entrails (covering half the plate) by the table as a mark of our disgrace.

"That was a nice little pizza and empanadas," said Liz.

Echoes of Wales

Down on the bottom right hand side of South America, a little bit of Wales has been pasted onto the desert steppe. Those who went there were looking for a better life, while the founders were idealists.

The Welsh migration to Patagonia was small, but the move was driven by economic hardship, harsh landlords and religious differences. A man called William Jones provided the idealism. He wanted a Welsh colony where the colonists could live a traditional way of life, speaking their own language, without the pernicious influence of the English.

The idealists pushed a rather one-sided view of Patagonia, portraying it as being like parts of Wales. Settlement in Patagonia had been encouraged because the only occupants were native Indians who tended to ignore the government. When the Welsh first arrived, there was no sign of the Indians because they followed the herds of guanaco and nandu. When the Indians returned, there was mutual respect and trade.

Early harvests were poor and the hard times were exacerbated by bad weather and the distance to the port. The arrival of more settlers provided the impetus and manpower to improve irrigation. It was to be the turning point and exports of wheat and livestock grew.

The community was self-governing, with chapel at its heart and flourishing school and artistic activities. The government in Buenos Aires took a dim view when the Welsh offered protection to the Indians who were in conflict with the government. There was further trouble when President Roca wanted to integrate the Welsh into the rest of the country. Moves that were particularly unpopular were mandatory military service on Sundays and the teaching of Spanish in schools. A flood and increasing immigration from other countries reduced enthusiasm further and the Welsh eventually became outnumbered. After 1900, hundreds left for Canada and Australia. Even so, of all colonies settled by the Welsh, Patagonia retained its Welsh character far longer than any other.

We left the Andes behind us at sunset and drove east across the country, arriving at Trelew at six in the morning. We caught a local bus an hour north to Puerto Madryn where the first Welsh settlers had landed in 1865. It was daylight and we drove along a straight road. As far as the eye could see was a mesmerising landscape of sandy soil covered in tussock and scrub moorland. Had I been one of those newly arrived Welshmen, I would have experienced a deep and immediate longing for the green valleys of home.

It was humid and oily cloud poured across the sky. Big blobs of rain started to fall. We drove west up the Chubut valley to Gaíman on gravel back roads past farms sheltered by poplars. There would be surprisingly rich patches of green but also areas that had gone wild. The desert was very close.

Gaíman was a sleepy town with wide streets laid out in the usual Argentine grid pattern. We had trouble getting anyone to answer the door as we tried successive guest houses and decided that all the owners were at a meeting to work out ways of drumming up business. In the end we found Dyffrn Gwyrdd which apparently means Green Valley, run by the affable Pablo.

Some of the buildings dated to 1880. One of these was Plas Coed, a tea house and bed and breakfast. Its slightly unkempt garden was full of rose bushes and would have looked at home in a British village, but here it stood out. Many houses were serving tea and each one flew the Welsh flag next to the Argentine one.

We had a beer with Pablo. He was 34 and originally from Trelew. He told us he had been married for eight years, then pulled a face. We never saw his wife, so we presumed it had not ended well. He had trained as some kind of technician, and had worked in Buenos Aires for five years. Then he moved back to Trelew where, amongst other things, he sold tyres and managed a supermarket. He had been running this hosteria for 18 months, but his dream was to own a campo in 10 years, a farm over near Esquel. He showed us photographs of him in a gaucho hat with his uncle and on a fishing trip in the Gulf of Madryn complete with large fish, as well as other memories of his competitive horse-riding and rugby days.

The rose gardens were a thin veneer on the desert. We walked up to the cemetery on the edge of town on the side of a valley where the scrub started again. On the far side of the valley beyond poplar trees and green fields were desert bluffs. Many of the graves were Welsh and written in Welsh. There were two young Jamiesons,

227

both written in English. One said "A blessed relief after suffering" and there were Italians too. The scrub stretched on behind it and the place would have had a desolate, windswept feel were it not for the trees planted around the graves.

The regional historical museum had a distinct smell of old building. It was housed in the former railway station, now on the side of a street without a railway. We met the curator, a man with a mop of dark, curly hair, a beard and glasses. His mother had been an English teacher with the maiden name of Roberts and his own middle name was Trevor. His English was good and he also spoke Welsh. His English accent was a curious mix of Spanish and Welsh, especially in the pronunciation of words such as "chapel" and "happy". He sang in the local choir with which he had visited Wales ten years before.

We caught a late bus out of Madryn and on through Comodore Rivadavia. I awoke to a landscape of tussock grass. On one occasion this was broken by a few pink flamingos in a lake. We stopped briefly at a town called Buena Piedra lying beside a wide river. It squatted low in a depression. There were no trees except in town or serving as windbreaks to the occasional estancia. The landscape was fascinating in its sheer emptiness. Even the few sheep we saw seemed to be keeping close to the fences by the road, as if the vastness beyond spooked them.

We approached Rio Gallegos down a wide valley marked by steep bluffs under a mostly blue sky. The outskirts of town had an outpost feel. These kinds of places in the middle of nowhere fascinate me; there is something quite compelling about that feeling of isolation.

The centre of town was like others we had seen in Argentina. The square was full of trees, in the middle was a pointing soldier on a rearing horse, and there were shops and supermarkets. It had a cathedral which was a tiny wooden building with a red tin roof, barely the size of an English village church. The inside was wood panelled and it had an octagonal tower. It had a homely, peaceful feel despite the door which rattled in the wind. The clear windows had net curtains and there were pot plants on the side altars.

We drove on. In the distance the Andes reappeared, pointed outlines which seemed to rise straight out of the grasslands. The sun shone beneath the day's cloud and turned the valley bluffs golden and black in light and shadow. Rain showers, lit by the evening sun strode across the steppe like giant phantoms, their heads touching the low, grey cloud. Nearing the tourist oasis of El Calafate, we drove down the edge of a valley of exposed strata, carved into the steep sides of a wide valley. There were hazy, cloudy mountains at its head and a wide lake. The late afternoon light gave it all a wild look, ancient and alien. It was all a very long way from Wales.

World of Paine

It was Liz's silly idea to go horse-riding a few days before we were to head out trekking and my sillier idea to go along with it. Lynn agreed, despite having just flown in the previous day. Perhaps she was simply being agreeable. She was a friend of Liz's I did not know well. She in turn was a little worried about embarking on a long hike as a third party with a couple.

We rode out from the outskirts of Punta Arenas on horses that meandered at so slow a pace we were an hour late returning from our four hour ride. The only other speed I got out of my horse was a trot and I could feel Mum's chances of being a grandmother again diminishing with every step. Not so much the Magnificent Seven as the Rather Crap Three. Our guide did not seem too bothered. He was a large chap with a head moulded from a sand castle bucket and a physique that looked as though he would change a tyre by picking up the car with one hand and swapping the wheel over with the other. We rode out to some hills above town with views across the Magellan Strait to Tierra del Fuego. As far as I was concerned, that was just a place in a book.

By the end, we were sore and both my knees were painful. We still had a couple of days before starting the walk doing the circuit of the Paine massif. I bought some walking poles and they turned out to be worth every peso. We also bought supplies for the trek. We spread them out on a double bed in the hostel and negotiated who should carry what. Lynn was not used to carrying a pack; I had bad knees. This left Liz as the strongest amongst us. She rolled her eyes. We had about eleven days' food each. Having removed anything unnecessary from our packs, we shared out the food and then picked up each pack in turn to compare weights, dividing it again until we were all satisfied.

The weather had been gloriously sunny and windless for over a week, so it was typical that the morning we were to set off was blanketed with grey cloud. One of my knees was hurting more than it had done for days. The ache eased over the two hour drive to the national park across rolling pampa and as we set off on the start of the walk, the grey was even clearing from the Paine massif. We had glimpses of the towers, the Torres del Paine, through ragged cloud. A high glacier appeared through a gaping hole like a magic land of ice in the sky.

The pain in my knees was faint on the first day and I made good speed with my poles over about twelve miles. We climbed the side of a hill and came down into the valley of the Rio Paine, walking along grassy river flats with rocky hills around us. We spent the night camping under a starry sky and set off again into a similar landscape before climbing a steep shoulder of rock which at last gave us views of the mountains and a distant glacier. By this time, my knees had started to hurt. I got to the stage of thinking that the sensible thing would be to turn back. I walked through the pain for the rest of that day, deciding to see what it was like the day after. I hated the idea of going back and spending a week watching people come and go from the trek.

Our second campsite near Lago Dickson looked straight towards a sheer, high wall of rock across the valley. Beyond the trees sheltering the site, the Dickson glacier calved icebergs into its lake in rumbling explosions. The third morning dawned sunny and we waited until lunch to continue. I felt better after the night's rest as this was to be a shorter day.

We had a steep climb onto a ridge and the main valley opened up in front of us again – huge rock walls, distant glaciers and a blanket of beech forest in the valley. We walked through this in dappled sunlight, weaving amongst the trees and sometimes near a rocky, rushing river. When Lynn came to any log across the track, she was glad she had left her dignity behind. She is not a tall person and her bulging pack altered her centre of balance, so she would throw a leg over the log and then teeter helplessly, straddling it with neither foot touching the ground, unable to heave herself one way or the other because of the weight of her pack. She would just laugh as I hauled her off.

Emerging from the trees, we climbed to the top of a windy moraine from which we could see the Los Perros glacier sliding into a small lake filled with icy flotsam. A few hundred yards further on was our home for the next two nights and our first without a hot shower. Instead, there was a cold shower fed through a pipe by water from the ice-filled lake. Liz, as impervious to cold water as ever, had a shower.

Chatting with other campers, our conversation kept returning to food that was not available. Our typical meals were either mashed potato (from flakes) made with a powdered soup for flavour, or a flavoured rice containing dried vegetables and herbs. Both we would cook with soya protein, sometimes adding a sauce made from a dried soup using half the amount of water. Not all that bad.

We occupied our rest day with chatting and going on a peg hunt (Lynn had borrowed a tent which was missing some).

Thanks to our day's delay, we had good weather for climbing the pass. I also felt at my fittest for years. By this time, Liz had found herself a couple of sticks as she had seen how they helped me. The first part of the pass was through a muddy mire filled with the twisted roots of stunted trees. We came out onto steeper rocky slopes. Black pointed peaks lined the valley on one side, wisped with cloud and opposite, another glacier crumpled down the slope.

From the gusty pass, we looked onto a world of white. Several thousand feet below and four miles wide was the Grey Glacier. It filled the valley in every direction. Half a dozen other glaciers fed it from the mountains opposite and it appeared out of the Southern Ice Field, covering the southern Andes, from under mystical white cloud billowing over the mountains. It was an exciting view; you could almost see the ice river easing its way around the valley sides, folding and creasing into seracs and crevasses.

An icy wind blew off it and we pulled out our windproofs. We headed down the extremely steep valley sides towards the glacier. A lack of recent rain made it much easier to negotiate the dusty tree roots that grew larger as we descended. I moved much faster than my short-legged companions. I felt like I was trekking with hobbits.

The El Paso campsite was nothing more than vaguely flat gaps in the trees, mostly occupied by a team of military conscripts working for the park rangers.

As she was going to bed, Lynn found a spider trying to get into her tent. It looked capable of carrying off baby animals and small children and probably Lynn herself, but being vegetarian, she was squeamish about murdering it. On the other hand, I took one look at its crawling silhouette in the light of a head torch and was reaching for a hefty boot. Most other night visits we heard about (other than one puma) were from voracious mice. We hung everything in trees at night, but several trekkers had their toothpaste nibbled. I had visions of giggling mice pulling faces at each other to show off their shining teeth.

It rained all night. The army presence showed its benefit the next day as they had been working to improve a couple of ravine crossings up the track with makeshift ladders propped against the steep gravel sides. You notice the weight of a pack when climbing a ladder. The other times you notice it is how it affects your balance on a log or suspension bridge.

That day was fairly short, but a bit of a workout with lots of ups and downs and heaving over rocks which Lynn found particularly tricky. We came through forest to the snout of the glacier and our first shower for days. I emerged from it dancing. We slept with icebergs floating past the tent.

We made good speed the next day over relatively easy terrain, evading the bitter wind off the glacier as we rounded the south side of the mountains and camped at the base of French Valley. We walked up it as a day hike the next day, gratefully leaving our packs behind for the first time. The previous day the Horns of Paine had appeared dramatically from behind a hill, lit in the late sun just like a postcard. These are like three massive square fortresses squatting on cliffs above the valley. In the morning however, the sun was on the opposite side of the valley and the high walls of Cerro Paine Grande, a monster capped with what were probably hundred foot cliffs of ice. The valley opened into a wide semicircle of cliffs and peaks with ice trickling between gaps.

The next morning, we took the boat out to the bus and Liz left her sticks at the refuge at the trailhead for someone else, despite having named them Brian and Trevor we discovered. It was the ninth day. Amazingly, after 75 miles we were all blister-free and had no problems walking.

As we sat on the ferry watching the Horns of Paine drift away, Lynn said to me: "I thought your crap jokes would annoy me, but actually I've really enjoyed them."

We spent a few days in a bed and breakfast. It had views across the Sound of Last Hope to the Balmaceda Glacier which wound from the summit to the sea. On the first day, a storm whipped up. It rocked the building in a "Am I dizzy or is this building moving?" kind of way. We had been very lucky with the weather.

Living in New Zealand
2004 – 2009

New Zealand is threatening to become usual. I have to keep reminding myself that, for example, volcanoes are not normal. While it felt odd to travel from New Zealand, we managed to find an even less populated country in Namibia and I had the strange experience of a trip to the UK as a visitor.

The barber of Parnell

The barber appeared with his newspaper and grunted at me when he saw me waiting outside his shop. He let me in and I sat down in the well-used barber's chair while he brought his bike in.

"How old's this chair?" I asked, seeing a natural way to open conversation.

"Don't know," he replied curtly. Maybe he had been asked that question a million times before. Or maybe he was just grumpy this morning. I watched him in the mirror as he leaned his bike against the wall, then put the sheet around my shoulders. He did seem to be a grumpy, so I decided not to try any more conversation and sat in silence while he pushed my head around to the desired position.

"Been busy at work?" he asked suddenly.

"Yes, last week was, but hopefully this week will ease off."

It had been such an obvious conversational opener that I didn't feel like continuing. He wasn't interested; he was just being the barber chatting to his customer. He continued cutting my hair in silence a little longer. Then – "Weather's packed in again," he said. Another classic.

"Yes, I thought it might finally clear up, but it's not looking like it now. Looks like the farmers are going to cop it again."

We were silent once more. Well he was trying, I thought, although we weren't getting anywhere. I felt like it had to be my turn this time. I searched for something to start us off.

"So what do you think of the mayoral election?" I asked, wondering whether politics was the right subject; some of the candidates for Auckland mayor were currently involved in a childish slanging match.

"Not that bothered," he said. "I live in Manukau." So his council was different. Oh well, I had had a go. But then he continued, telling me who their mayor was and how he had no opposition.

"So you haven't got the nonsense we've got here?" I encouraged him. It worked: he went off. He compared the current mayor to Winston Peters, a notoriously divisive MP, saying they both modelled themselves on Muldoon, a notorious prime minister of the seventies and eighties. All were tyrants, he reckoned. It seemed I'd given him the perfect topic on which to vent his grumpiness.

Playing with TNT

The most endearing feature of TNT as a cricket team was the flurry of puns on their name that exploded on the field from time to time. I had been pointed in their direction by a work colleague who occasionally played for them. He added that he was finding himself increasingly attracted to playing friendlies with an over forties side rather than this league which played by the speedway track in Onehunga.

I had gone to a few pre-season nets and the team seemed likeable enough. They had a surplus of bowlers and the batsmen enjoyed hoiking the ball out of the nets. Each Saturday, all ten teams in the league would play on the same ground, occasionally ducking each other's boundaries.

My first game was their second of the season. I missed the match against the Samoans who, I was told, play with a plank of wood in the islands. When there isn't one available, they make do with a bat. This makes for a very entertaining, albeit frequently short, game. In each of the two games I did play, TNT collapsed for less than a hundred. In each I played a valuable innings of one run holding up the other end while skipper Mike knocked off a few valuable last runs. He took his captaincy very seriously for the level he was playing, but no one else in the team was prepared to take on the chore of putting together a team each week.

With such a small total to bowl at and a large number of bowlers in the side, I didn't expect to get a chance as the new boy, so in the first game at least, did my best in the field, saving a number of boundaries. TNT had an excellent seam bowling attack. There was a tall, fiery Irishman called Dan who had the opener's traditionally grumpy disposition. And then there was JK from the Cook Islands. His father used to play too but these days preferred to lounge on a deckchair in the shade and hurl abusive advice at his son from the boundary. JK himself was mountainous. Shaking his hand was like shaking someone by the thigh. From his towering height he would

239

somehow unleash the ball at great speed despite a run up of a casual trot. These two would make short work of the opposition.

As a team, they lacked the sportsmanship I was used to from playing with the Mystics and Magicians at home. I had grown accustomed to a magical class of banter in the field, rather than straight abuse, and a mystical level of sportsmanship. Take for example the time when one of TNT's opposition was struck on the side of the helmet by a bouncer. My immediate reaction would have been to apologise, especially because it would have been an accident since none of my balls are ever that short deliberately or fast enough to bounce that high without the aid of a divot. What happened instead was that most of the team complained bitterly when the umpire signalled it as a no ball for bouncing over shoulder height.

At the end of the second game, since he had overs to spare, skipper Mike let the opposition's twelfth man bat to reward him for giving up his Saturday afternoon to join his hung-over student mates. And because it no longer mattered, he let me have a bowl. Of course with no pressure it was like batting in the nets for these guys and they proceeded to hoist me over my head for several boundaries.

"Those were good balls," someone consoled me afterwards, but I didn't think much of my chances of ever bowling for them again.

Kiwi spring

The country narrows to a few kilometres in Auckland where a wide creek cuts in from the Hauraki Gulf, almost meeting Manukau Harbour on the west. Weather is a constant source of conversation in Auckland. It rolls in off the sea with nothing to stop it, so it behaves as if it were still at sea. One day, an hour north of Auckland, we drove into a cloudburst so heavy, it was like driving underwater. I pulled over, unable to see.

New Zealand is a land of rainbows. Squalls blow in, flying over the city like some vast airship, trailing downpours and leaving bright sunshine in their quiet, damp wake. It is not unusual to be able to stand and watch the weather pass by, or for the top of the space station-like Sky Tower to fade away into cloud, out of which at night, lights glow like ghostly lamps.

There are many viewpoints in the city, small volcanoes born of explosions thousands of years ago, each with deep summit craters and views over city, bays, headlands and islands. One of these islands straddles the horizon in the Gulf, the youngest volcano of them all: the low cone shape of Rangitoto which last erupted only six hundred years ago.

Turn your eyes the other way and on the skyline are the Waitakere Ranges, steep and covered in a dense rain forest. Mighty kauri, with still a few old enough to have seen Rangitoto's last eruption, tower above the rest, trunks straight and branchless until more than half way up their height. Hairy epiphytes rest in the crooks of their branches. Below are kowhai, spindly rimu, flax glowing green in the sun and prehistoric punga, the tree ferns that seem to conjure dinosaurs out of the dense undergrowth. Streams weave amongst the hills and waterfalls topple over edges hidden in the rainforest. Then the waves of hills break upon the crashing Tasman sea, meeting the misty spume in high cliffs that drop down to wide beaches of dark sand. Swamps lie where streams leak onto the shore. Here too were once volcanoes, the sea cliffs are all that is left, with lava vents still visible as angles of dark rock in their faces.

On clear mornings, the light is crisp and golden and it washes over plants crowding the front gardens of Parnell's wooden villas as we walk to work. The grand War Memorial Museum sits proudly on the hilltop of the Domain behind the house above imported oak trees which will soon be billowing with green as spring bursts over the city. Already there are splashes of blossom and the mornings and evenings are warmer as the short winter is falling behind.

Far south the mornings are still frosty and the mountains from Fiordland to the Central Plateau are snow-covered. But below them, especially in the rich, rolling farms of the Waikato, the land is green and calves and lambs fill the fields. As the spring creeps south, so the snow will creep up away from the warmth, leaving just the cold, broken tentacles of glaciers reaching down from the summits.

One weekend we walked in Tongariro National Park amongst the scrub and tussock. The path rose up successive ridges of old lava flows and crossed streams until we climbed a steep shoulder to a ridge above the twin blue Tama Lakes, lying in their ancient explosion craters. On one side, the snowy skirts of Mount Ruapehu folded over themselves, dropping out of the low cloud. On the other, suddenly lit by an invisible sun, the perfect white cone of Ngarahoe almost managed to separate itself from the white cloud that seemed to give birth to it in front of our eyes. Snow was at our feet, but beyond, the scrub country ran off into the distance into low ridges lying across the land in layers of blues and greys, broken only by the occasional shattered hill.

Later we walked through forest where gnarled trees clothed in sheer suits of soft moss, stood watching each other. Old cobwebs hung like circus nets filled with fragments of twig and torn leaf. Through gaps in the trees we could sometimes see the wide rocky floor of the Tongariro River, shallow channels of water a foamy blur behind the slow motion stillness of the woods.

The sun emerged as we drove home, gleaming off wide Lake Taupo, the site of a cataclysmic volcanic explosion in the late second century and now a major resort destination for those who love to sail and fish. We drove through craggy country blanketed with conifer plantations and into the gentle hills of the Waikato, looking like a half remembered dream of England. Cambridge, Hamilton and Huntly passed beneath our wheels and then the

Bombay Hills appeared lumped across the road. To be south of them is the Aucklander's 'north of Watford' for a Londoner.

We entered the suburban sprawl in three lanes of traffic until the spike of the Sky Tower, lit by coloured lights, beckoned us home and we slipped off at Khyber Pass Road and sneaked round the back of Newmarket and the dark Domain to home.

Flying to Wellington

We were soon above the clouds, leaving Auckland behind and flying just off shore from the crumbling cliffs of the Waikato coast. I saw Raglan's natural harbour and the old volcano of Karioi which Liz and I had climbed. Between it and town I saw the beach where I had proposed to her afterwards.

A layer of cloud spread inland, but in the distance, Ruapehu rose above it, its summits looking like peaks of meringue that had been whipped up out of the cloud with which they merged. We flew over the Whanganui River and I looked down at the hills. They were typical of New Zealand: steep sides and narrow ridges, as if the country were a piece of paper that had been screwed up tight and then flattened out again. There are only a few places in the North where the land has been ironed flat as flood plain.

We started to descend after we had crossed the bulge of the Taranaki and flew down the Kapiti coast. We flew wide over the Cook Strait, the Marlborough Sounds a series of hazy islands and peninsulas in the shining sea, and curved around to make our approach from the south into the northerly breeze. The sun was low and the rugged south west coast was layers of hills diminishing in clarity as they disappeared into the sun.

Symonds Street morning

The air is crisp and still as I close the gate behind me and walk up the street. I go past the knife shop and the motorcycle show room and cross the road that leads down to the Victorian prison with its fortress walls carved from the quarry below Mount Eden. A little wooden church stands on the corner.

Further up the road, a break in the buildings reveals how high the road is at this point, giving views across to the Waitakere ranges, a hazy blue at this time of the morning lapped by the mist lying at their feet. I walk by Galbraith's Ale House, a solid Victorian building that serves some of the best beer in town. Then I reach wide Symonds Street, which runs all the way down the long hill for a mile and a half, almost as far as the port. Most shops are still closed and trees down the centre of the road are leafless. Unlike the trendy suburbs, Parnell and Ponsonby, which ride ridges on either side of the city centre, this part of town feels like an inner city.

I walk past cafes, takeaways, a launderette, a cobbler, a corner store and a shop selling medieval antiques, models and costumes that makes me wonder how the owner can possibly make a living. I come to the bridge over the motorway and the view widens to look eastwards over the Hauraki Gulf, the sun rising beyond the distant Coromandel Peninsula and nearer Waiheke Island. Buses go by, obscuring my view. As I cross the bridge, five pass me, the first two each bearing an advertisement for *X-Men 3*.

I reach the old cemetery, sitting in permanent gloom beneath twisting pohutukawa, an evergreen still in full leaf. It is a place of stillness and quiet despite the busy roads bounding it on four sides. I come to another crossroads. To my right is narrow Grafton Bridge over the gully of the same name through which the motorway now runs. To my left is Karangahape Road, usually known as K Road. It is the bohemian end of the city centre, where interesting people can be found wandering the streets and sitting on benches amongst the cafes, and shops selling bric-a-brac and colourful clothes.

Now the office blocks and new apartments begin to rise up. There is the plush Langham Hotel and the offices of global companies such as Oracle and SAP. I go by a sad war memorial where the statue of a woman reaches up to the monument, trailing her forgotten flag on the ground. In summer at this time, the early sun would be catching her, but not on this mid winter morning.

I am amongst the university buildings now. There are students about. I cross the road by the university marae, its red painted carved gable looking out of place amongst the big concrete buildings. I turn left, still downhill, and cut across Albert Park, my favourite part of the walk. It was one of Auckland's volcanoes and the site of the old barracks, but now it is an ornamental park, centring on a bandstand. For a moment, under the European trees, I could be in England, but then I notice the fig trees with their huge buttress roots and full canopy of leaves.

After the brief respite from the traffic, I emerge by the Metropole Hotel, the modern high rise towering over its original neo-classical façade. I have heard that, once, they discovered a body of a man in the thick foliage below and assumed he had jumped from a high floor. A wide, marble foyer is briefly visible as I walk down Chancery Lane and pass some car-parking spaces that, if purchased, could buy a decent house in some parts of the country. No one is sitting outside at the cafes yet, although it won't be long with this day's promise. People are picking up coffees and huddling with them as they go up to their offices in the lifts.

I have a lift to myself and shoot straight up to the fifteenth floor. Few people are in the office. I greet Navin, sat by the windows with the port spread out below him. The sun hits the summit of Mount Victoria on the North Shore and rising behind it, the amazing low triangle silhouette of Rangitoto Island. I find a desk, plug in my laptop and start my latest day at the office.

New boots

The Hump Ridge Track was having an earthquake sale. We were told about it when we found out that our intended track, the Kepler, was covered in too much snow, while the Milford and Routeburn tracks, which we had already walked, were suffering from landslips and washed out bridges caused by a recent earthquake. The lesser known Hump Ridge had decided to take advantage of the situation and was offering a free shuttle service to the trail head.

In 1988, the local community in the Southland town of Tuatapere had decided it needed to do something to bring in more tourism. Their solution was to build a track over the Hump Ridge and join it with the Southern Coastal Track run by the Department of Conservation. They raised three million dollars to build it and it opened in 2001.

It started on an easy path through pleasant bush. After forty-five minutes, there was a long, steep flight of steps down a cliff to the beach. This led to a long swing bridge over the White River then down a four wheel drive track which ran behind the beach. It was filled with puddles of varying depths that we either went through or walked around on stones and logs. Liz had only just glued her boots back together and wanted to keep them as dry as possible.

After two hours and six kilometres of this, we passed a few simple holiday cabins on a low hill above the beach and, crossing another swing bridge, entered dense bush where a well made track went up and down through forest. At a high point above the beach, a sign pointed to Okaka Hut and we turned inland and uphill.

Initially the going was easy: a gentle slope, lovely bush of podocarp, matai and the odd rimu with broad-leafed ferns filling the forest floor. There was a long section of boardwalks, part of eight kilometres of them on the fifty-three kilometre track.

We began to tire, although knowing we had an eight hour walk ahead of us had not helped from the start. At Water Bridge, the last water before the hut, we still had several hours of steep walking up a side spur. My feet were hurting in my new boots which were clearly not as broken in as I had thought they were.

We would rest on fallen logs breathing in the enveloping peace of the bush, a joy spoiled by knowing we would have to stand up and climb again. "The only way is up," sang Liz. But we still managed to appreciate the forest as the sun went in and out of clouds creating a constant change of colour and light.

At last we reached Stag Point, a clearing in the bush still an hour from the hut, but we could see it not too far above us. In the other direction were the Takitimu mountains which, according to Maori legend, are the upturned hull of one of the country's founding waka. Looking the other way was the wide sweep of Te Waewae Bay with Stewart Island hazy in the distance.

We entered goblin forest of twisting trees and moss and realised we had reached the Hump Ridge which fell away into bush and hills towards the south coast. Okaka Hut snuggled below the ridge, a set of buildings perched in a cirque. We dropped our packs at the junction and carried on up boardwalks to a collection of tarns and sandstone tors and the view west.

It was after six o'clock and the light was soft beneath high cloud. We looked into Fiordland and the snowtopped line of the Princess mountains and Lake Poteriteri behind them backed by more mountains. The tors on the ridge were bleak and sculpted. Snow clung to the sheltered edge of a pool and the rocks around it created striking reflections of light and dark.

Back at the junction we met Nicolas, a skinny, bearded Frenchman from Grenoble. He had done the walk in five and a half hours compared to our eight. He joined us in the hut which had views into Te Waewae Bay, cutlery, crockery and pillows in bunkrooms of only four beds. This was luxury, even compared to the huts on the Great Walks.

The wind was picking up as we went to bed and it howled through the night. I lost count of how many times I thought it might have blown over as it calmed briefly only to start again. Sometimes the hut would shake on its stilts planted in the rock. I was glad we were on the leeward side of the ridge.

I ran to the toilet block in the morning in the bitter wind and horizontal hail. I was not looking forward to climbing onto the ridge. Then I received a text message from the Track Office: "It might pay to stay another night if it's bad up there."

So we stayed for the day, sitting by the gas fire – another luxury – reading, playing games, sleeping, eating. We played Ludo and Pick-up-sticks and Nicolas taught me Otello. I watched the clouds rush past the hut and down the slope, trying to compare their speed to cars. I decided on 50-60km/h with gusts at least half that again. It would have been very unpleasant, not to say dangerous, to walk along the ridge. The wind calmed somewhat in the afternoon and the cloud lifted above the mountain top.

The next morning it was raining steadily, but not heavily. The thought of the rain slowed our preparations and it was nearly 10am before we left. Nicolas has already gone on his way. The rain pattered on our coat hoods. The wind was much calmer, but there were still a couple of times when gusts almost knocked me off balance. There were only a couple of places where a fall from the boardwalk would have been far enough to cause injury. Usually it would have been a soft landing into bog, providing you did not fall awkwardly or become impaled on a branch. As we walked, I realised being blown off our feet was not the only danger we had avoided the day before: the track was littered with branches of all sizes and even the odd tree.

The ridgewalk went in and out of bush until, after nearly two hours, we arrived at Luncheon Rock and obediently stopped for a sandwich. This was where the steeper section began. Much of it was on boardwalks, but on other sections, we picked our way around mud and puddles. There were showers of rain and hail and sunny spells and it became flatter and after a further two hours, we emerged onto the South Coast Track. This was the old logging tramway and so was wide and flat. Three great wooden trestle bridges spanned valleys. The first and third were about fifty metres long and twenty-two metres high, but the second was a hundred and twenty-five metres long and thirty-six metres high. All were solidly built from Australian hardwood. Ferns crowded the bottom of the valleys through which brown streams flowed.

When we had joined the coastal track, a sign had said it was three hours to the hut. Twenty minutes further on, another sign said it was only two hours. We were cheered, but still the track seemed interminable. My feet were sore and despite being flat, the track was hard going. It was either firm and hard on the feet, or the rain and streams had taken over and we had to climb along narrow

249

muddy ridges or step from old sleeper to branch to stone. Eventually I just walked through the shallowest looking points.

When, by my timing we were almost there, a sign told us there was still another forty minutes to go. The inconsistency in the signposts was very bad for morale.

Nicolas was already settled in by the time we arrived. The huts occupied part of the site of the once thriving logging township of Port Craig. It closed around 1930 and what was not dismantled became overgrown as the bush returned.

Pearl the hut warden was from Essex, via the Isle of Wight. She and her husband had come out to New Zealand for a quieter life and bought five acres. When their neighbours had heard they wanted a few animals, they had received donations of some lambs, calves and chickens. They moved a house onto the section and put solar panels on it as the $6000 it cost was the same as the lines company was going to charge to connect them to the national grid.

We made ourselves dinner and the four of us chatted until it became dark. During the storm, Pearl told us, the wind had been so strong that they had found it hard to shut the doors on the huts.

The next morning dawned sunny. We left Port Craig and went up and down on the trail where streams flowed down small valleys to the sea. Nicolas overtook us and strode off with a handshake. Up and down we continued and twice came out onto a beach. Waves rolled in, sparkling in the sunshine as they crashed over a reef just off shore.

When we came to the Okaka Hut turn off, a sign told us there was three hours left to go. Forty-five minutes earlier, a sign-posted had yet again given us false hope by claiming the same thing. We knew the next part had taken us two and a half on the way in. We had a quick lunch and started on the last eight or nine kilometres. We only skirted one large puddle this time, ploughing through the others regardless and taking to the beach in the end which was flatter. By this time I was limping from a blister on my left foot and my left calf muscle was strained. We walked past the now empty cribs. One was called *Miles Away*.

As we reached the swing bridge over the White River, we saw there was yellow and black danger tape across it and a sign warning it was unsafe and should not be used. Our only other option was to wade the river. It did not seem too deep at first, so I plunged in, quietly amused about how careful we had been not to get our feet wet over the previous few days. Soon I was up to my knees and treading carefully to keep my balance against the force of the water on the large rounded stones at the bottom. I could see it went deeper still. I reversed and we tried further down at the edge of the beach but it was no better. I am no expert in river crossings, but from what I could remember, you should not go above your knees in fast flowing water. Having tested it, I understood why and with Liz's short legs sporting correspondingly lower knees, she would have found it even harder going.

We retreated to the bank. Finding I had cell phone coverage, I warned the Track Office that we would be late for the shuttle pick up. They told me the man from the Department of Conservation who had closed the bridge had said he would probably use it himself, but that it should be crossed carefully, one at a time.

"It's at your own risk," she counselled.

"So's crossing the river," I replied.

We tried the river one last time before going to look at the bridge. It was thirty or forty yards long and twenty feet above the river. It did not *look* as though it were about to disintegrate. Steel cables made up the framework and sides of the bridge with planks set lengthways to walk on. Which of us would go first? Liz was smaller and lighter. Was it better that I went over first, testing it with my heavier weight or that she went over first as her weight was less likely to be the final straw?

"I don't know," said Liz.

"I'll go first," I decided. "I don't want to have to watch you plummet into the river."

I started across. The bridge did look as though it had been thrown about in the winds. The sides were loose and some of the planks had popped their nails. I trod carefully, watching where I put my weight on the cable railings on either side. I wondered what I would do if it collapsed. I decided I would hold on as the river was neither that far down nor very deep. The bridge appeared more likely to give way to one side so I looked more carefully at the cabling as I went, finally stepping with relief onto solid ground.

Then it was Liz's turn. She followed gingerly but more confidently. Once across, we celebrated with some chocolate. I realised the thorough soaking my boots had received in the river had made them much more comfortable to wear. I should have been walking through every puddle on the track, but setting off again, I automatically walked around the next puddle I came across.

Soon after were the killer steps and the stroll through the woods to the waiting shuttle. We drove back into town along the road by the beach which was looking at least as sorry as it had before where recent storms had eaten away verges where people used to camp.

Back in the guest house in Te Anau, the owner gave us a copy of the previous day's Southland Times. It described the effects of the storm, including roofs ripped off and gusts of 130 to 160km/h. In particular he pointed out we had made the front page: "Hikers on the Hump Ridge Track were advised to spend an extra night at the Okaka Hut rather than risk being blown off the boardwalk or struck by falling branches."

Fame at last.

Help in the desert

We did not realise we would need all the daylight we could find. If we had, we would not have been so casual about leaving Tsumeb in northern Namibia. The road was uninteresting: straight with blond vegetation backed by low reddish bush.

We arrived at Otjiwarongo with its bustling shopping centre where music blared from clothes shops, and people shouted to each other across the wide main street. I bought a few groceries in the supermarket. We dropped the tailgate to pack them and a man came over and tried to sell us some model animals made from wire and beads. He set giraffe, crocodile, elephants and others on the tailgate for us to look at. We were tempted but resisted, although he dropped his price from N$30 to N$20. We had no idea of the right price and were reluctant to pay too much.

He went away and an artist called David came up to show us his portfolio. N$150, he said, then N$100. We said nothing and showed no interest and the price plummeted to first N$70 then N$50. He tried another tack: he hadn't sold all morning. Just buy one and he could go and buy himself some lunch. "It's good to help one another in the desert." He knew all the lines. We were even less interested in the paintings than we had been in the animals so resisted again and wished him good luck. But he hadn't finished. Did we have any old shoes – he had just seen our boots in the back of the truck – or an old tee-shirt? I looked at him. He was dressed much smarter than most of the clothes I had with me and would have been decidedly unimpressed with anything I could have offered him.

About 40km out of town, we saw a car stopped on the side of the road. The woman flagged us down so I pulled up behind them. As we did so, the man crossed the road and relieved himself on the verge. The woman mimed a spanner and a pump. Her husband, once he had returned, spoke some English and confirmed that they had a jack, but that they had no spanner to remove the wheel. The pump was to put more air in their spare.

Our spanner was a great success, but when they asked if we had a pump, they were initially puzzled when we lifted the bonnet on the engine, thinking we had misunderstood. However, we had a compressor in the engine to which we attached an air hose and, hey presto, his tyre inflated. He said he needed to get to Otjiwarongo before the meat spoiled and gestured to two black bin liners on the ground. A pair of horns and some neck emerged from them.

We gave them a toot and a wave as we drove off and felt pleased with ourselves. After all, as David the artist had said, you always help each other in the desert.

We took a detour to see what is known as the Arizona of Namibia. It took us down a wide, dusty side road between rounded scrubby hills emerging in a valley that cut through a plateau. Red cliffs gave onto rocky slopes and in front of us was the narrow finger of rock called the Vingerklip together with a couple of other buttes, backed by a mesa. It really did look as though we had found a back door into the American West. The valley floor contained small trees and a farm. Above us, looking over it all, was a lodge whose round roofed chalets looked like covered wagons. As we drove back out to the main road, a solitary figure was silhouetted on a hilltop by the road. "Indians?" I wondered.

We returned to the main road. We had been thinking of getting to Palmwag or perhaps Sesfontein in the wild north western Kaokoveld of Damaraland, but it was four o'clock and we were still miles from Khoraxis, the next town. It had an uninteresting sounding campsite and Liz found another in our guidebook called Abu Huab which seemed to be about seventy kilometres beyond Khoraxis. It was a gravel road, so it would be slower, but we estimated we would get there soon after nightfall. This worried us a little because with both wild and domestic animals attracted to car headlights, it is advised not to drive after dark.

Khoraxis turned out to be small and uninteresting and we had no qualms about driving straight through. The tar seal ran out on the other side, but the gravel road was still good and I was able to do 80 to 90km/h most of the time. What slowed us down were the many shallow dips caused by occasional streams in the wet season. When there were several close together, they gave the impression of being at sea as we rose up the crest and dipped into the trough.

We passed the sign to the fossilised forest, a notable tourist attraction in the area. But others were keen to capitalise on this local asset and we passed a number of other less official looking signs painted on scraps of wood which also advertised a fossil forest. There were rickety roadside stalls of wood and branches nailed together which, as far as we could tell in the fading light, displayed stones. There was no one about and few buildings. Driving past others on another day, we saw Herero women at these stalls, many in the traditional native dress based on the long Victorian frocks of German missionaries, holding up necklaces as we drove past, while children danced around their legs.

Driving west, the low sun made it difficult to see the shallow dips in time to brake. It also created light and shade on the pale grass in the folds of the land. We topped a rise and the sun was setting behind lines of flat topped hills, the road a ribbon into the distance.

It was all but dark when we arrived at the Twyfelfontein turn off expecting Abu Huab to be just near the junction, but it wasn't. There was a building which was both local bar and car mechanic and a few huts and a lamp post creating a pool of light above a patch of ground. A sign pointed to a place called camp Doro !Nawas. We drove on a little further and passed a group of cattle making their own way home along the verge. A little way behind them strolled a languorous bull with long horns and hump. There appeared to be nothing for miles, so we turned back and tried the turn off to Doro !Nawas. We juddered a few kilometres down a track and came to a set of chalets surrounding a dark building on a central hill. We saw a man carrying a tray and towels. He told us there was no camping: it was just a lodge. Deflated, we bumped back down the track to the main road.

We had to decide what to do next. Palmwag was another ninety kilometres in the dark. Returning to Khoraxis was almost the same distance. We found out two days later that Abu Huab was about half an hour down the Twyfelfontein road opposite *another* turn off. At this time, not wanting to retrace our steps, we decided to push on to Palmwag.

The glow behind the mountains was already fading as we headed off. Now the sun was gone it was easier driving with headlights, although even the main beam did not light up much – there was nothing for it to shine onto. It took some concentration, peering into the night, intent on that patch of lit road, sometimes creeping up to 80km/h and slowing for the bends and dips.

On one hill, straining as we reached the top, I started to turn the wheel to the left, following where the road appeared to go, only to find it went right. I had a pain in my left shoulder blade from my tense posture and I was tired. I found the miles went faster if I didn't look at the odometer. I passed the time checking my calculations for when we would arrive and estimated it would be at about 8pm. We passed lights on isolated native buildings and signs to luxury lodges which can charge anywhere from US$350 to US$600. We drove through some kind of settlement. Not far now, maybe 10km or less.

Suddenly up ahead we saw hazard warning lights. As we came closer, we could see about eight people clustered around a Toyota Hilux. They were waving us down.

"Don't stop," said Liz.

We had seen only two or three other cars in the last hour and we were nowhere. It was potentially dangerous, but something told me it was safe to pull over. Still a little suspicious, I wound down the window. A tall bespectacled man in a coat approached.

"Good evening," he said.

It turned out they had had two punctures and needed a pump. I turned the car round and pulled up right behind them. We took out our lantern and rummaged behind the driver's seat for the compressor hose for the second time that day. They were impressed. They inflated the first tyre to try to find the hole.

They were on their way to a meeting. Liz thought he had said it was about birth control. He asked where we came from. New Zealand, we told him.

"That's near Australia isn't it?" he asked. We compared our temperatures; they seemed to be similar as he said their summer temperatures only reach the early thirties too.

"But we don't have elephants," I said.

"What animals do you have in New Zealand?" he asked. He was surprised, as would be most people, to find that it had only two native mammals, both bats. We were amazed that he had heard about the recent large Treaty settlement giving a huge tract of forest back to Maori. He was impressed that a government would return so much land to native ownership.

Meanwhile, one of the men had located the hole in their tyre, stabbing it with what looked like a corkscrew without the screws. Then he took a stick of plastic a few inches long from a bag, placed it on another skewer, coated it with a gluey substance and plunged it into the hole, sealing it. They pumped up the tyre again and after we had waited a few minutes for the compressor to cool off, they followed the same procedure on the second wheel. We discovered this was the usual tyre repair method in Southern Africa.

"How can we thank you?" asked our friend. I said I was sure he would help someone else along the way. Besides, Namibia seemed to be the kind of place where you help people you find on the road.

"You always help each other in the desert," I chuckled.

He said that in other parts of Southern Africa it might be dangerous to stop to help people who appeared to be in trouble because they might really be criminals and not really need help, but not in Namibia.

We explained that we were trying to find a campsite.

"Just as well for you," I added, "or we wouldn't have been along to help you."

They assured us it was not far and it was after 8pm when they waved us off. I felt refreshed after the break and we were pleased to have given a tiny bit back to the country. Of course this was not to help our consciences when we would later sail past hitch-hiking locals, as instructed by our car hire firm so as not to invalidate our insurance.

We drove a few more kilometres and came to a large gate in a fence which marked the boundary between native herders and the big ranches, the veterinary control fence. We sat waiting. A lad in orange overalls sauntered up. He leaned in the window, said his name was Ricardo and asked Liz's name. He said his mother was also called Elizabeth.

"When are you coming back?" he asked.

On our way back, we found out he was asking so that he could prepare some personalised baubles to try to sell us. Meanwhile a woman had appeared from the house opposite and opened the gate for us. She came up to the car and, despite our ongoing conversation with Ricardo, tilted her head sideways towards the open gate, as if to say "I've opened the gate, so get a bloody move on so I can go back inside out of the cold."

Not far on the other side was the turn off down a bumpy track to Palmwag. There were campsites lining the bank of a dry river bed. Ours had a shelter with a roof of branches for shade, a bench and a sink. Next to it was a building made from bamboo containing a toilet and hot shower which looked out over the river. We had a campsite with en suite!

We were too tired to cook dinner, so had a bowl of cereal and a biscuit. Cleaning my teeth, I looked out over the river bed. Palm trees and distant hills were just visible as shapes against the clear sky. The Milky Way arced overhead and dived down to the horizon, looking like someone had dipped a brush in a pot of white paint and shaken it at the wall of the night.

Air Force One

"That can't be right," said the chief flight attendant looking at the manifest after I told her my seat number. I peered over her shoulder. Next to my seat at the front of the plane was the name J. Key. Could it be that I had been placed next to John Key, New Zealand's newly elected Prime Minister?

"I can sit on the aisle if you want. I promise not to harass him."

"The PM usually gets the whole row. I don't know how this happened," she replied.

John Key came on board accompanied by an ape with a buzz cut and a tight fitting suit. The PM and I said "Good morning" and I stood up to let him take the window seat while the ape stowed our leader's briefcase in the overhead compartment.

"Are you sitting there?" I asked the ape, indicating the seat next to the PM.

"I certainly am," he threatened. The suit became even tighter when he sat down.

The cabin door was closed and the ape lifted his arm up and spoke into his cuff.

"Thanks Fred and Bob. We're all set now. See you later."

I toyed with asking him to turn off his sleeve in case it interfered with the aircraft's navigation systems.

John and the ape settled in to read their newspapers and to my disappointment did nothing interesting during the short flight from Auckland to Wellington. Once we landed, everyone stood up to leave and I was out of my seat quickly to allow the PM off first so that I did not interrupt the smooth running of the nation. At this point it became clear that the front of the plane at least was full of National Party voters.

"Congratulations, John."

"Well done!"

John Key smiled and nodded his acknowledgement in a way that would have been sufficient if he were actually walking off the plane. The trouble was that there was a hitch with the air bridge and we were in limbo, half out of our seats. Everyone continued to mutter congratulations, smile and nod at each other.

As the delay stretched into a couple of long minutes, things became more awkward. The congratulations had run out and there was no time for further conversation so everyone just tried to avoid looking at anyone else. Once or twice eye contact was made by accident and this resulted in a nod and a quick lift of the eyebrows that offered congratulations and returned thanks without the need to repeat the words.

Suddenly the door opened with a sigh of relief, giving everyone something sensible to look at. The PM and his ape were met by a suited woman, who took his case, and an elderly policeman, who strolled a few yards in front. That appeared to be the entire security operation.

I smiled to myself. It is a delight to live in such an insignificant and inoffensive country.

Return to England

There were no fanfares. It was dark and still as we flew into Heathrow. Once on the tarmac I peered out at my country, but airports give little away. I was half afraid of being homesick and half afraid of not being.

An English colleague had returned to New Zealand after a couple of years back in the UK. "It can be very depressing listening to the incessant moaning," he had said. So were the English really all miserable? On the Tube from Heathrow, I studied my fellow passengers. They did look a little glum...but then it was half past six on a cold, dark winter's morning and they were on their way to work. It was easy to forgive them for not dancing down the middle of the carriage. Auckland and Wellington commuters would have looked the same.

I had time to wait at Euston station. I noticed a new type of policeman, a Community Policeman. He was wearing a fluorescent vest covered in bulging pockets. Fascinated by them, I took a few surreptitious photographs. He saw me take the last one and strolled over. He asked why I had taken it and took me up on my offer to delete it. I did not tell him about the others. When my brother arrived he was outraged. The police take photographs of people without asking them at the smallest demonstration, yet complain if someone takes a photograph of them, he exclaimed. He was active in the campaign against identity cards in the UK, a policy which had already wasted millions of pounds of tax payers' money in developing systems. Britain is said to have the world's greatest surveillance and I noticed many cameras around roads and public buildings.

The Pendolino train rushed us north on newly improved tracks reducing a journey I remember as being nearly two and a half hours by nearly an hour. I looked out at the green fields and bare trees under a flat grey sky. It was all so familiar. It did not feel like five years since I had left it behind.

Mum met us at the station, delighted to have both her boys home for Christmas. The house felt smaller than I remembered. After lunch we went for a walk across the fields to the canal. The smell of the damp earth, the shape of trees and the colour of grass were all different from New Zealand.

Town was busy with Christmas shoppers. Woolworths was in its last few days before it closed down, a victim of the recession already hitting the UK hard. I listened to the accents. While most of the English I knew in New Zealand were northerners, it was still odd to be surrounded by so many strong accents.

I loved the way the light fell across the town and how the church towers and rooftops faded into a haze. I had forgotten, or never realised, how many churches and pubs there were. It occurred to me that I was seeing my own country through the eyes of a visitor.

I went for walks in the Peak District on crisp sunny days. The bare trees fascinated me with their shapes, their silhouettes and the way the sun lit their trunks and branches. The dry stone walls and stone bridges clothed with moss were like accidental works of art. I had missed the low winter sun and its frail golden light; the way it created shadow and shapes. On a morning outside Glossop, we drove up over the tops and looked back below us to the sun shining through mist in the valley. Each layer of hills rose from a ghostly white haze. In the Goyt Valley late in the day, the sun lit the grass on the hillsides a burnished bronze and it shone against a line of dark grey cloud behind it. Heavy morning frosts turned each tree and bush into a crystal statue, glistening in the clear morning sunshine.

Being away for five years gave me a whole appreciation for the passage of time. Friends seemed to have passed from being just themselves to being adults. Maybe it was seeing people successful and well settled in their careers, or married and living in real houses, living lives like real people do.

I had been afraid that my friends and I would have drifted apart. Despite email and cheap international phone calls, we had not communicated often, but old friends were still old friends. It was frustrating how I had spent years getting to know all their boyfriends and girlfriends and then several had gone and married someone I had never met. One had a new baby.

Friends did not appear to have aged much. It was in the children where the passage of time was clearest. They were all so much bigger. Some were teenagers. "Blimey, you're enormous!" was the first thing I said as I walked into one house to see a very tall lad. That evening, he and his little brother listened with amusement as his father and I reminisced about our university days, the amount of Old Speckled Hen we consumed attempting to sabotage our attempts to keep the stories appropriate to the young audience.

I had mixed feelings about Nottingham. Perhaps it was because I was already used to visiting Macclesfield, but Nottingham was my other home and where I still owned a house. Once more it was good to see friends, but Nottingham had changed in subtle ways. The city centre had at least one grand new building, it was my first sight of the new trams, and bus stops had digital signs showing arrival times. Mini supermarkets abounded; rebranded and smartened up Co-ops competing with Tesco Metro. There was a CityCard that you could load up to pay for bus journeys, visits to the leisure centre and record your library borrowings. It felt as though I had returned to the future. I was pleased to see that Broad Street, which contained the art house theatre, had not only acquired an excellent new Indian restaurant, but also two late night cafés sufficiently in the Wellington style to please Elizabeth were we ever to return.

It was inspecting my house, now tenanted, that really led to the mixed feelings. Considering it had been tenanted for five years, it was faring well, but it was still sad to see it cluttered with strange furniture. My memories were of it on cosy evenings or filled with laughter during dinner parties. A bed had gone missing and the garden was overgrown and uncared for, a small urban wasteland where once I had watched plants flower through the seasons. I comforted myself that these were all cosmetic and if we returned it would only take a little time and money to put it all to rights. It did not help that the day I looked at it was a damp, grey day, probably the only one of my visit.

Cities provided a contrast to New Zealand. They sprawled and were filled with people. We hit Birmingham at rush hour and met with impatient drivers as we tried to find our way. On New Year's Day, Manchester was half dead as most people stayed in or nursed hangovers. I admired the new shopping centres, the understated thirteenth century cathedral and the spaciousness of Salford Quays with Manchester United's Old Trafford ground squatting in the hazy distance. From the upper floor of my friend's townhouse in Liverpool, we could just see the modern gothic tower of the Anglican cathedral and the crown of thorns of the Catholic one, together with the city's other icon, the Liver Building.

Lincoln's old quarter was as beautiful as ever. The cathedral with its triple towers sailed majestically above the town. A row of terraced houses backed right onto the medieval walls of the castle. In another example of people living side by side with historic monuments, I turned a corner in Lewes's high street and walked underneath the archway of the castle's barbican.

The pull of the old became another fixation. My eye wandered over the ancient stonework of Manchester cathedral and the gothic woodwork of the choir stalls. In Lincolnshire I visited a couple of parish churches. Both had grand tombs for the local nobility, one of which recorded the early death of two children "by wicked practise & sorcerye".

I spent the last weekend in Sussex. The south country is so different to the north. The hills are not so bleak, the cottages are flint or brick. They are the romanticised village England, harking back to an imagined rural idyll, while the stone cottages on the high moorlands of the north are something quite different. Parish churches were different too. In Sussex they had towers and were low and simple. Lincolnshire churches had sky-piercing spires.

The parting with the family on the station at Haywards Heath was silently emotional. From there, I was on my way and did not go outside again as I was shuttled through stations and into Heathrow.

My last view of winter was moonlit snowy fields somewhere over central Europe. My next sight of land was gliding down amongst fluffy white canyons of bubbling cumulous into Kuala Lumpur. The sun rose slowly over Australia and it was lunchtime as we came into Auckland from the north. It was warm, people were in shorts. There were faces from the Pacific islands.

At the top of our driveway, I took the mail out of the letterbox and looked across to One Tree Hill. This was home. For now.

Epilogue:
Companions

My first travelling companions were Canadian sisters Camie and Ria. I met them in 1986 when they were looking for people to share petrol for a two week journey from Adelaide to Perth. Their favourite exclamation was "Holy cow!" I left them in Perth with a song I had written called *Canada was built on pumpkin pie*, a fact they had assured me was true.

I met Camie again in 1988 before she was married her then boyfriend and afterwards in 1997. We went out on his hobiecat and were becalmed in the lake. We had to lie on the hulls and swim our way back to the shore.

By this time, Ria was with a solid, likeable guy called Richard. We went to his house in the backwoods and I slept on the floor in the living room, surrounded by the heavy breathing of a Great Dane and a Rottweiler who would both bark threateningly if anyone dared to walk past the house. In the morning, the Rottweiler came over to my face and rolled on her side to have her stomach rubbed. Obediently, I gave her a rub until my arm was sore. She looked at me, clearly pointing out she had not given me permission to stop. Trussed up in my sleeping bag like a tasty sausage roll, I felt I had little choice.

Camie is divorced now with two teenage daughters. Ria also has children and is happily married to Richard. Camie and I still exchange Christmas letters from time to time.

I met Jim in Zagreb in 1987. Four of us went to a bar one night and drank strong Croatian beer. We had each bought a round when the landlady came over with a tray of drinks.

"Chesny has bought you a shout," she said.

That was a very nice of Chesny, we thought. Then, realised she had not been speaking English before, so she must have been speaking Serbo-Croat. What had she said? We never did pay for those drinks.

I was walking through the street in Istanbul a few weeks later when I bumped into Jim again. He had told me in Zagreb that he was going to Istanbul too, but it was still a surprise. We decided to travel together through Turkey. On the bus out of town, I discovered he had found the raincoat that I thought I had lost.

We watched the sun set and rise over Nemrut Dagi and I looked after him on a bus where, sick with food poisoning, he had suddenly felt the urge to vomit. I alerted the driver's assistant, trying English, German and French to get my message across, before pointing at Jim and miming what he was about to do. The man performed a comic exclamation and rushed to fetch a tiny plastic bag. Jim paused long enough to look at it with incredulity before accurately vomiting a correspondingly small amount of liquid into it.

He came to visit me at university in Sheffield and he later caught hepatitis C in Edinburgh. I first visited him in the US in 1990, then in 1997 and again in 2001 when I went to a conference in his hometown of Minneapolis. The weekend I arrived, we drove up to Duluth. On the way back, the sky suddenly darkened with a big Mid-Western storm. Jim started to look worriedly at the sky and I told him not to worry about lightning, we were safe in a car.

"I'm looking for tornadoes," he explained.

I started scanning the sky too.

It was at a bus stop in Benbecula in the Outer Hebrides that I started chatting to an Australian woman called Dale. It turned out her mother was from near Kurri Kurri where Mum was born. She was a fascinating and eccentric woman. She made films and would talk to anyone who stood still for long enough. I introduced her to my parents who were a little bemused at my friendship with a woman old enough to be my mother, but we are still friends. She visited me in Nottingham, I saw much of her, her daughter and her ex-husband when I lived in Australia. He was known as John B and to my surprise no one else had ever thought to call him "The Sloop". It stuck and years later, it is his email address. Dale came to my wedding and I have stayed with her daughter where she lives near Venice.

On one of my travels, I proposed. She was a Chinese Canadian called Tammy and we had met in a backpackers' hostel in Brugge where I stayed regularly on my way to and from Ostend. We were walking around the town when she noticed a Canadian flag flying on a building and asked me to take a photograph of her in front of it. To get the angle right, I had to kneel down.

"While I'm down here," I joked, "will you marry me?"

She started laughing: two elderly ladies walking behind me had paused to hear what her answer would be.

She had a few days to fill and I suggested she go to Bouillon in the Belgian Ardennes, a deep forested valley containing the castle of Duke Godfrey, one of the leaders of the First Crusade. I later received a postcard telling me about the wonderful time she had spent there. I visited her in 1997 in Toronto and we canoed across a lake in Algonquin National Park in the pouring rain. Every now and then we still write. She has lived overseas, but has since returned to Toronto with a husband and at least one child.

In China, I travelled with a Welshman called Ade. His website recounts the travels of Ade the Nomadic Welshman. On a visit from his adopted home in Sydney, he came to see me in my hotel in Solihull where I was working and over a few beers showed me photographs of his time in Mongolia where he had gone as a mountain guide. He later went to Antarctica which he said was the most amazing place he had ever been. For a while it even took away his enthusiasm to travel because nowhere else could possibly compare. He continues to make me very jealous by travelling in beautiful mountainous areas and getting paid for it.

I was travelling with Ade when I met two New Zealand girls called Fiona and Liz. It was in the Himalayan town of Zhongdian that Ade and I borrowed a book from Fiona to learn about a route it referred to as the Chengdu Backroad. I do not remember talking to Liz. Two weeks later, travelling on my own again, I came across them in a café in Dunhuang, an oasis town in the Gobi Desert. We were heading the same way and I spent the next two and a half weeks with them exploring the wonders of the Silk Road and the Karakoram Highway into Pakistan before I flew home.

We had a reunion in Ely, after they had reached England, at the home of an eccentric Englishman called John who had been with us during some of that time and who had flown back to Manchester with me. We continued to meet up and I would chat often to Liz on the phone in Edinburgh. As time went on, we became more than friends. We have since travelled in many countries together. She is now my wife and the mother of our two sons.

Travel can change your life.

We are all travellers in the wilderness of this world, and the best we can find in our travels is an honest friend.

Robert Louis Stevenson

Enjoy this book? You can make a big difference

Reviews are hugely powerful when it comes to getting attention for my books. As an independent author, it's one of the few ways I can try to compete with the big publishers.

Honest reviews of my books help bring them to the attention of other readers.

If you've enjoyed this book, I'd be very grateful if you could spend a few minutes leaving a review (it can be as short as you like) at your favourite retailer.

About the author

Find out more about KA Barron at www.kabarron.com.

You can also connect with him on Twitter at @kabarronauthor, on Facebook at www.facebook.com/kabarronbooks and if you feel like it, send him an email at kevin@kabarron.com.

Also by Kevin Barron

Travel and humour

Into the blue

Half-planned travels of an amateur vagabond

Kevin Barron feels guilty if he stays at home and does nothing. His solution is to visit other countries and do nothing there instead. An added benefit is that writing about it gives him something to do at home.

Lose your ticket before you've even set off, find out what whalers think of Greenpeace, dodge dive-bombers, meet dangerous truckers, interview a tennis star, witness horror, walk all night, fish for your dinner, watch sunsets in the wilderness, ride legendary highways, stargaze in the Rockies, hitch-hike through the outback, be rescued by an angel, become Robin Hood, escape from Colditz.

This collection of stories covers more than a decade of travel, so throw your backpack over your shoulder and head off...into the blue.

Tales of Socks and Splendour

The Grumpete is a disgusting yet warm hearted character who lives alone in a land beyond the Ocean of Spleg. Embarking on an adventure one day, he encounters the Kazza Princess in a distant castle and their lives are never the same again.

Join the foul-bummed Grumpete and the kimmering Kazz as they shine, explode, wander, flatulate, burn, run, reproduce, eat and fight their way through a series of far-fetched adventures in glorious nonsense verse.

Whether read out loud or quietly to yourself where no one will find you, these fast-moving and humorous poems are sure to entertain children of all ages...apart from perhaps those of a delicate disposition.

Novels (as KA Barron)

Light Funnel

A father in despair. An ancient destiny. A darkness that can change everything.

Fear has kept ancient enemies apart for centuries, but the Archbishop has made a discovery which will overturn the balance of power.

Falling between worlds, young Charlie Denham and his father Richard find themselves on opposite sides when war looms. The descendants of lost crusaders now face a decisive conflict with the Delf who wield demons of fire.

As darkness pours from the earth and armies gather, Richard and Charlie will face the nightmare from a lost past which threatens to consume both worlds. They must find each other, and escape the approaching storm, if they are to have any hope of staying alive or returning home again.

Light Needle

In dreams, something is stirring.

Eight years have passed since the events described in Light Funnel. An uneasy peace has existed between the Order and the Delf. Now, rumblings of dissent threaten a return to war.

Inspired by dreams, Jack Silver searches for the descendants of the adventurers who left Outreterre centuries before and never returned. With their help, the Delf could be overthrown forever.

Former adversaries Berwick, Rodon and Raul secretly follow Silver and his protectors across the sea; Solimo, still haunted by his experiences, is about to face his greatest fear, while a footloose Charlie Denham will soon be fleeing for his life from forces he does not understand.

For an old enemy has found a way out of Limbo and will stop at nothing to purge the worlds.

When he returns, a great city will burn and a society will be torn apart. Only a fragile web of alliances, old and new, stands before the terrible new power emerging from Limbo.

In this second book in the Light Funnel series, multiple storylines weave together culminating in a climactic confrontation.

Later books in the series will be:
Light Cradle
Light Mage

Business

How to Run Facilitated Workshops

A pragmatic guide to successful meetings

Are your meetings a waste of time?

Get productive.

We've all had those moments of wondering about the point of meetings. People wander off topic, take over, tune out...

Perhaps you have run some workshops, but want some ideas about how to deal with specific situations.

In today's fast moving business environment, you need to make the most of people's time, energy and knowledge. This book is aimed at people in organisations who have limited time and budget to achieve their objectives, but need to be inclusive, consultative, yet efficient.

It provides pragmatic advice of immediate use to both novice and experienced facilitator. It can be read end to end, or you can dip into it depending on your need.

The book is packed full of advice and techniques to help you prepare for, run and follow up on facilitated workshops. Not only is the process described, but there is advice for dealing with problems along the way, notably managing behaviour that can kill productivity and collaboration. There is a focus on planning the workshop and setting out the agenda. A set of sample agendas covering a wide range of project scenarios is included.

With the advice in this book, gleaned from twenty years of experience in industry and consulting, you can pre-empt problems and be well on the way to saving time and achieving usable outcomes that will accelerate your projects.

275

Kevin Barron has worked in industry and consulting for more than 25 years. He has led teams, worked on projects and delivered training across many sectors including banking, media, retail, wealth management, telecommunications, transport, IT services, utilities, local and national government, and manufacturing. He has facilitated hundreds of workshops in the UK, Australia, New Zealand, Sweden and Germany. He is also an experienced business analyst and agile practitioner.

CPSIA information can be obtained
at www.ICGtesting.com
Printed in the USA
LVOW01s1441040417
529579LV00011B/1102/P